Karen Brown's

New England

Charming Inns & Itineraries

Written by
JACK BULLARD and KAREN BROWN

Illustrations by Vanessa Kale
Cover Painting by Jann Pollard

Karen Brown's Guides, San Mateo, California

Karen Brown Titles

Austria: Charming Inns & Itineraries
California: Charming Inns & Itineraries
England: Charming Bed & Breakfasts
England, Wales & Scotland: Charming Hotels & Itineraries
France: Charming Bed & Breakfasts
France: Charming Inns & Itineraries
Germany: Charming Inns & Itineraries
Ireland: Charming Inns & Itineraries
Italy: Charming Bed & Breakfasts
Italy: Charming Inns & Itineraries
Mexico: Charming Inns & Itineraries
Mid-Atlantic: Charming Inns & Itineraries
New England: Charming Inns & Itineraries
Pacific Northwest: Charming Inns & Itineraries
Portugal: Charming Inns & Itineraries
Spain: Charming Inns & Itineraries
Switzerland: Charming Inns & Itineraries

To each of you who have enriched my life in so many ways
through so many chapters
I thank you

Front cover painting: Dunscroft by the Sea, Harwich Port, Massachusetts.

Editors: Clare Brown, June Brown, Karen Brown, Tony Brown, Courtney Gaviorno, Debbie Tokumoto, Yvonne Sartain.

Illustrations: Vanessa Kale.

Cover painting: Jann Pollard.

Technical support and graphics: Michael Fiegel, Gary Meisner.

Maps: Michael Fiegel.

Copyright © 2005 by Karen Brown's Guides.

This book or parts thereof may not be reproduced in any form without obtaining written permission from the publisher: Karen Brown's Guides, P.O. Box 70, San Mateo, CA 94401, USA, email: karen@karenbrown.com.

Distributed by Fodor's Travel Publications, Inc., 1745 Broadway, New York, NY 10019, USA, tel: 212-751-2600, fax: 212-940-7352.

Distributed in Canada by Random House Canada, 2775 Matheson Boulevard East, Mississauga, Ontario, Canada L4W 4P7, tel: 888-523-9292, fax: 888-562-9924.

Distributed in the United Kingdom, Ireland and Europe by Random House UK, 20 Vauxhall Bridge Road, London, SW1V 2SA, England, tel: 44 20 7840 4000, fax: 44 20 7840 8406.

Distributed in Australia by Random House Australia, 20 Alfred Street, Milsons Point, Sydney NSW 2061, Australia, tel: 61 2 9954 9966, fax: 61 2 9954 4562.

Distributed in New Zealand by Random House New Zealand, 18 Poland Road, Glenfield, Auckland, New Zealand, tel: 64 9 444 7197, fax: 64 9 444 7524.

Distributed in South Africa by Random House South Africa, Endulani, East Wing, 5A Jubilee Road, Parktown 2193, South Africa, tel: 27 11 484 3538, fax: 27 11 484 6180.

A catalog record for this book is available from the British Library.

ISSN 1535-4059

Contents

INTRODUCTION	1–14
About Inn Travel	2
About Itineraries	10
ITINERARIES	17–68
Driving Itineraries:	
Boston: A Grand Beginning	17
Cape Cod, Nantucket, Martha's Vineyard & Newport	23
PLACES TO STAY	69–247
Connecticut Inns	69
Route 7 & Much More	41
The Byways of Coastal Maine	51
New Hampshire Beckons	65
Maine Inns	87
Massachusetts Inns	119
New Hampshire Inns	183
Rhode Island Inns	199
Vermont Inns	209
INDEX	247–256
MAPS	
Places to Stay and Itineraries	Color Section at Back of Book

*We are proud to present
as our 2005 cover painting,
Dunscroft by the Sea
in
Harwich Port, Massachusetts.*

Introduction

Because of its history, its special relationship with the sea, its back roads and scenic beauty, its changing seasons, and the great diversity between traveling the coast and the valleys and mountains, New England is a wonderful travel destination at all times of the year—though many consider that it is most glorious in the fall. New England is comprised of the six states in the northeast corner of the United States. The upper portion of New England encompasses Maine, New Hampshire, and Vermont; while Connecticut, Massachusetts, and Rhode Island make up the lower portion. The traveler to New England, more often than not, visits either the northern three states or the lower three, since touring the entire region, with all its many and diverse attractions, requires a considerable investment of time.

About Inn Travel

We use the term "inn" to cover everything from a simple bed and breakfast to a sophisticated resort. A wide range of inns is included in this guide: some are great bargains, others very costly; some are in cities, others in remote locations; some are quite sophisticated, others extremely simple; some are decorated with opulent antiques, others with furniture from grandma's attic; some are large hotels, others have only a few rooms. The common denominator is that each place has some special quality that makes it appealing. The descriptions are intended to give you an honest appraisal of each property so that you can select accommodation based on personal preferences. The following pointers will help you appreciate and understand what to expect when traveling the "inn way."

BATHROOMS

While the majority of guestrooms have connecting or *ensuite* bathrooms, you'll want to make certain when you make your reservation. Some inns offer guestrooms that share a bath with other rooms, or rooms that have a private bath but locate it down the hall. We usually do not specify whether the bath is equipped with stall-shower, tub-shower, tub only, or Jacuzzi; so you'll need to ask about that, too.

BREAKFAST

A welcome feature and trademark of many inns is their morning repast—many cookbooks have been authored and inspired by innkeepers. Breakfast is almost always included in the room rate, and the "coffee cup" icon on the hotel's page will confirm this. Although innkeepers take great pride in their delectable morning offerings, know that breakfast can range from a gourmet "waddle-away" feast (as proudly described by one innkeeper-chef) to muffins and coffee. Sometimes breakfast is limited to a Continental in your room or a hot breakfast with others in the dining room, and sometimes both. Breakfast times vary as well—some innkeepers serve a hot breakfast at a specified time, while others replenish a buffet on a more leisurely schedule. Breakfasts are as individual as the inns themselves and are something to look forward to.

If you have any special dietary requirements, most innkeepers will gladly try to accommodate your needs. Not having a fully stocked refrigerator as a restaurant would have, innkeepers usually plan a breakfast menu that features one entree and have those ingredients on hand. Therefore, it is best to mention any special requests at the time of making your reservation, both as a courtesy and from a practical point of view, so that the innkeeper can have on hand items such as special, low-fat dairy products, egg substitutes, sugar-free syrups, etc.

CANCELLATION POLICIES

Although policies vary, inns (by definition) have only a few rooms and when a reservation is made, the owner/innkeeper counts on receiving that revenue. Most inns usually require you to cancel at least a week in advance of the arrival date, and some inns charge a small fee if the reservation is canceled in order to cover their administrative costs. If you cancel within a specified number of days prior to your planned arrival, you may be required to pay the first night if the room cannot be re-rented. Some inns have even more stringent policies, so be sure to inquire at the time you make your reservation.

CHECK-IN

Inns are usually very specific about check-in time—generally between 3 and 6 pm. Let the innkeeper know if you are going to arrive late and he will make special arrangements for you, such as leaving you a door key under a potted plant along with a note on how to find your room. Also, for those who might arrive early, note that some inns close their doors between check-out and check-in times. Inns are frequently staffed only by the owners themselves and that window of time between check-out and check-in is often the only opportunity to shop for those wonderful breakfasts they prepare, in addition to running their own personal errands.

CHILDREN

Many places in this guide cater only to adults and do not welcome children, or welcome children only over a certain age. They cannot legally refuse accommodation to children, but, as parents, we really want to stay where our children are genuinely welcome. We would always recommend that you inquire about the inn's policy when making your reservation. In the inn descriptions on our website (*www.karenbrown.com*), we have an icon that indicates at what age children are welcome.

COMFORT

Comfort plays a deciding role in the selection of inns recommended: firm mattress, a quiet setting, good lighting, fresh towels, scrubbed bathrooms. The charming decor and innkeeper will soon be forgotten, if you do not enjoy a good night's sleep and comfortable stay. Be aware, however, that some inns in areas with hot summers, especially those in older buildings, do not always have the luxury of air conditioning. If air conditioning is of prime importance to you, look for the appropriate icon at the bottom of the description and verify that the inn has it when making a reservation.

CREDIT CARDS

Whether or not an establishment accepts credit cards is indicated at the bottom of each description by the symbol ▣. Even if an inn does not accept credit card payment, it will perhaps request your account number as a guarantee of arrival.

CRITERIA FOR SELECTION

It is very important to us that an inn has charm. Ideally an inn should be appealing—perhaps in an historic building, beautifully decorated, lovingly managed, and in a wonderful location. Few inns meet every criteria, but all our selections have something that makes them special and are situated in enjoyable surroundings. We have had to reject several lovely inns because of a poor location. Many are in historic buildings, but remember that the definition of "historic" may depend on the century in which the state came into being. Many inns are newly constructed and may be in buildings built to look old. Small inns are usually our favorites, but size alone does not dictate whether or not a hostelry is chosen. Most are small, but sometimes the only place to stay in a "must-visit" area is a splendid, larger establishment of great character and charm. We have tried to include properties with a variety of size, decor, and ambiance to suit a variety of tastes and pocketbooks.

ICONS

Icons allow us to provide additional information about our recommended properties. When using our website to supplement the guides, positioning the cursor over an icon will, in many cases, give you further details. For easy reference an icon key can be found on the last page of the book.

We have introduced these icons in the guidebooks and there are more on our website, *www.karenbrown.com*. ❋ Air conditioning in rooms, ⏉ Beach nearby, ☕ Breakfast included in room rate, ⚛ Children welcome, ♨ Cooking classes offered, 💳 Credit cards accepted, ☎ Direct-dial telephone in room, 🐕 Dogs by special request, 🛗 Elevator, 🏋 Exercise room, 🔥 Fireplaces in some bedrooms, ⓨ Mini-refrigerator in rooms, **P** Parking available, 🍴 Restaurant, ⊘ Some non-smoking rooms, ✳ Spa, ≈ Swimming pool, 🎾 Tennis, 📺 Television with English channels, 💍 Wedding facilities, ♿ Wheelchair friendly, 🏌 Golf course nearby, 🚶 Hiking trails nearby, 🐎 Horseback riding nearby, 🎿 Skiing nearby, 🌊 Water sports nearby, 🍷 Wineries nearby.

MEMBERSHIP AFFILIATIONS

If a property is a member of either Select Registry or Relais & Châteaux, we reference this on the hotel description page. These associations impose their own criteria for selection and membership standards and have established a reputation for the particular type of property they include.

PROFESSIONALISM

The inns we have selected are run by professional innkeepers. We recommend only inns that offer privacy for their guests, not places where you'd have to climb over family clutter to reach the bathroom.

RESERVATIONS

The best way to make a reservation is changing. We used to just pick up the phone and call, but with the advent of the worldwide web, it is now possible to view many properties, including the bedrooms, "on line" and then make a reservation electronically. Email links are published on the individual hotel pages on the Karen Brown Website. Phoning is still a good way to discuss the various differences in available accommodation and the inn's policies. As a courtesy to the innkeepers, however, keep in mind that staff is often limited, and during certain periods of the day, such as the breakfast hour, they are busier than others—flipping pancakes, checking out guests, helping plan activities. Also, inns are often homes, and you might be waking up the innkeeper if you call late evenings or early mornings. Another convenient and efficient way to request a reservation is by fax. If the inn has a fax, we have noted the number in the information line next to the telephone number. As a final note: when planning your trip, be aware that the majority of inns in this guide require a two-night stay on weekends and over holidays.

RESPONSIBILITY

Our goal is to outline itineraries in regions that we consider of prime interest to our readers and to recommend inns that we think are outstanding. All of the inns featured have been selected solely on their merits. Our judgments are made on the charm of the inn, its setting, cleanliness, and, above all, the warmth of welcome. Each property has its own appeal, and we try to present you with a very honest appraisal. However, no matter how careful we are, sometimes we misjudge an inn's merits, or the ownership changes, or (unfortunately) sometimes inns just do not maintain their standards. If you find an inn is not as we have indicated, please let us know and accept our sincere apologies.

RESTAURANTS

A bonus to staying in a New England inn is that of dining in its restaurant. Your meal will be a great one and will feature regional fare ranging from seafood like lobster, clams, and bluefish to the wild game of pheasant and quail. The heritage of New England is turkey, and Thanksgiving dinners generally include the presentation of this bird with a variety of family stuffing recipes, from oyster to corn bread, to traditional herb bread with seasonings. At the end of a day of touring, you'll find that the fireplace in the inn's tavern, and another in the dining room, will lure you to both warmth and good dining. If a property has a restaurant, it is indicated by the fork and knife icon. In the inn descriptions on our website (*www.karenbrown.com*), we have an icon that indicates which meals are served.

Introduction–About Inn Travel

ROOM RATES

It seems that many inns play musical rates, with high-season, low-season, midweek, weekend, and holiday rates. We have quoted the 2005 high-season general range of rates for two people (singles usually receive a very small discount) from the lowest-priced bedroom to the most expensive suite including breakfast. The rates given are those quoted to us by the inn. Please use these figures as a guideline and be certain to ask at the time of booking what the rates are and what they include. We have not given prices for "special" rooms, such as those that can accommodate three people traveling together. Discuss with the innkeeper rooms and rates available before making your selection. Of course, some inns are exceptions to our guidelines, and whenever this is the case, we mention the special situation (such as breakfast not being included in the rate). Please be aware that local tourist taxes are not included in the rates quoted and can be very high.

SMOKING

Most inns have extremely strict non-smoking policies. A few inns permit smoking in restricted public areas or outside, but, in general, it is best to assume that smoking is not appropriate. If smoking is of great concern, be sure to ask the hotel specifically as to their policy about smoking in the garden, on the deck, or in a specially designated public area.

SOCIALIZING

Inns usually offer a conviviality rarely found in a "standard" hotel. The gamut runs all the way from playing "cozy family" around the kitchen table to sharing a sophisticated, elegant cocktail hour in the parlor. Breakfast may be a formal meal served at a set hour when the guests gather around the dining-room table, or it may be served buffet-style over several hours where guests have the option of either sitting down to eat alone or joining other guests at a larger table. Then again, some inns will bring a breakfast tray to your room, or perhaps breakfast in the room is the only option. After check-in, many inns offer afternoon refreshment, such as tea and cakes or wine and hors d'oeuvres, which may be seen as another social opportunity. Some inns set out the refreshments buffet-style where guests are invited to meander in and out, mixing or not mixing with other guests as they choose. Others orchestrate a more structured gathering, often a social hour, with the innkeeper presiding.

WEBSITE

Please supplement this book by looking at the information provided on our Karen Brown Website (*www.karenbrown.com*), which serves as an added dimension to our guides. Most of our favorite inns are featured on the Karen Brown Website (web participation is an inn's choice). On their web page, you can usually link to their email, so making a reservation is a breeze. Also featured on our site are comments, feedback, and discoveries from you, our readers; information on our latest finds; post-press updates; contest drawings for free books; special offers; unique features such as recipes and favorite destinations; and special savings offered by certain inns.

WHEELCHAIR ACCESSIBILITY

If an inn has *at least* one guestroom that is accessible by wheelchair, it is noted with the symbol ♿. This is not the same as saying it meets full ADA standards.

About Itineraries

Though the same thread of "Yankee" (as defined by many) culture is woven throughout all six states, there are distinctive differences between the states themselves. Within each state, there are areas that are markedly different in terrain, weather patterns, and tourist attractions. These differences make for delightful trips. This book guides you on journeys that show off this diversity, and gives you the opportunity to choose the experiences you most want to have.

Boston: A Grand Beginning describes our recommendations for what to see in this wonderful gateway city to New England. Four detailed driving itineraries, (*Sturbridge & The Connecticut Shore, Byways of Coastal Maine, Cape Cod, Nantucket, Martha's Vineyard & Newport, Route 7 & Much More and New Hampshire Beckons*), describe routes through the various regions of New England, so that you can choose a journey through an area that fits both your time and travel constraints. The itineraries are outlined on the hotel state maps found at the back of the book in the color map section and on the individual, more detailed, black-and-white map that precedes each itinerary. The overview map will help you visualize the routes of the various itineraries as they navigate a course through the New England states. Tailor these itineraries to meet your own specific needs by leaving out some sightseeing if time is limited, or linking several itineraries together if you wish to enjoy a longer vacation.

Though several itineraries use Boston as their point of origination, and this is a logical starting point for travel to Cape Cod and the Berkshires, they may be accessed at any point en route and from any of the various points at which you may arrive in the northeast. Your entry into New England will probably depend on your destination—Manchester, New Hampshire—for ease of access into Maine, New Hampshire, and Vermont; Providence, Rhode Island—for visiting Cape Cod, the islands of Nantucket and Martha's Vineyard, and the small but activity-rich areas of Rhode Island; Hartford, Connecticut—for trips to the western portions of Connecticut and Massachusetts, and north into Vermont and New Hampshire; and Albany, New York—for alternative access to the western parts of New England. Although New York City is located at least an hour's drive (more if you travel during congested commuter hours) from Connecticut and the start of the itinerary travels up the western side of New England, its airports may provide the best airfares and schedules for the international traveler, as well as the more distant U.S. traveler.

ANTIQUING

If you have a passion for antiquing, you might already know that New England is full of treasures to satisfy almost any desire to start or add to a collection. Most of the antique shops in New England are small and privately owned, but in the last several years, "collectives" have become very popular. These are group shops representing a few antique dealers, or maybe as many as a hundred dealers. In the larger shops, there is a greater chance of finding the elusive object you're searching for. Antiques are generally divided into objects of significant value and collectibles, the latter having less dollar value, but not necessarily of less interest-value to the buyer. Fortunately, in New England there is a wealth of both antiques and collectibles, and the real challenge is finding the shops in which those treasures you have always wanted will be waiting for you. To aid you in this, a good reference is Sloan's *Green Guide to Antiquing in New England,* a compendium of 2,500 shops. Since no dealer can be familiar with the value of all objects in all categories, and generally has items in stock not within his general line of expertise, you may have an opportunity to purchase an overlooked treasure at a real bargain.

CAR RENTAL

Our itineraries are designed for travel by car. If you are staying in any of the major cities at the beginning of your trip, it is not necessary to pick up a rental car until you leave the city or just before any daytrips you can make only by car, since public transportation systems are so convenient and all of the cities are great for walking. Ask your hotel if there is a car rental office nearby—if so, you might find out if that particular company can give you rates as competitive as any other. If you are really lucky, as with some of the rental companies, you might even have your car delivered to your hotel. There is no question that the less time you have to spend getting to your car and then turning it in at the end of your trip, the happier you will be. Inquire when you make your car reservation about all the add-on charges, and don't be surprised at how much they increase the total rental cost. Do check to see if your home or car insurance or your credit card will provide you with coverage in the event of an accident.

DRIVING TIMES

New England is not particularly large—in the central portions six hours of driving will generally take you from east to west or from south to north, unless you stretch out New England and try to go from southern Connecticut to the tip of Maine (more like a ten-hour trip). We have indicated in our itineraries a daily pace that we believe will make for a pleasant and comfortable trip, allowing you time to enjoy not only the scenery, but also the historic sights along the way. Allow more time if you want to do a lot of shopping, or if you have a special interest in any particular area.

FALL FOLIAGE

While routes are picturesque in any season, our four fall driving itineraries weave through some gorgeous regions, where the richness of your day will be matched not only by the color of the foliage, but also by each passing farm with pumpkins and gourds piled high, and cornstalks tied to fence posts. Fall Foliage highlights are referenced in the introductory pages of each itinerary, but if you were to choose the most traditional Fall Foliage route, you might want to consider the itinerary, *New Hampshire Beckons*.

New England is special at any time of the year, but there is simply nowhere on earth where you can experience nature's changing colors as you can here. When the days become shorter, the nights turn cool, the first frost coats the lawn, and the roof shingles sparkle with their early-morning ice, New England prepares for the magic season of fall foliage. Trees, shrubs, flowers and weeds all begin the transformation that changes their color from green to multiple hues of red, orange, and gold—and a million shades in between. It's simply a time of magic! It's also the time when nature performs a brilliant display reminiscent of fireworks on the fourth of July. It's a time to be in New England.

Fall foliage is generally at its peak in the first two weeks of October after the first bite of cold temperatures, and seems to be best when there has been the proper amount of rainfall during the spring and summer. This season of changing colors generally begins in the far northern reaches of New England (unless you happen to be on a winding lane in the Connecticut valley alongside a quiet pond where the cold air of the night has settled in and painted everything in sight with a vivid brush of intensity). The turning of the colors generally wends its way southward, unless it happens to turn west, or unless you happen to be on the peak of a mountain enjoying views for miles around. Remember, each rule about the timing of fall foliage has an exception.

This special time in New England. Unless the weather is unusual, it will perform as it has for hundreds of years. Do not worry excessively (or perhaps at all) about being on exactly the perfect road at the precise moment when the foliage achieves its peak and the golden and red leaves fall from the trees. Generally, plan to be in New England between mid-September and mid-October—farther north in the middle of September, and in Massachusetts and Connecticut in the month of October.

Reservations: The northeast's fall foliage is without a doubt one of the most popular tourist attractions in the U.S. Finding places to spend the night is sometimes difficult, so reservations are a must. Hopefully, you'll be able to find a place to suit your preferences among the inns recommended in this guide. If there is no room available, ask the innkeeper for his or her recommendation of an alternative accommodation—most innkeepers recommend only places where they themselves would stay, so you'll be safe with their suggestions. Nonetheless, making a reservation as soon as you book your airplane ticket or plan your road trip is well-advised.

MAPS

A total of five colored maps are to be found at the back of the book. The overview map outlines our recommended driving itineraries as they cross through the New England states. The overview is followed by a series of four detailed maps that show the itinerary routings, and places to stay by geographic state groupings. Fronting each itinerary is a black-and-white map that outlines the suggested route, detailing sightseeing suggestions and roads. These are simply renderings and not necessarily to scale. For detailed trip planning, it is essential to supplement these with comprehensive commercial maps. Rand McNally maps are available for purchase on our website, *www.karenbrown.com*.

PACING

At the beginning of each itinerary, we suggest our recommended pacing to help you decide the amount of time to allocate to each one. The suggested time frame reflects how much there is to see and do. Use our recommendation as a guideline only. Choreograph your own itinerary based on how much leisure time you have, and whether your preference is to move on to a new destination each day or to settle in and use a particular inn as your base.

WEATHER

There's a saying in New England "If you don't like the weather, just wait a few minutes." While the weather may be changeable, there are certainly some guidelines that will be helpful to the traveler in planning a trip. In the winter months of December through March, you can expect everything, from snow and ice to sleet and freezing rain. Temperatures often get down to zero and below, and there may be days, even weeks, when there is little snow and just brisk cold weather. Traditionally, in the latter half of January, there is even a period of warm weather, deceiving everyone into believing that winter is over. The spring months of April, May, and June are wonderful—with all of New England sprouting forth with bulbs of every description, and flowering shrubs and trees. The newness of everything with the green freshness of spring green is hard not to love. However, occasionally in the spring there is a taste of winter weather that will remind you that the decision to bring a coat on your trip was indeed a very good one. Summer is a lazy time of year and generally has lovely weather, but there will be rain showers. Summer can also get hot and humid—on those days you'll welcome the pair of shorts and short-sleeved shirt that you brought, and you'll be grateful that your rental car and your hotel are air-conditioned. Many a traveler will say that New England is best in the fall when the days are long and warm, the evenings are cool, and the foliage begins to turn.

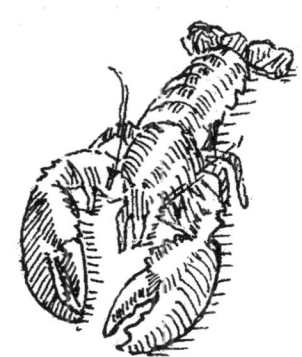

Boston: A Grand Beginning

Boston, the economic and intellectual center of New England and, historically, America's cradle of liberty, is the stage on which much of the drama of the earliest years of our country took place. It is here that the Colonies, which evolved into the present United States, were first established. The capital city of Massachusetts, Boston was first settled in the 17th century, but it was the 18th century that saw the growing rift between the English Parliament and the colonists in what was referred to as the Bay Colony. Many of the historic sites and buildings in Boston, and the towns surrounding it, are associated with this period of separation from the Crown.

Beacon Hill, Acorn Street

Recommended Pacing: Plan to spend at least three nights and four full days in Boston, and you will be able to pick and choose among the many things to do and come up with a program tailored to your interests. Touring Boston is not only desirable, but really a necessary element to fully experience New England. In fact, if you want to see in-depth everything there in the way of historical, cultural, and educational importance, you may never leave Boston at all!

Old State House

Getting Around: Boston has a good public transportation system, so the best way to explore the city is by subway. Visit Park Street station (one of the main downtown stations) to obtain a map of the color-coded subway lines and information on Boston Passports, which provide unlimited subway travel for 1, 3, 5, and 7 days. If you are planning on taking daytrips to Lexington or Marblehead, you can do so from North Station (on the subway system). For further information, log on to *www.mbta.com*. Do not pick up a rental car until you leave the city.

In Boston, you should not miss walking along the **Freedom Trail** in the heart of the city, marked by a red brick path in the pavement (this takes at least two hours). The trail leads to the sites where many of the history-making events that created the new country took place—be sure to include the **Old South Meeting House**, the **Old State House**, **Faneuil Hall**, and **Quincy Market**. A detour onto **Beacon Hill**, an area where early merchants built homes and where the **Capitol Building** is located, is well-worth the time. If you would like to do some shopping as a break from all the history, just walk across the Boston Common and proceed, with credit card in hand, down **Newbury Street**, where you find the city's finest boutiques, art galleries, antique shops, and some of the best restaurants.

Charles Bullfinch, one of the principal architects of many of Boston's historic buildings, completed the **State House**, with its golden dome, in 1786. Nearby, another example of his talent, the **Harrison Gray Otis House**, today serves as the headquarters of **SPNEA** (Society for the Preservation of New England Antiquities). Throughout New England, there are 37 houses and gardens owned by SPNEA, displaying the furnishings and decorative arts of the region's past. Telephone 617-227-3956 or visit their website at *www.spnea.org* for information on these historic properties.

The New State House

Back Bay, with its commercial and shopping areas, begins at the **Boston Common**, a 50-acre park in the center of the city. The adjacent **Public Garden** (the first public botanical garden in the country), with its guide-pedaled swan boats and wonderful duck statues found along its network of paths, is a treat for children who have read and loved *Make Way for Ducklings*. Not to be missed in Back Bay are **Copley Square**, **Trinity Church**, and the **John Hancock Tower**, from whose 60th-floor observatory you get splendid views in all directions. **Commonwealth Avenue** retains much of the grandeur of a residential street with its center mall lined with elm trees.

In the colorful part of Boston known as the **North End**, there are many Italian bakeries, restaurants, and street markets. The **Paul Revere House**, downtown Boston's only 17th-century house (now a museum), was the starting point for his famous ride to Lexington and Concord to warn the patriots of the coming of the British.

Boston's **financial district** is centered around one of its major transportation hubs, South Station. Within a few blocks' walk are the Aquarium, Chinatown, the theatre district, and many shopping opportunities in the larger department stores.

Boston, home since the early years to some of our nation's most prominent educational, medical, and research institutions, is equally famous for its cultural activities. Here you find important international museums including the **Museum of Fine Arts** and the **Isabella Stewart Gardner Museum**. While each is very different from the other, they both have world-renowned art comparable to the best museums anywhere. In the Museum of Fine Arts, our favorite galleries would include those devoted to American and European art; but major collections of Asiatic, Egyptian, Nubian, and Near-Eastern artworks, as well as sculpture and photography, are there to enjoy. At the neighboring Isabella Stewart Gardner Museum, the art objects collected by Mrs. Gardner are displayed exactly as they were in her lifetime, making a tour of this museum a very intimate experience. At the heart of the museum, you find a renowned courtyard with plantings changed throughout the seasons, and concerts are held regularly in the Tapestry Room. Just south of the city, reachable via public transportation, is the **Museum at the John Fitzgerald Kennedy Library**, which houses the archives of the former president.

For children, there are two museums of particular note: The **Boston Museum of Science**, located by the Charles River, offers an array of educational exhibits that invite active participation in the world of science and technology. (This museum is fascinating and I urge you to make time for it in your program.) The **Children's Museum** at Museum Wharf is a wonderful, interactive, educational museum that will delight adults as well as children, and also has an area for toddlers and preschoolers.

Back Bay Skyline and the Charles River

The **Boston Symphony Orchestra**, one of the world's most famous, performs throughout the fall, winter, and spring seasons in Symphony Hall and during the summer at Tanglewood in the Berkshires. The **Boston Pops**, with its programs of lighter music, performs in summer at Symphony Hall and in free concerts on the Charles River Esplanade. There's nothing like a summer night under the stars listening to music with a picnic supper. (I suggest that you bring a blanket and enjoy this very special treat.) Boston has a **theater district** just south of Boston Common and not far from the financial district—most of the theaters are on Tremont and Boylston Streets. Here you can find many pre-Broadway and current Broadway shows, as well as a ballet company, which performs seasonally.

Across the river, neighboring **Cambridge** is home to **Harvard University**, **Radcliffe College**, and the **Massachusetts Institute of Technology**. Around these academic communities has developed a maze of commercial and residential neighborhoods, artists' studios, and theaters. On the Harvard campus, sites worth visiting include **Harvard Yard** with its student residential buildings, **Memorial Church**, **Harvard Museums of Cultural and Natural History**, and the **Botanical Museum,** which houses the world-renowned collection of Blashka glass flowers. These pieces were created between 1877 and 1936, and represent more than 780 species of flowering plants—an absolute must for garden enthusiasts. To this day no one has been able to recreate the processes used in producing these magnificent examples of floral beauty.

For adults and children alike, the **New England Aquarium** is a special place to visit. Its center exhibit is a four-story 187,000-gallon ocean tank re-creating a Caribbean reef, and there are also exhibits encouraging children to handle crabs, sea urchins, and starfish.

The *USS Constitution*, the oldest commissioned warship afloat, which participated in a number of sea battles in disputes between the American colonies and the British, is berthed in Charlestown, and reached using public transportation unless you are up for a very long walk.

There are many other varied attractions for the visitor to Boston. More information can be obtained from the **Greater Boston Convention and Visitors Bureau** located at 2 Copley Place, Suite 105, at the intersection of Tremont and West Streets (1-888-SEE BOSTON, *www.bostonusa.com*).

Full descriptions and details of the hotels we recommend in Boston are given in the *Massachusetts Places to Stay* section of this book.

 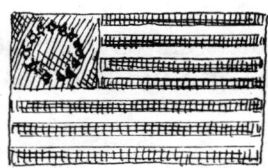 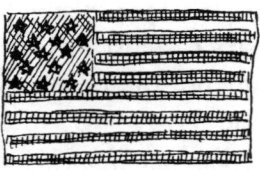

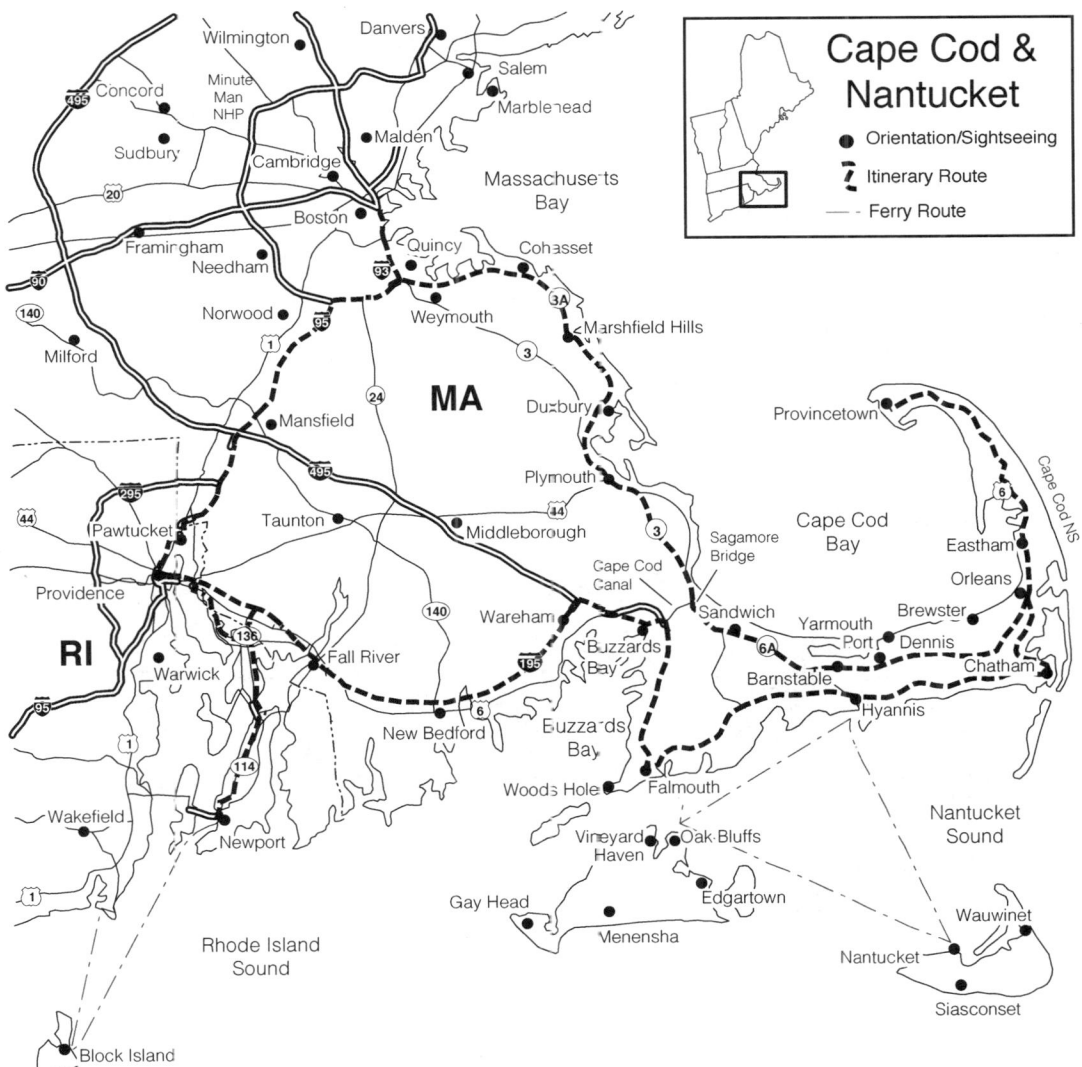

Cape Cod, Nantucket, Martha's Vineyard & Newport

Travel south from Boston—to the coastal villages and fishing harbors of Cape Cod, out to the enticing islands of Nantucket and Martha's Vineyard, on to the gracious mansions of Newport—and back to Boston. Along the way, you have ample opportunities for antiquing, and you'll come to love the weathered architecture that gave its name to the "Cape" style of building. The north shore of the Cape along Route 6A is my favorite. It's much quieter, less populated, and much less commercial than the towns along Route 28 to the south, and there is a real sense of community here. In the warm months, flower gardens thrive on Cape Cod, especially roses, which seem almost to engulf the houses in early June.

Nantucket

Recommended Pacing: The routing for this itinerary is also outlined on Map 2 (in the back section of the book). This itinerary can be comfortably followed in its entirety in six or seven nights, though you can, of course, adapt it to fit your individual interests. On day one, head south along the coastal route, visit Hingham, Duxbury, Plymouth, and stay overnight in Duxbury. On day two, cross the Sagamore Bridge and stay overnight in Sandwich. On day three, drive along the north side of Cape Cod to the Cape Cod National Seashore and the artist community of Provincetown, spending the night in Orleans, Eastham, or Chatham. Day four takes you south along the coast to Hyannis, where you take the ferry or fly to the islands of Nantucket or Martha's Vineyard. One day (minimum) on each of these islands provides time to see the villages and to absorb the culture of the seafarers who arrived as early as the 18th century. On day six, a flight or boat trip back to Hyannis and a drive to Newport, Rhode Island provide an opportunity to see the grand summer cottages of the "rich and famous" residents, built in the first quarter of the 19th century. Spend the night in Newport, and then a second night, if your interest in touring the mansions of Newport has absorbed an entire day. From Newport, head north back to Boston, stopping off en route to explore Providence, the capital of Rhode Island.

The Cape Cod Canal is only an hour's drive from Boston if you take the Southeast Expressway out of Boston and pick up Route 3 to the Cape. The bridge onto Cape Cod can also can be reached via the winding Route 3A, a slower road, which takes you through the coastal communities whose history and charm will make their way into your heart. (Note that the towns located along the 3A and Cape Cod are best and most easily visited outside commuter hours.) From Boston, follow signs onto the Southeast Expressway (I-93) to Quincy; and then take either the faster Route 3, or the more leisurely Route 3A, to the Sagamore Bridge and the beginning of the Cape.

On Route 3A, the towns of **Quincy**, **Cohasset**, **Duxbury**, and **Plymouth** are quaint: their main streets have been traveled for the last two centuries by horse, carriage, and now sport utility vehicle. It's worthwhile to stop in Plymouth at the historical sites of **Plymouth Rock**, where the Pilgrims first landed and see the replica of *Mayflower II*, the ship that brought the Pilgrims to Plymouth in 1620, and **Burial Hill**, the graveyard where many of the first settlers are buried. It is interesting to note that the fear of Indians at the time was so great that in order to disguise their dwindling numbers, settlers were buried in the dark of the night. The last gravestone dates to 1620. Take a stroll down Leyden Street, the oldest street in New England, and look across to Clark's Island, where the sick were once quarantined. Handsome, old homes still line the street, seemingly very little has changed from days gone by. You can almost envision someone walking down the street with a lantern, signaling the island that the mail and supplies are on the way, and to meet the boat at the halfway point. There are two museums, the **Mayflower Society Museum** and the **Pilgrim Hall Museum**.

Located three miles north of town on the Plymouth waterfront, the **Plimoth Plantation** is an absolutely incredible, living history museum that is a "must-see" and warrants no less than a half-day's visit. A re-creation of a 1627 Pilgrim village with homes, storehouses, animal pens, and fields planted for harvest stretch up the hillside from the water's edge and also includes the neighboring Wampanoag Indian community—**Hobbamock's Homesite**. To give you a perspective of time, the Mayflower landed seven years earlier than the date of this village, and Boston would not be founded for another three years after. If you have had an opportunity to visit Sturbridge or Williamsburg, they would not be settled for another 200 years. The docents that live and work at Plimoth Plantation are not just day actors, but rather, termed Time Travelers, who have dedicated years to studying a particular character. Admission to Plimoth Plantation is to experience their world. Talk with them about their passage, their hardships, their battles, their joy, and their lives. I promise you will believe you have traveled back in time. Note: It is possible to purchase an admission ticket valid for the Plantation, the Homesite and the Mayflower II. For more information, visit *www.plimoth.org*.

The **Sagamore Bridge** spans the **Cape Cod Canal**, which is used by shipping and pleasure craft to avoid circumnavigating the entire Cape on journeys between Boston and the coasts of Rhode Island, Connecticut, and states to the south. This is your entrance onto **Cape Cod** with its scenic character and unique charm. Almost immediately after crossing the bridge, exit Route 6 (the continuation of Route 3) onto Route 130, then 6A to the town of **Sandwich**, an excellent place to stop for the night (be sure to make advance reservations in season). The town is a charming one for wandering the streets and has two outstanding museums. The **Sandwich Glass Museum** (closed in January) displays the glass produced in Sandwich between 1825 and 1888—lamps, candlesticks, tiebacks, doorknobs, vases, and much more, which have become collectors' treasures. The **Heritage Plantation Museum**, founded with the generous contributions of the Lily family, has collections of early-American historical artifacts and folk art. There are extensive collections of firearms, cars, as well as folk art and an old-fashioned carousel. On the museum's grounds is an extensive rhododendron garden, which blooms each year from mid-May to mid-June—a "must" if you have an interest in gardening.

Leaving Sandwich, get onto Route 6A, the northern route along the upper coast of Cape Cod. It's a delightful road to follow as it winds its way through the lovely, historical towns of **Barnstable**, **Yarmouth Port**, **Dennis**, and **Brewster**. These old seafaring communities with their lovely main streets, beautiful homes, and colorful harbors make for a wonderful day of browsing, antiquing, and for just absorbing the atmosphere of the Cape. Continuing north through the towns of **Orleans** and **Eastham**, you come to the **Cape Cod National Seashore**, where you can take a fabulous dunes tour from April through October—a perfect way to see the ever-changing face of the sand dunes of this portion of the Cape. Farther on, at the tip of the Cape, is the artist community of **Provincetown**. **Chatham**, protected by the sandy, offshore barrier of Nauset Beach, remains an active fishing port.

Head south and travel along the south shore of Cape Cod on Route 28, which brings you into the more commercial area of the Cape—more traffic, more shops, and more restaurants, but also many inns and places to visit. **Hyannis** is the major shopping center for Cape Cod's residents and also the **summer home** of former president **John F. Kennedy**, where there is a small museum of photographs of the Kennedy family on summer vacations.

Before you return to the mainland, take the time to visit the enchanting islands of Nantucket and Martha's Vineyard. Leave your car in the parking lot at any one of the various departure points (Hyannis, Woods Hole, Falmouth, or New Bedford) from which airplane or ferry services (but not necessarily both) are available. Some ferries are catamarans and make very fast trips. The frequency of both air and ferry service depends on the season and the weather (on the day I was to go to Nantucket, fog prevented me from flying and I ended up taking the one-hour ferry from Hyannis). You can fly to Nantucket or Martha's Vineyard from Hyannis (the best and most frequent service), Providence, and Boston with Cape Air (800-352-0714), Island Airline (508-228-7575), and US Airways (800-428-4322). Ferries to Nantucket run from Hyannis (alternative departure points include Harwich Port and Martha's Vineyard). Hy-Line (508-778-2600) has a one-hour, high-speed catamaran, and the Steamship Authority runs a high-speed catamaran and other boats that take somewhat longer (508-495-FAST).

Nauset Light House, Eastham

Ferries to Martha's Vineyard leave from Falmouth, Hyannis, Woods Hole, New Bedford, and Nantucket. I suggest that you ask the staff at the inn where you are planning to stay for their recommendation of the best and fastest routes.

The two offshore islands of Nantucket and Martha's Vineyard were major whaling industry seaports from 1740 to 1830. The wealthy tradesmen who were associated with this very profitable venture built many of the magnificent homes along the streets of the seafaring ports of both islands.

Nantucket is perfect for exploring on foot or by bicycle (bicycles may easily be rented from one of the many shops near the ferry landing). The **Nantucket Historical Association** sells combination tickets to the historic houses and museums it manages, which include the **Whaling Museum**, the **Old Mill** (a 1746 windmill still being used to grind corn), **Old Gaol** (the original jail with its four cells), and the **Oldest House** on the island. Tickets are available at any of these locations. Along the town of Nantucket's cobblestoned, elm-shaded Main Street are many shops, art galleries, and very good restaurants, the latter specializing in the locally caught seafood. Of particular note are the **Three Bricks**, three stately mansions built by a wealthy merchant for his three sons. Nantucket is one of my all-time favorite places—I have been there in the summer; I have enjoyed a vacation in a rented cottage in October; and I have spent a New Year's weekend there. Each occasion was very special. Nantucket is simply one of those destinations whose ambiance and charm vary with the mood of the season—it is improved only by your having more time to spend there.

When it comes time to leave Nantucket, go on to Martha's Vineyard by boat or by plane, or return to the mainland.

Martha's Vineyard has a greater number of villages, so unless you are going to restrict your visit to the village where the ferry docks, you will either have to rent a car (my suggestion if you are planning to make more than just a brief visit) or take taxis to reach the various parts of the island. Of course, you can also rent a bicycle, but remember that the villages, which appear to be so close together on the map, are really several to many miles apart. If you fly to Martha's Vineyard, you will need to rent a car since the airport is some distance from the island's points of interest.

The ferry (from Wood's Hole, Hyannis, Falmouth, or Nantucket) will bring you into one of the three principal townships on Martha's Vineyard. Vineyard Haven, Oak Bluffs, and Edgartown are distinctly different from one another, although they are all fishing villages. **Vineyard Haven**, the principal entry point to the Vineyard and a source of rental cars or bicycles for touring the island, has a group of shops and restaurants, but very quickly changes into a rural landscape stretching along the coast with homes built in the 19th century. There is particular charm in the settlement of **Oak Bluffs**, a meeting place for Methodists in the late 19th and early 20th centuries. Around the meeting ground and the tabernacle that was built for these religious gatherings, a colony of small, wooden cottages decorated with gingerbread (Victorian lace-like) trim were built and painted in wonderfully vivid colors. **Edgartown** was the seaport from which the whalers left to hunt the elusive whale, and the island's mansions were built in this area. Be sure to visit **Gay Head** with its clay cliffs, which have stood high above the sea for the last 100 million years—their colors and majesty are memorable.

Returning either by boat or by plane to the mainland, drive west on Route 28 through Falmouth, picking up Route 25, which in turn connects to I-195. Look for the exit to Route 136 south and then Route 114 into **Newport**, Rhode Island. The homes built there in the 19th century for the wealthy to escape the oppressive summer heat of the south became the center of a social life never seen before or since. Today many of these homes are open to the public and tours give you a glimpse of the opulence of a bygone era. You can tour many of these homes. If you plan on visiting several, purchase a ticket that will allow you to visit two or eight of them. Among the "must-visit" mansions are: The Breakers, home of Cornelius Vanderbilt, The Marble House, built for William Vanderbilt, The Elms, and Rosecliff, used for the filming of *The Great Gatsby*. For details and tickets call 401-847-1000.

Take a bracing walk along the oceanfront, which hearkens the image of those halcyon days. This is a very special experience and you should plan to take an hour or several hours (perhaps as I did with a bottle of wine, some cheese, and a loaf of good bread) to enjoy this oceanfront path. With the ocean on one side and the fabulous homes on the other, this is a memorable experience. Today, many festivals take place in Newport including a music festival during the summer months.

Leaving Newport, head back north on Routes 114 and 136 to I-195 into **Providence**. With a concerned effort to bring back the ambiance of yesteryear, Providence is quickly becoming one of New England's most popular cities because of its historical charm. This is the capital city of Rhode Island. Three rivers weave a course through the heart of town and segment the key districts: the university quarter, the business, convention center and mall, and the seat of government with its **Capitol Building** and **State House**. The educational institutions of **Brown University** and the **Rhode Island School of Design** are located in a tree-shaded, residential neighborhood where there are many small cafés, bookstores, and little shops. At the Rhode Island School of Design, there is a museum with collections ranging from medieval to contemporary pieces; and in the nearby **John Brown House,** you can take a guided tour of this 18th-century brick museum with its fabulous collection of furniture belonging to the family. Business is the focus at the heart of town with the convention center, larger hotels, principal shopping mall and the Capitol Building dominating the northern hillside. If your visit falls on a weekend night in summer, you will be fortunate to experience **Waterfire**. A crowning tribute to Providence's renaissance, Waterfire is a living sculpture. An award-winning creation by sculpturer, Barnaby Evans, Waterfire pays homage to the importance of fire in human civilization as depicted in Greek mythology. Volunteers, clad in black, act as firetenders and ply the waters of the Woonasquatucket and Moshassuck Rivers in boats named after the gods, traveling from one of the 42 braziers to the next, igniting the wood set in the sculptures, sparking bonfires that crackle above the water passage. With a backdrop of enchanting music and the aromatic fragrance of wood smoke, this is a hauntingly memorable experience.

Leaving Providence, drive north on I-95 to Route 128, the circumferential route around the city of Boston, and follow the signs to Boston. This is about an hour's drive, unless you hit rush hour.

If you plan to connect with another of the itineraries in the southern part of New England, drive southwest from the Providence area on I-95 along the coast of Connecticut into the area of the Connecticut River Valley.

Sand Dunes on the Massachusetts Shore

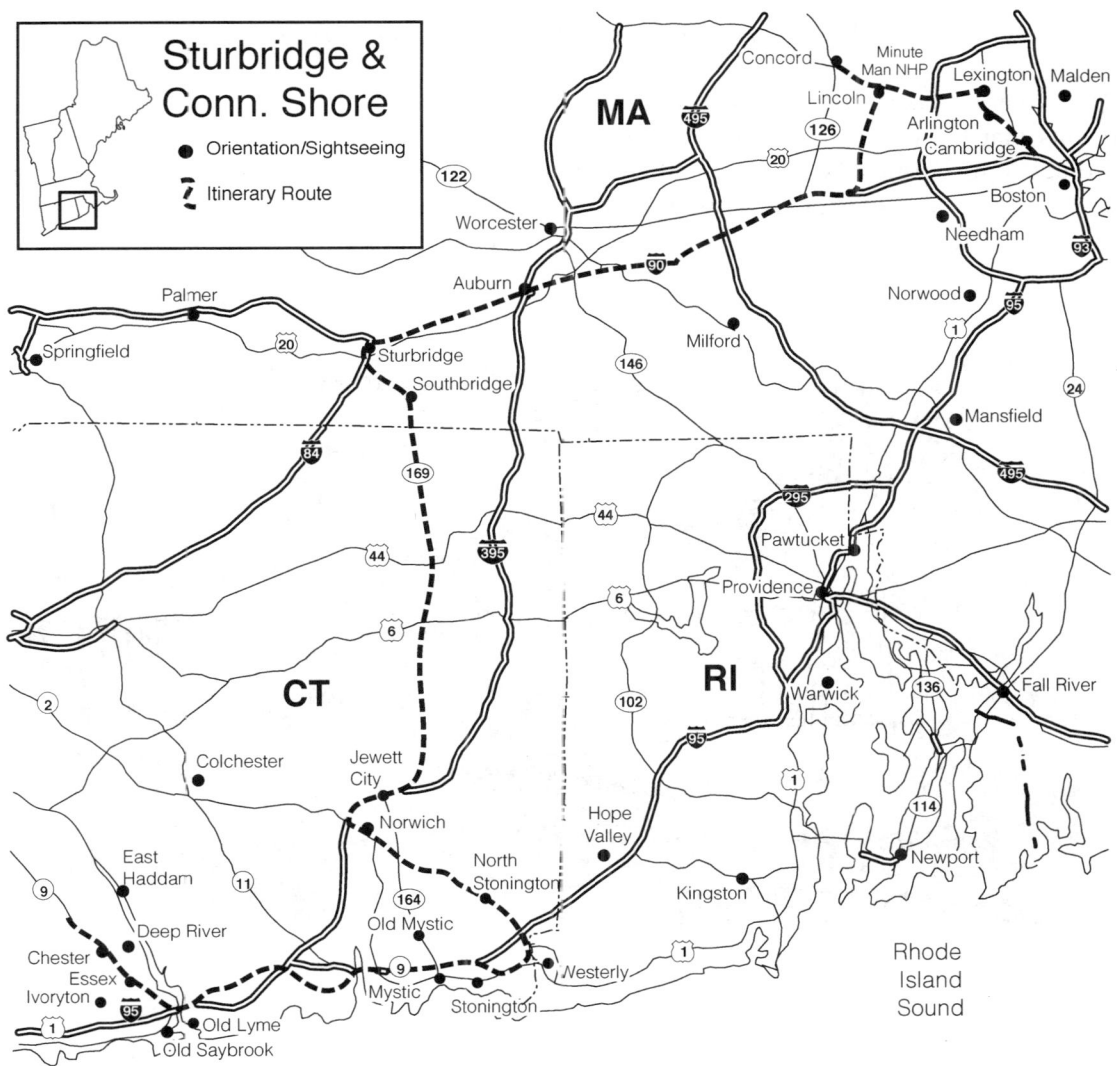

Sturbridge & the Connecticut Shore

This itinerary takes the traveler from Boston to Lexington and Concord, sites of historical events that led to the founding of the Colonies, and from there, westward to Sturbridge Village and south to the Connecticut shoreline, with a visit to Mystic Seaport. This is an especially good route for those with children, since the historical sites have guides who theatrically depict the events that took place in days of yore.

Mystic Seaport

Recommended Pacing: (The routing for this itinerary is also outlined on Maps 1 and 2 at the back of the book.) The Lexington and Concord portion of this itinerary is an easy daytrip from Boston, since this area is only about an hour's drive from the city. Alternatively, you can overnight here or go on to Sturbridge, a little less than an hour away, and sleep there. Plan on spending one full day in Sturbridge before heading for the Connecticut shore, about an hour and a half beyond Sturbridge. You will definitely want to include at least one night based on the coast in order to adequately explore the towns of Essex, Old Lyme, and Mystic with its wonderful "living museum," Mystic Seaport.

Fall foliage touring in this area is ideal for those who want to do a day trip to see what New England is so famous for. There is no prettier area for seeing color in the trees than in the towns to the West of Boston. Couple the history of this area with the beauty of the countryside as the leaves begin to turn, and you have a very special itinerary. This foliage trip can also be the beginning of a visit to areas beyond the towns west of Boston, down into Connecticut, and to the shore towns along the Connecticut River.

Today, Lexington and Concord are residential suburbs of Boston, but their place in history has linked them together for over 200 years. It was here, in April 1775, that the Colonial troops fought with the British in skirmishes that eventually led to the **American Revolution**. That story comes alive in the preservation of the sites and monuments, and in the annual April 19th re-creation of those important events. In areas now designated as national parks, guides relate the events that led to the revolution giving the visitor, young and old, a graphic understanding of what took place during that momentous time. Perhaps the most famous story is that of **Paul Revere's** horseback ride from Boston to Lexington and Concord—to warn of the impending attack by the British—which enabled the colonists to meet the challenge and drive them back.

To reach Lexington, leave Boston on Storrow Drive and then follow signs to Route 2, which takes you from Boston west through Cambridge and Arlington. Exit Route 2 in Arlington on Route 60 to Route 2A, which will take you into the center of **Lexington**. Lexington's village green, with its several monuments to the April 19th rout of the British

The Old North Bridge

who fled back to Boston, is surrounded by lovely homes. There are a few shops and restaurants where you can refresh yourself after walking around the historic area.

Leaving Lexington, continue along Route 2A to **Concord** and visit the area where the battle at the **Old North Bridge** between the British and the Minutemen took place. The **Minutemen**, so called because of their willingness to pick up arms on a minute's notice to defend against injustices inflicted by the British government, drove the British soldiers back through Lexington and on to Boston. At the **Old North Bridge Visitor Center** there is a replica of the "bridge that arched the flood" and a national park ranger recounts the story.

The **Minuteman National Historic Park** between the towns of Lexington, Lincoln, and Concord has a Minuteman Visitor Center showing a movie that re-creates that period.

The **Concord Museum**, in the town center, houses 19 galleries with furnishings of the revolutionary period and the century that followed. What is particularly interesting in this museum is that each room represents a different period. As you tour these various rooms, guides explain the evolving style of decoration and life as it was lived at the time. Other interesting stops include **Orchard House**, home of Louisa May Alcott, author of *Little Women*, the home of the poet **Ralph Waldo Emerson**, and **Walden Pond** where Henry David Thoreau lived and wrote. **Sleepy Hollow Cemetery**, the ancient burial ground for many of these famous citizens, is a suitable finale to the Concord tour.

From Concord, Route 126 leads south to the Massachusetts Turnpike (I-90), which is the fastest way to reach **Sturbridge**, less than an hour away. The town itself is worth a stop. Beautiful, old houses line the common or central lawn, the old tavern still serves fine food in an ambiance of the past, and the cemetery with tombstones that date back hundreds of years identify and lend tribute to many of the original settlers. On the outskirts of town is the **Old Sturbridge Village**, a living-history museum, you should allow a full day to explore the re-creation of life as it was lived in the first half of the 19th century. Costumed actors inhabit the village by day, wandering the streets, manning the stores, and tending to the tasks of yesteryear. They bring history to life.

There are more than 40 staffed exhibits, homes, craft shops, mills, and farm buildings on more than 200 acres of fields and farmland. Among my favorite buildings is the clock gallery where many different types of timepieces are on display. In addition to the one-room schoolhouse, the mills, and the demonstrations of shoemaking and cooking over a wood fire, there are seasonal exhibits of sheep shearing, apple pressing, and maple sugaring. For children, there is a special educational program providing hands-on activities. Be sure to wear comfortable walking shoes.

From Sturbridge, the scenic Route 169 leads south toward the Connecticut shore. However, if time is of the essence, I recommend Route 20 from Sturbridge northeast to Auburn, picking up I-395 south to Jewett City, and then Route 164 into **Mystic Village Seaport**, a stop that appeals to both parents and children alike. Ever since the 17th century, Mystic has been the area's center of shipbuilding and of maritime commerce. It is now a museum village depicting life as it was in this earlier time. At the visitor center a movie is shown that introduces you to the town—an excellent way to begin your visit. Many clipper ships were built in this port in the middle of the 19th century and here you find several examples of the vessels of that era. Of the three fully rigged sailing craft moored at the docks, particularly interesting—and open for tours—is the ***Charles W. Morgan***, the last of the 19th-century whaling ships surviving today. Don't miss the shops of the craftsmen who made the materials used in the construction and the sailing of these vessels. There is a **Children's Museum** where you can enjoy the activities and games played on board ship.

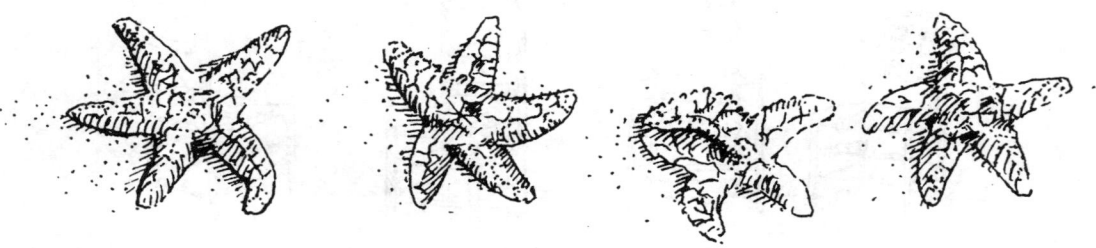

In the **Stillman Building**, visitors can watch a ten-minute film describing the adventure of whale hunting on the open sea.

If you have time, a drive through the **Connecticut River Valley** is most relaxing. To reach the towns along the Connecticut River, take I-95 south to Route 9 north, and exit immediately for Essex. The valley has along its banks a number of lovely Colonial seafaring towns where white clapboard homes, churches, and town greens are still very much in evidence. There are old shops and pubs, and a number of art galleries reflecting the love that so many artists have for this area. Be sure to visit **Essex** and drive the broad tree-lined main streets of **Lyme** and **Old Lyme**. In season, there is a steam train running from Essex to **Chester** (about an hour's trip) enabling you to enjoy the Connecticut River Valley at its best. A riverboat trip from **Deep River** to **East Haddam** can be either a separate trip or combined with the train excursion. In the town of East Haddam, during the months of April through December, the **Goodspeed Opera House** is the home of musicals being previewed for the legitimate theatre and revivals of some of America's most beloved plays.

You have several options at the end of this itinerary: return to Boston going northeast on I-95 along the Connecticut and Rhode Island coasts through Providence (about two and a half hours); go north to I-91 to visit northern New England; or travel west on I-95 along the coast of lower Connecticut to Norwalk, where you can join the itinerary *Route 7 & Much More* through the western part of Connecticut, Massachusetts, and Vermont. If you are leaving New England, continue southwest along the I-95 to the airports of La Guardia and Kennedy.

Sturbridge & the Connecticut Shore

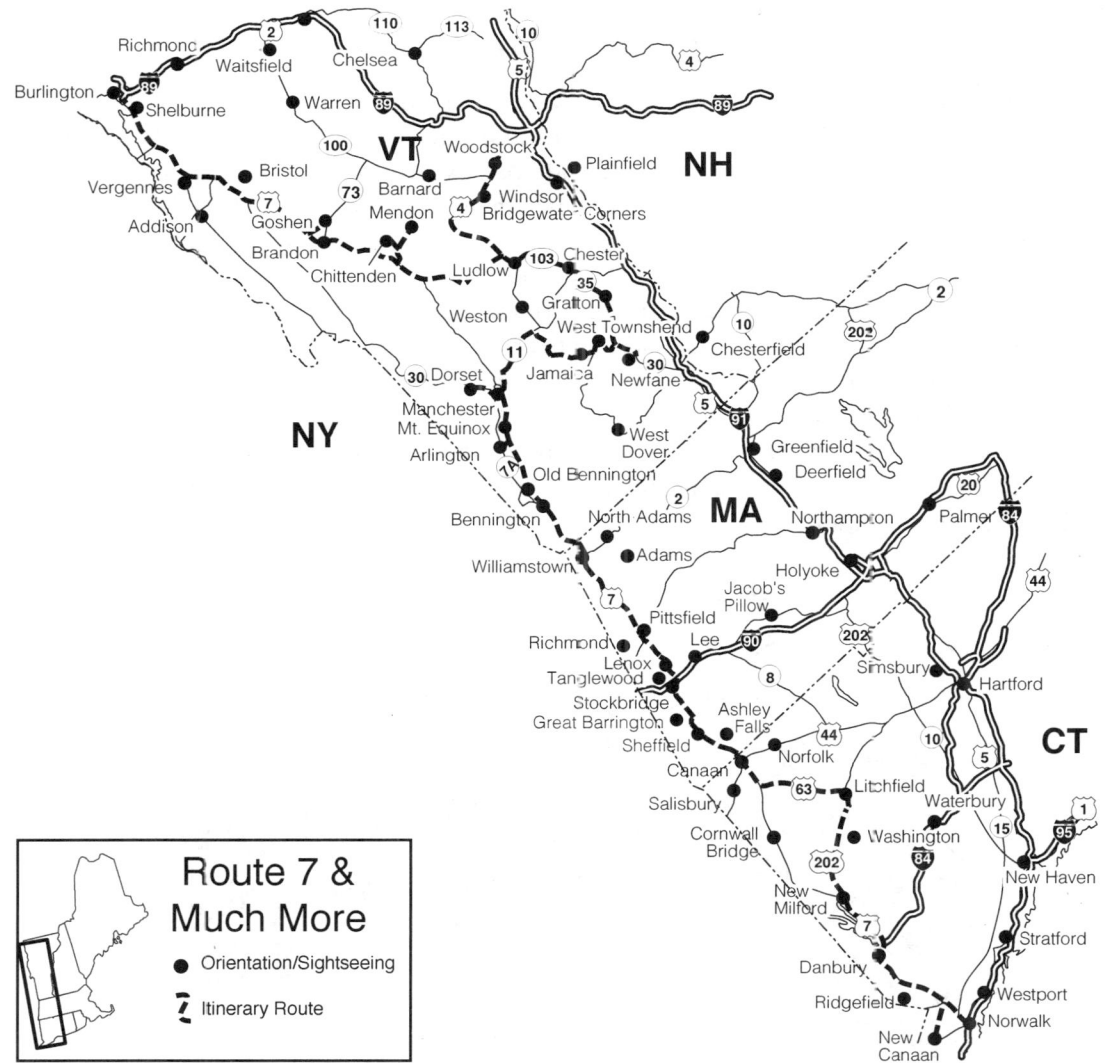

Route 7 & Much More

A trip to New England should include a drive along the western edge of the region through the states of Connecticut, Massachusetts, and Vermont. Fortunately, Route 7 follows the contours of this western edge almost exactly and is the backbone of this itinerary. The "much more" portion comes in when you cross the Green Mountains to visit the towns of Newfane, Townshend, and West Townshend. If you're interested in antiques, there is no drive with more "opportunities" waiting than this one. If what appeals to you is the charm of countryside, field, and farm; the rural character of this route will delight you. Pretty, little towns appearing around bends in the road after miles of countryside present farmhouses, stately mansions, and summer cottages—each with its own brand of charm. Plan on being in one of these towns to share the experience of Memorial Day or the Fourth of July; when the schoolchildren parade, the girl and boy scouts march, the high-school band plays, the hardware store mans a float, and the fire engine screams its presence.

Route 7 & Much More

Recommended Pacing: (The routing for this itinerary is also outlined on Maps 1 and 3 at the back of the book.) Allow five nights to complete this itinerary, four if you do not cross over the Green Mountains but continue up Route 7. Spend the first night in the northwest corner of Connecticut in Norfolk. Then the following day, continue north across the border into Massachusetts, luxuriating in the beauty of the Berkshires. Settle for the night in Stockbridge or Lenox. Continue north to Williamstown, and then into Vermont to overnight in Manchester or Dorset. Cross over the Green Mountains and visit the towns of Newfane, Townshend, and West Townshend. Plan to spend the night in one of these towns where there's an inn that is certain to appeal to you. On day five, conclude this itinerary either by driving north and east to Woodstock, or to Shelburne with its wonderful museum.

It's important to realize that the number of miles to be driven during any one of these days is not great—to emphasize the point they are noted below (all approximate):

Norwalk to Norfolk—80 miles
Norfolk to Stockbridge—30 miles
Stockbridge to Manchester—70 miles
Manchester to Townshend—40 miles
Townshend to Woodstock—65 miles
Townshend to Shelburne—160 miles

This itinerary has no prescribed "sightseeing" or "timetable," rather, it affords the opportunity to "experience" New England. You set the specifics. You can decide to meander along at a leisurely pace—pause in front of the post office and walk through the village; look at the plaque that dates a home; go into the local drug store where, if you are lucky, there will be a row of counter stools to sit and have an ice-cream soda. Wander into the antique stores for the experience of seeing your grandmother's pitcher or the old kitchen spatula. Buy a postcard to send to a friend, a gift for a loved one, or a memento to take home.

If your trip is focused on fall foliage, there can be no better route to follow than this one, for as the leaves of the trees change from green to red, yellow, and orange, you can follow the line of frost and the magic of a countryside in vivid color.

This is New England at its best. This is not the New England where great events of history shaped the founding of the Colonies, or the New England where you walk the beach and squiggle your toes in the sand, dodging the breaking waves. This is the heart of the New England states: where farmers grew their crops, where school was in one room, where the inns usually had a pub, and where having a meal at the place you slept was customary.

Join Route 7 at its southernmost point in **Norwalk**, Connecticut. If you have just completed the itinerary that ends in the Connecticut River Valley, it will take no more than two hours to reach Norwalk and to begin the route north. If shopping in an upscale suburban community is what you feel like during the morning, go to **New Canaan** on Route 106 and visit galleries, antique stores, and other high-end shopping. New Canaan is the home of the **Silvermine Guild of Artists** with studios for studying and creating many different forms of art. Every May and June the Guild exhibits works by its members. Taking Route 106 from New Canaan back to Route 7 will put you on the path to Ridgefield, which will be the second detour—and you've hardly begun! **Ridgefield** is only an hour north of New York, but you would never know it from the rural character of this lovely town. Old trees line the streets and front the gracious homes, many of which date back to the 18th and early 19th centuries. Here you will find the **Aldrich Museum of Contemporary Art**, where changing exhibits display the work of today's contemporary artists.

Back on Route 7, proceed north through Danbury and above New Milford take Route 202 to **Litchfield**. With its village green and surrounding homes dating back to the 18th century, there is no prettier town in all of Connecticut. The **Litchfield First Congregational Church** is an architectural treasure, and if you are traveling here in the autumn, the church framed by the seasonal color of the trees will be one of your most memorable photographs. Return north on Route 63 to South Canaan and Canaan, then drive west on Route 44 to **Salisbury**, yet another charmer.

The Berkshires

Cross into Massachusetts and in the towns of **Ashley Falls**, **Sheffield**, and **Great Barrington**, you find a bounty of antique shops. Referring to a local guide, available in most of these shops in the Route 7 area, will enable you to concentrate on those stores most likely to have the treasure missing from your collection. If you're not an antique lover, enjoy the towns—stop and wander about, have coffee or a bite to eat at one of the local eateries, and just absorb the charm. Ashley Falls is tiny, Sheffield is mid-size, and Great Barrington tends to be the "papa bear" of these three towns and the convenient center with a hardware store and larger supermarkets.

Just 7 miles north of Great Barrington is **Stockbridge**, that grand old dame of the Berkshires. Whether you stay here or in one of the surrounding towns matters not, for there is much to do in this area. The village of Stockbridge, with its broad Main Street, lovely old trees, and one beautiful old home after another, is worth a full day. At the top of the list is a visit to the **Norman Rockwell Museum**, which houses the largest collection of the work of this famous American artist. Many pieces were used on the covers of the *Saturday Evening Post* and his depictions of everyday life ring true and close to home with any viewer. Smiles are difficult to repress! In a totally different vein is **Chesterwood**, the estate of Daniel Chester French, the creator of the monument to the Minutemen in Concord, Massachusetts and, more importantly, the sculpture of Abraham Lincoln in Washington, D.C. If you want to enjoy the music of the Boston Symphony Orchestra at the **Tanglewood Music Festival**, held each summer since the 1930s, then you need to make plans to extend your stay. There are several halls in which these musical events take place, but there is nothing like sitting on the lawn with a picnic supper and a bottle of wine for a relaxing summer evening enjoying beautiful music. This is an experience not to be missed. Also in this area are the **Jacob's Pillow Dance Festival**, the **South Mountain Concert Festival**, and summer theatre at the **Berkshire Playhouse** in Stockbridge. The **Williamstown Theatre** is a little more than 30 miles to the north, also on Route 7.

Head north toward the border of Massachusetts and Vermont. Along the way plan to visit the **Hancock Shaker Village**, located outside of **Pittsfield**, and then (one of my all-time favorites) the **Sterling and Francine Clark Institute** in **Williamstown**. This treasure, built by its donors in a town far away from urban centers that at the time might be threatened by war, has collections ranging from the Renaissance to the great American painters of the 19th and 20th centuries. There are also displays of furniture and porcelain, and (my particular favorite) a wonderful collection of English and American silver. Do find the time for this visit as it's an extraordinary one—a major museum in a spectacular countryside setting.

Leaving Williamstown, cross into Vermont and head for **Old Bennington**, a charming village dating back to the 18th century and steeped in Colonial history, which lies 9 miles to the west of the commercial town of **Bennington** on Route 9. Allow time for the walking tour (maps available at the Chamber of Commerce) including the **Old First Church**, the **Bennington Battle Monument**, and the **Grandma Moses Schoolhouse**, where you can see several paintings of the well-known artist who started painting at the age of 70 and continued painting until she was 101. As a fan of folk art, I find that the primitive-style paintings of Grandma Moses with their naïve renderings of farm and country life (particularly those in winter) to be extraordinarily charming.

Continuing north on Route 7 brings you into the town of **Arlington**. At this point, take Route 7A towards Manchester, detouring for a short sidetrip along the scenic Equinox Skyline Drive, a 5½-mile drive to the top of **Mount Equinox**, the highest point in the Taconic Range. Views from the summit are especially wonderful in the fall when the foliage is at its best. **Manchester** and **Manchester Center** have lovely old homes sitting along their main streets. In Manchester Center, there is now a grand array of brand-name outlet shops. From Manchester Center, follow Route 30 for 8 miles into **Dorset**, a small village with lovely, white clapboard homes, church, and village green (a favorite of mine). Whether you're visiting in winter with the town dressed in white, in summer with the fragrance of freshly mown grass in the air and the Dorset Playhouse presenting summer theatre, or in fall when frost coats the pumpkins and turns the leaves into magical colors, you're in for a special treat when you visit Dorset.

Leaving Dorset, you pass through more of the same bucolic countryside—farms and fields, rolling hills and valleys, rushing streams, sturdy stone walls, and towering trees—a photographer's paradise at any time of the year. Take Route 11 to Londonderry and turn south on Route 100 to **Jamaica**, **West Townshend**, **Townshend**, and on to **Newfane**. Retrace your steps back to Townshend and head north to **Grafton**, **Chester**, and **Ludlow**. This is a winding and relatively narrow route that will enhance your appreciation of the special, unique qualities of Vermont villages. The **Green Mountains** are home to some of New England's oldest and most famous ski areas—many a youngster has learned ski technique here. Each mountain has its own distinctive style of skiing and skiers often will have their favorite. Studying the individual ski area descriptions of elevation, number of trails, degree of difficulty, and overall size should make a decision easier as to which to visit. As always, the mid-week package lift ticket is the most economical way to enjoy skiing on any mountain. Don't count these areas out at other times of the year—many of them run their ski lifts for visitors in the fall when the foliage can be enjoyed from a unique perspective on high.

From Ludlow, you can easily conclude this itinerary in **Woodstock** by driving north on Route 100 to West Bridgewater then turning east on Route 4. Ever since the 18th century Woodstock has been a magnet for merchants, professionals, and those who wish to live in a sophisticated community. The homes, of many architectural styles, are a legacy of those prosperous citizens. Today this village is not only the commercial center for this area of Vermont, but also provides upscale shopping in its many stores and galleries.

If you are staying with this itinerary, turn west from Ludlow to Route 7 following it north towards **Burlington** on Lake Champlain and detouring along the way to visit **Mendon**, **Chittenden**, and **Goshen** before arriving in **Shelburne**. Be sure to visit the **Shelburne Museum** with its incredible collection of folk art and displays of the crafts, furnishings, art, and tools used in the early years of the 20th century. The complex consists of 37 buildings on a 45-acre setting that is open from late May to late October. A visit to this museum is all but a must, if you can add this extra day to your itinerary. There is the Circus Parade Building, the Shelburne Railroad Station, the *Ticonderoga* (a side-wheeler steamship), the Stencil House displaying decorative wall stenciling, the Colchester Reef Lighthouse with its collection of marine art, the Stagecoach Inn, and the Electra Havemeyer Webb Memorial Building with a re-creation of rooms from the Webbs' Park Avenue apartment. With this small sampling of the contents of the Shelburne Museum, you can see that it would be easy to spend more than one day exploring even a portion of what's here for your enjoyment. You can overnight either in the Shelburne area or nearby **Warren** or **Waitsfield**.

This itinerary ends here, but if your travel time permits, consider continuing to the east and spending time in New Hampshire.

Marblehead Harbor, Maine

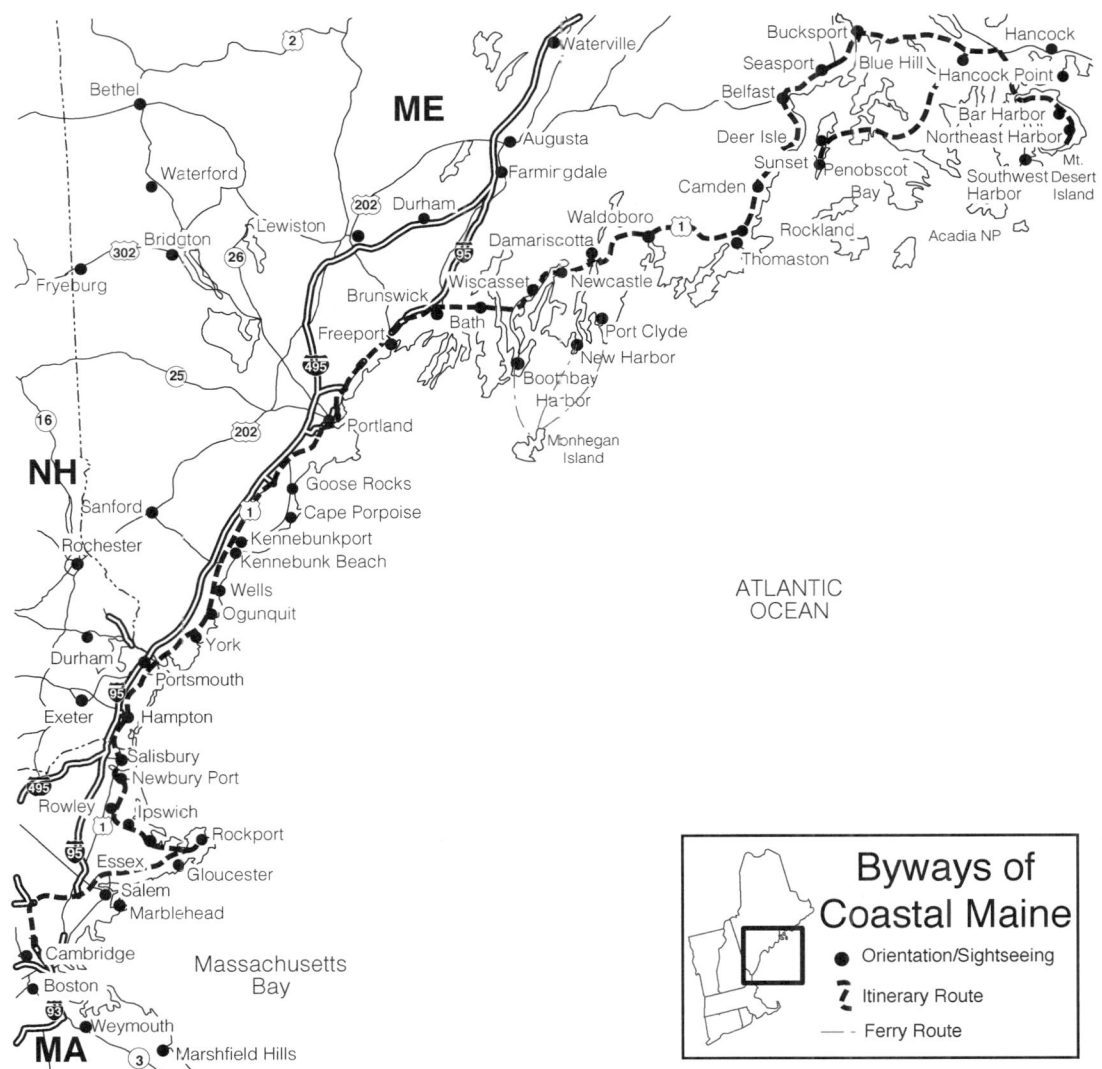

The Byways of Coastal Maine

There are many wonderful itineraries in New England and none are more different than the trip up the coast of Maine with its rugged beauty and picturesque charm. In the lower portions of the coast, the seaside villages are all relatively near the road, while above Portland the geology of the ice age created long fingers into the sea as the ice retreated, and you have to travel miles down winding backcountry roads to reach the tips of some peninsulas. What makes this itinerary so special is the fact that your pace is, by necessity, very leisurely since the roads wind from one lovely town or harbor to the next. You couldn't drive fast if you wanted to—and, believe me, you won't want to.

The Byways of Coastal Maine

Recommended Pacing: (The routing for this itinerary is also outlined on Map 4, as well as briefly referred to on Maps 2 and 3—all at the back of the book.) There is no perfect way to follow this itinerary. Where you spend your time will be dictated by your personal interests. Allow a minimum of six nights—five, if you do not visit Salem and Marblehead. If you choose to visit Salem and Marblehead, spend your first night here. Day two takes you to Rockport and Gloucester and the small villages in the northeastern part of Massachusetts. After which you enter New Hampshire and quickly cross over the Merrimack River into Maine, where you stay overnight in the area of York or Kennebunkport. Continue north through Portland and Bath to the lovely village of Wiscasset and spend the night there. The following day, your drive takes you through Rockland to Camden, a favorite spot on the Maine coast and one of the most charming towns in which to spend the night. Conclude your itinerary in Bar Harbor with a two-night stay, allowing time to explore the Acadia National Park.

Magnificent, old trees sit beside the roads with their branches hanging over the passing vehicles; houses are white and old barns have mellowed with the weather to soft browns and grays; and, everywhere, there are views down saltwater inlets, views that change with the rise and fall of the ocean tides. These wonderful trees open their bright, green leaves later in the spring than in the more southerly parts of New England, as winter and its snowy ground cover continues its hold in this northern territory. It's said that to plant before the last full moon in May (generally around Memorial Day weekend) is foolish indeed, as there is always that one last frost which will nip your early gardening enthusiasm.

Fall foliage along the coast of Maine is often interspersed with the Maine pines, which tend, in the more southerly areas of the State, to predominate. It is only when one reaches north of Portland that the traveler gets the best of both, the craggy coast with its tiny inlets and sparkling blue waters, and the rippling colors of trees as they begin to turn into brilliant, autumn colors.

As you travel on the back roads and byways of Maine, be sure to stop at the farm stands which open in the late spring with strawberries, garden peas, and sweet peas, and

The Byways of Coastal Maine

continue into the bounty of summer produce, and then in the fall with the arrival of pumpkins, Indian corn, and interestingly shaped gourds.

However, before you reach this magical coast of Maine, you must take the time to visit Salem and Marblehead, where history buffs will find much to enjoy while walking the streets and learning about the lives of the citizens who lived in these communities over two centuries ago. Rockport and Gloucester offer visitors the opportunity to see the arts, antiques, and scenic harbors that make this part of Cape Ann so charming. Leave Boston on I-93 north, turning onto the circumferential Route 128 and I-95. Shortly after you have turned east on I-95 and are headed towards the north shore of Massachusetts, you find signs that will take you, via Route 114, towards Salem and Marblehead.

Salem, famous in the late 17th century for witchcraft hysteria, is well known now as the home of the **Peabody Essex Museum**, a superlative museum where you can easily spend several hours viewing the exhibits on the maritime history of the Massachusetts Bay Colony. The focus is on objects collected by the ship captains of Salem on their voyages delivering the colony's goods to the capitals of Europe and Asia. Of particular note is the Asian export art collection (decorative art made in Asia for export to the West), considered to be the most complete of any in the world, featuring 17th- through 19th-century decorative and utilitarian objects used in homes and businesses. There is also a great collection of maritime art, as well as a focus on Asian, Oceanic, and African art, and Native American arts and archaeology. The **Witch Museum** offers exhibits and a sound and light show with vignettes of the witch trials of 1692. **Chestnut Street** is lined with mansions built by ship captains that reflect the wealth of that era and the shipping trade. Salem is also famous as the home of the **House of Seven Gables**, where tours bring to life the scenes from Hawthorne's famous novel of the same name. **Pioneer Village** (open from May through October) is a re-creation of buildings that existed in the early days of the settlement of Salem. There are houses with thatched roofs, dugouts, and a wigwam. Interpreters dressed in costume explain the daily life of Salem's early settlers.

A visit to the North Shore would not be complete without a drive to **Marblehead**, and a walk in the historic district dating back to the 17th and 18th centuries when Marblehead's harbor was, as it is today, a hive of activity. In fact, Marblehead is known as the sailing capital of New England. On summer weekends, you can see sailing yachts of every size and description racing and cruising in the waters of the harbor and nearby ocean from many vantage points.

If you've spent the night in the Salem and Marblehead area, you'll now be facing the choice of a second day on the North Shore or moving onward into Maine. I recommend that you drive to **Gloucester** to visit **Beauport**, the **Cape Ann Historical Museum**, and, if time permits, the **Hammond Castle Museum**. My favorite of these three is Beauport, the 40-room home designed and decorated by Henry Davis Sleeper. Beauport is open from May to September and guided one-hour tours are available. If decor is of interest to you, this visit would be one you'll never forget. This is one of the many fine houses that are owned by the **SPNEA** (Society for the Preservation of New England Antiquities) and a tour of several of these properties throughout New England would be well worth an itinerary all of its own. For details contact SPNEA at 617-227-3956, or visit their website at *www.spnea.com*.

After you leave Gloucester, take Route 127A to **Rockport**. This part of **Cape Ann** is the site of an artists' colony and its galleries. Surrounding shops are very busy during the summer months with visitors enjoying the scenery of the old fishing village and harbor. In the harbor, one scene of an old fishing building and wharf has become so famous that it is known as "Motif # 1" to artists around the world.

Leaving the Cape Ann peninsula on Route 133, you drive through the town of **Essex**, famous for its several antique shops, where you may find some treasure to take home. If traveling on a Wednesday or Thursday between May and September, you would be well rewarded to detour out to **The Great House** on the 2,100-acre **Crane Estate**. Presiding over rolling hills, quiet woods, open meadows, salt marshes, and miles of sandy beach and estuary islands, this 59-room mansion was built by Richard Crane and is preserved as a National Historic Landmark. (Note: the gate house of the Crane Estate has guestrooms available to travelers. See the Hotel Section for its description and more information.)

From Essex, Route 133 connects to Route 1A through the town of Rowley and onto **Newburyport** with its magnificent High Street, another town made famous by its shipping history and the homes of those associated with that very prosperous trade.

Exit the Maine Turnpike (I-95, the fast interstate highway) onto Route 1 (the road that connects one old historical town to the next) as soon as you can—the exit from the turnpike in York is a perfect place to begin this journey. In this lower part of Maine you will find yourself less than a mile from the coast, so driving in and out of the little coastal villages is quick and easy. If you can begin this itinerary in Maine with a drive through **York** and **York Harbor**, it's a nice way to start to relax and see the sights, and experience the sounds and smell of the ocean. You'll also begin to see some color in the foliage of the deciduous trees in these charming villages. There are a number of **antique shops** all along Route 1. Lower Maine has several collectives (where several dealers, rather than one, display their merchandise) in the York area.

Continuing north from the Yorks brings you to **Ogunquit**, which, in the language of the American Indian tribe of the Algonquins, means "beautiful place by the sea." The long, narrow harbor is especially scenic, and while you may not see the lobster boats depart early in the morning, you can catch them returning in the afternoon with a following of inquisitive sea gulls seeking a free dinner. Because of the attractiveness of this area, many artists settled here—the subjects for their art are everywhere. The Ogunquit Playhouse offers theater performances on summer evenings.

Traffic along Route 1, as you drive north to Wells, can be especially tedious—even more so on a foggy or rainy day, when all the tourists are searching for entertainment and are visiting the concentration of outlet shops at the southern end of this route. I'd suggest, if at all possible, avoiding this drive at the beginning or the end of the beach day, when those who have spent the day on the sand and in the ocean find their way to restaurants, grocery stores, and back to their overnight accommodations.

In the town of **Wells** there's a real concentration of antique shops offering formal and country furniture and decorative objects. Just north of Wells, Route 9 breaks off to the town of **Kennebunkport**, and I strongly recommend that you drive into "the Port," as the locals call it. This is a storybook village, but was originally a fishing port. In the fall, the ancient trees on its main streets pour forth with gorgeous colors of red, yellow, orange, and everything in-between. You can still see the lobstermen go out to sea each day to empty their traps and to bait them for the next day's catch. Kennebunkport has become a tourist mecca, especially for its shops. To absorb the charm of this town with its lovely stately homes and elm-tree-lined streets, allow time to include a walking tour of the town center. Afterwards, find a spot to have a cup of New England clam chowder or a Maine lobster. One of the sights outside the town is the **Wedding Cake House** on Route 9A, which, as the stories go, was decorated with all manner of gingerbread trim by a sea captain who was called to sea immediately after his wedding.

Just north of Kennebunkport, taking Ocean Avenue first east and then north from the village, you come to the **summer home** of the 41st president of the United States, **George Bush**. Shortly thereafter, along Route 9, you reach **Cape Porpoise**, which exudes all the ambiance of a tiny fishing community with houses set on hills looking down on its lobster boats and other small craft. It's tiny and will take only a short time to visit, but it's charming. Make sure to take the time to drive through the village and out to the point from which you can see the lighthouse just off shore. Back on Route 9, you continue north a few miles to a barn on your left with a clock tower and a somewhat confusing sign on your right that points to the beach called **Goose Rocks**. With one tiny store, this beach is a magnificent 2-mile-long stretch of sand—a rarity on the rocky coast of Maine. If you're able to linger here, you become immediately aware that the tides on this northeast coast rise and fall 10 feet or more with each change of tide, so the beach you walk at low tide will become much narrower as the tide comes in. If you put a toe into the water, you quickly learn that swimming on the coast of Maine takes a degree of courage!

From Goose Rocks, drive north on Route 9 to Route 1 north, and then take I-95 onward to Portland. With its population of about 65,000, the city of **Portland** is the largest town you come to as you go northward along the coast. The port is an important one for the fishing industry and the city has become the center for commercial business in northern New England. This is a city that is perfect for sightseeing on foot since all the interesting spots are within a short distance of one another. There is also an advantage to walking as the pace allows you to study the architecture and permits the occasional glimpse into a hidden garden here and there. The downtown area of Portland has been revitalized and many of the historical buildings have been rehabilitated. There are many great restaurants and lots of shopping in boutiques known for their handcrafts. Portland has a great historical area and is a regional center for the arts. The **Museum of Art** focuses on artists of the state of Maine, and there are wonderful paintings by Winslow Homer, Andrew Wyeth, Edward Hopper, and John Marin. For those interested in seeing more of **Casco Bay**, there are seasonal, daily trips by boat to view the islands, though it is not always possible to disembark.

Portland Head Lighthouse

From Portland, you can take a ferry to Nova Scotia; but unless your time is very limited, I suggest you continue a little farther north by car along the coast to Bar Harbor. This is well worth the time, and from there it is a much shorter sea trip to reach the maritime provinces.

About 12 miles northeast of Portland, off the I-95, is the town of **Freeport**, made famous by the **L. L. Bean store** which is open 24 hours a day. Here you can find everything from a canoe or camp stove to a ski cap. This famous institution has now expanded into selling almost anything you can use in your home. Freeport has also become home to more than 120 brand-name outlet stores of every type. If shopping is your thing, this is the place to "shop till you drop." Of greater interest to me is the **Desert of Maine**, a phenomenon of former forest where the winds of time have laid bare more than 500 acres of sand, now formed into sand dunes—in an area nowhere near the sea. To reach and view this phenomenon (open from early May until mid-October), take I-95 to exit 19 and then drive 2 miles west on Desert Road.

North of Freeport is the community of **Brunswick**, home of **Bowdoin College** and the **Bowdoin College Museum of Art** with its collections of early-American portraits and (annually from mid-May until mid-August) a display of the paintings, etchings, and memorabilia of the artist Winslow Homer. The particular focus of much of his work was the coast and lore of Maine, so this becomes a topical experience for those interested in the work of this very famous American artist.

Just north of Brunswick, Route 1 begins its coastal-hugging path toward Bar Harbor, still 150 miles to the north. Long fingers of land stretch out into the sea, and a trip down any of these will bring great pleasure as you meander along winding, tree-lined roads between one small fishing village and the next. The village of **Bath** has been a shipbuilding center for hundreds of years, and its harbor hosts the relics of schooners from long ago. You can see ships in dry dock being repaired, in mothballs, or in the process of being built. As you view the wide harbor, it's easy to imagine a time when commercial ships sailed from this port to the European capitals, the Far East, and to the West Indies. In Bath, a visit to the **Maine Maritime Museum**, with its exhibits on coastal life, the shipbuilding industry, and the commerce of Maine, would provide an interesting diversion for both adults and children. There is a movie on the lobstering industry, as well as exhibits in a sail loft. During the summer, you can take a boat ride on the **Kennebec River** to observe the boat-building industry as it exists today.

Proceed north across the bridge to the town of **Wiscasset**, one of my very favorite villages in all of New England—I especially love its long street leading down to the water. There could be no prettier village in which to take in fall foliage that Wiscasset. Magically, the natural beauty of the homes along its streets are enhanced that much more when the colors of fall foliage play off the sparking white clapboard exteriors. This is a community with tree-lined streets, white churches, and lovely old homes dating back to the 18th century. It's also a terrific and popular center for antiquing, with an emphasis on country things rather than formal. In the winter, the pace is slower with the fickle weather, and some dealers open and others not.

Beyond Wiscasset, you are now in one of the most famous of all Maine regions— **Boothbay Harbor**. With a year-round population of only a couple of thousand, this is an area that can absorb the summer residents, the visitors staying the night, and those who will simply be passing through on the way north or south. Charm is at every bend in the road, as one scenic vista opens onto yet another and as one lovely old farmhouse with attached great barn and old faded-color siding leads to the next. Extraordinarily special are the little inlets from the sea with water shimmering so brightly that it almost blinds the eyes, wonderful green trees lining the banks. These saltwater extensions of the ocean bring the sights, sounds, and smells right up to the highway. With a dock here and there and a boat tied up, perhaps with a morning check of the lobster pots, this is a scene that will bring out your camera to capture a delightful memory. From the early spring green of new leaves signaling the end of winter, through the summer grasses and multicolored wildflowers, to the colors of fall, this is Maine at its best. Take the time to rent a bike and meander along the country roads that connect the little villages in the Boothbay area. Or at least park in a town or two, leaving your car under a red sugar maple so that you can smell the fall in the crisp air and collect a few leaves to press between the leaves of a book back home. There is no end to their shapes and colors; and by the time you've picked up a handful of chestnuts, you'll be wondering how to roast them over a fire back home. To all of this, add the flavors of seafood from the neighboring waters, especially lobster served boiled or stuffed, cold or hot with melted butter, and your visit is something special. While I was visiting, not only did I have my fair share of lobster in every form, but I also enjoyed the seasonal local clams, oysters, and Maine shrimp.

If you are interested in islands and the charm they provide, you can take a boat trip from Boothbay Harbor, New Harbor, or Port Clyde to **Monhegan Island**. Lobstering is the island's principal trade. The large number of artists who spend the summer here and work in the area augments the island's population. There are miles of trails for the hiker, and spectacular views from practically every vantage point. Any photographer would find that a visit here provides more subject matter than there is film.

Working your way north again along Route 1, you will come upon **Newcastle** and, just north of it, **Damariscotta**. Both are seafaring villages with restaurants, shops, and overnight accommodations. Everything's informal here, and you find the down-east Maine resident to be as special in his accent as in his friendliness.

Rockland, with its almost 8,000 population, is the next town of size. It has all the hustle, bustle, and commercial activity of a modern seaport from which lobsters are shipped throughout the world. Here you find the **Farnsworth Art Museum**, which is almost a required stop because of its 19th- and 20th-century paintings by Fitzhugh Lane and a large collection of paintings by members of the Wyeth family, who traditionally summered in Maine. Their ability to capture local Maine scenery and everyday events in oil and watercolor makes a visit to this museum a rewarding experience.

Farther north on Route 1 is another of my favorite towns on the Maine coast—**Camden**, which surrounds a protected harbor full of windjammer schooners moored on summer weekends, as well as gorgeous yachts cruising the waters of **Penobscot Bay**. This is a harbor of constant activity—an artist's dream from any angle. At the head of the harbor, high on the hill, is the **Camden Library**. From its windows and terraces, there are unforgettable views of all that lies below. In the fall when the foliage turns to red and gold, this view makes for one those indelible memories of your fall foliage trip. Be sure to leave time to drive on the back streets of Camden to see the displays of color and the fall gardens with their brilliantly colored chrysanthemums, asters, and other fall flowers.

Main Street, lined with white mansions and more New England churches, is a great place to stop for lunch if your meandering around the town has you there at that hour. Enjoy the lovely architecture of the homes around you. There are art galleries, shops, and restaurants. In summer, windowboxes and flowers thrive in the day's sun and the evening's cool temperatures. It would be difficult to think of a nicer place to stay than this delightful town. There is a good, little walking guide available locally, which I urge you to follow, for it will greatly enhance your visit to Camden.

Leaving Camden, travel northward along the coast through the towns of Belfast, Searsport, and Bucksport. From Route 1 take Route 175 south, and Route 15 down to **Deer Isle**, **Sunset**, and the incredible harbor of **Stonington**, one of the most photographed harbors anywhere. After visiting Stonington, take Route 175 north to the delightful village of Blue Hill–the heart of this Blue Hill peninsula. There are small restaurants, lots of antique shops, art galleries, and places that will entice you through their front doors to look for a treasure to extend the memory.

There's no way to return to the highway without taking another country road, but the Blue Hill Peninsula is wide enough to allow a different view from its eastern side. After the town of Ellsworth, you leave Route 1, taking Route 3 down into Mount Desert Island and the **Acadia National Park**. This park is an unforgettable experience and will cap your trip on the Maine coast, well-worth the effort of getting there. Plan on at least one overnight in this area if you intend to spend any time in the Acadia National Park (we have inn recommendations in Bar Harbor and Northeast Harbor). The smallness and compactness of this area allows for easy visiting of all that there is to do.

Mount Desert Island is about 108 square miles in size, its beauty lying in its granite quarries, mountains, pine forests, and freshwater lakes. From high on top of any of its mountains are panoramic views over the park and the surrounding islands. There are rocky mountains with exposed granite, and charming plants that seem determined to make the most of a short-lived season. Bright and diminutive wildflowers, blueberries, and plants with colorful leaves and berries will reward your camera with yet another photo opportunity. You can tour the park by car, guided bus, bicycle, or horse and carriage. You will want to

Mount Desert Coastline

linger and stop often, so I urge you to arm yourself with informational materials available at the National Park Headquarters and head off on your own.

Be sure to find and follow **Loop Road**, the park's main attraction, as it winds its way along the coast and up to Cadillac Mountain. There are many places to park, to gaze, to photograph, and to smell, and many birds to watch in this ever-changing landscape. Be sure to get to the top of **Cadillac Mountain** for the spectacular views. (Take a windbreaker with you to protect you from the chilly breezes.) Other points of interest include **Otter Cliffs** and **Thunder Hole**—the water rushing into this narrow cavern with the changing tide sounds like thunder. If you have time, be sure to walk the **Beach Cliff Trail**, and visit **Bass Head Light** and other areas of the national park located in the **Schoodic Peninsula**. In the fall, what you'll find here is not the towering maples and other deciduous trees with their brilliant foliage, but rather the beauty of small rock-hugging plants and the deep reds and russets that beacon forth from their tiny leaves. One of the most spectacular plants for fall color is the wild, Maine blueberry bushes—blushing with the brilliance of their unforgettable, red color.

The Byways of Coastal Maine

A visit to the village of **Bar Harbor** is more enjoyable in the summer when you will find it alive with activity and summer residents. After Labor Day, the pace in this part of Maine slows down and the night begins to turn frosty with everything covered with dew. The smells of fall are very special and the clear crispness can almost be tasted. In the winter, many of its shops are closed. However, then the pace is slower, and there is a special, quiet charm without the crowds. In the late 19th and early 20th centuries, Bar Harbor became a fashionable alternative to Newport, Rhode Island. Summer homes are grand beyond your wildest imagination and driving around Bar Harbor and down to either **Northeast Harbor** or **Southwest Harbor** will take you back to another era.

This itinerary ends at Bar Harbor, which is also the beginning of other journeys onward to Nova Scotia by boat and into the upper reaches of Maine and the Moosehead Lake region on the way to Quebec. If you're traveling here to see fall foliage, you'll need to plan to be here (normally) in late September, as fall color comes early here in this part of the Northeast. There is no doubt that a visit, and a stay, to **Greenville** would provide the traveler with unique experiences. Where else can you stay in one locale and go dog sledding, ice fishing, whitewater rafting, snowmobiling, cross-country or downhill skiing, participate in a moose safari, and have a guide instruct you in the fine art of fly fishing? Seaplanes are a popular mode of transportation in these northern parts, but if you're driving in the back woods on unpaved roads, a four-wheel-drive vehicle is good insurance that you'll arrive at your destination.

By heading west from Bar Harbor, you can take an alternative route across Maine into New Hampshire and Vermont, visiting the more northern areas of the **White and Green Mountains**. Herein lie small New England towns where farming and milk production are the principal industries, and where being off the beaten track is not an inconvenience, but rather a wonderful bonus. These small New England towns truly paint a picture and provide a poetic sense of New England, and there is much joy in finding an inn with a cozy fireplace, a nice dining room, and congenial hosts.

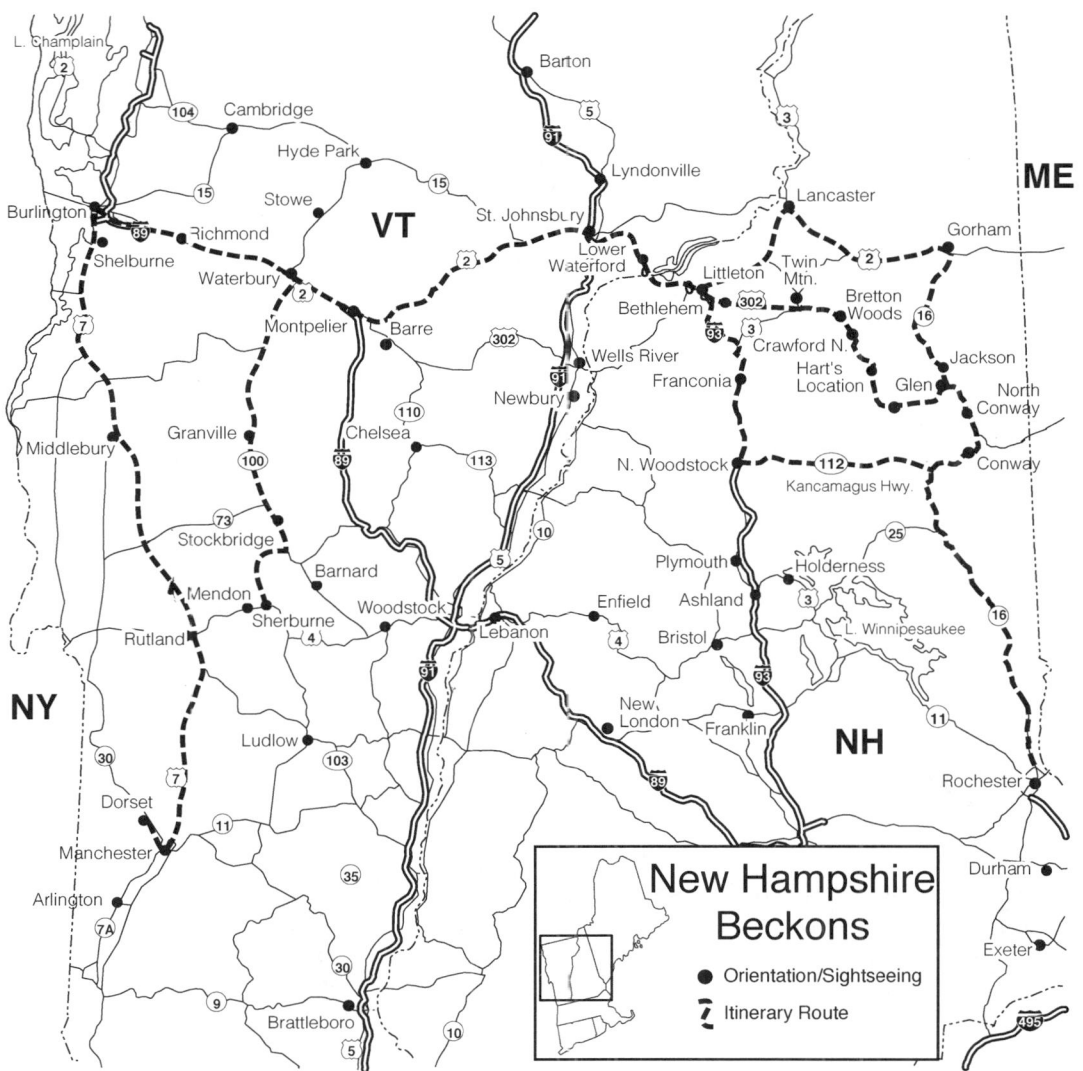

New Hampshire Beckons

Recommended Pacing: (The routing for this itinerary is also outlined on Map 3 and partially on Map 4, at the end of the book.) Two nights will enable you to cover the entire itinerary *at a leisurely pace* unless you decide to make this itinerary the center of your trip into this part of New England. The focus of this itinerary is the road trip north into Conway and North Conway—the heart of the Green Mountains. It provides the opportunity to explore several different spurs, then return back to the main route of the

itinerary. Deciding which of the spurs to pursue is analogous to having to choose one of your children, so let our descriptions guide you to the different alternatives. No matter which one(s) you choose, you will have a wonderful time. Let your day be open to new experiences and vistas and you'll be many times rewarded. Plan to use Boston or the Boston area as your point of departure going north on Route 95 through the northern part of Massachusetts into New Hampshire, where you will pick up Route 4 in Portsmouth, and then Route 16 north on the Spaulding Turnpike toward Rochester, and finally, north into the heart of New Hampshire.

To the west of Route 16 lies the grand Lake Winnipesaukee, at the southern portion of which is the town of Wolfeboro, the center of much boating activity on the lake, and the summer home for many who live in the cities of New England. This is a very popular area for vacationers, as there is nothing more idyllic than a week or two at the edge of a lake, swimming off the dock, fishing with your kids, or going out in a boat to explore the lakes' many coves and tributaries.

If you have resisted the temptation to go to Lake Winnepasaulkee, just continue along Route 16 on the very scenic route leading into **Conway** and **North Conway.** Whether you are traveling to enjoy the wintertime activities of the ski country of New Hampshire; the beauty of the unfolding spring with the flowering daffodils; the bounty of summer with the town fairs, the markets, summer theater, antiquing, or the fabulous colors of Fall—you are the beneficiary of the attributes that typify New England. In these mountain towns, you will find a ski area or two that will be running chair lifts during the fall season. This is a glorious way to rise above the trees and to gaze down, at first to the areas below you, and then from the top of the mountain to the vistas of the surrounding countryside. In many instances, these vistas include a blue lake lying below a swath of color, as if an artist were painting a brightly lit canvas.

The Conways, Conway and North Conway, and just to the north of them, the town of Jackson, are ideal locations for you to find a place to stay a night or two, and from which to take day trips into the surrounding countryside. From the Conways, there are three routes, resembling fingers, heading into the western portion of northern New Hampshire.

An excellent daytrip takes the northern finger out of North Conway, returning back in the evening via the middle finger. This northernmost finger follows Route 16 to **Jackson** and **Gorham**. Turn west at Gorham to connect with Route 2 to **Lancaster**, at which point pick up Route 116 south to **Littleton** and then east through **Bethlehem**. Follow Route 302 through **Twin Mountain**, **Bretton Woods**, **Crawford Notch**, **Hart's Location**, and **Bartlett** to **Glen**. Here you pick up Route 16 south, which returns you to North Conway.

An alternative to this more northern spur is to leave Conway via the "lower finger," turning west just south of town on Route 112, known as the **Kancamagus Highway**. This road rises through the **White Mountains** and is simply beautiful. It twists and winds, rises and falls, making every beautiful, scenic mile one to remember. The road ends in **North Woodstock** and from this point you head north via the I-93 to **Franconia**, **Bethlehem**, **Lower Waterford**, and **St. Johnsbury**, where you can leave the itinerary to travel south into Massachusetts on I-91, or continue on Route 2 to **Montpelier**, the capital of Vermont. The recently remodeled state capitol building is wonderful to tour.

This is the end of this itinerary, but certainly not the end of things to do in this area. If your plans call for a return to the Boston area, you can use one of the previous routes to reach Route 93, which will speedily bring you back south to either Route 2 or further south to Route 90, the Massachusetts Turnpike, and into Boston itself.

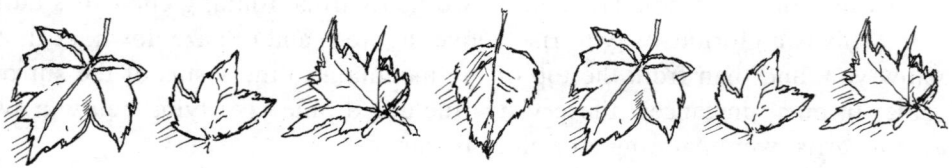

New Hampshire Beckons

Connecticut
Places to Stay

Essex — The Griswold Inn — Map: 1

The unspoiled Connecticut River Valley, with its delightful, historic river towns founded in the 17th century, is undoubtedly one of the most scenic areas in the state. None of these towns is more charming than Essex, and there is no more enchanting place to stay there than The Griswold Inn, known for its historic dining rooms with their collection of marine art and their inviting, cozy atmosphere, which encourages you to linger. There are many small dining rooms, which adds to the charm. A hostelry since it opened in 1776, it also offers most appealing accommodations—the owners have created in each of the guestrooms a level of charm and comfort that, like the dining rooms, makes for instant relaxation. The air-conditioned, pine-floored rooms and suites, of various shapes and sizes, are located in five buildings on both sides of the street. I stayed in a long, narrow suite above two shops with a great window seat looking out into the courtyard. The first floors of these separate buildings house little gift shops where you can find that perfect gift to take home. Essex's attractions include the Connecticut River Museum, which presents the history of the valley and its maritime heritage, a steam train and riverboat ride, taking a stroll along the quaint old riverfront, or just gazing at the river through your bedroom window. *Directions:* From I-91: exit at 22 south, follow Rte 9 south to exit 3 for Essex and the inn. From I-95: exit at 69, follow Rte 9 north to exit 3.

THE GRISWOLD INN
Innkeepers: Joan & Doug Paul
36 Main Street
Essex, CT 06426, USA
Tel: (860) 767-1776, Fax: (860) 767-0481
16 rooms, 15 suites
Double: $110–$230
Open: all year, Credit cards: all major
Select Registry
karenbrown.com/ne/griswoldinn.html

Greenwich — Homestead Inn–Thomas Henkelmann — Map: 1

Only a few inns anywhere in the world can begin to approach the level of accommodation and service offered by the Homestead Inn. Proprietors Thomas Henkelmann, a world-class, European-trained chef, and his wife Theresa, a truly talented designer, present the best of tradition and contemporary style. From the moment the valet opens your door, to the welcoming greeting as the front door opens to a small and charming lobby, the magical experience of your visit to the Homestead begins. The bedrooms have been ingeniously designed in the best of traditional decor with touches of spirit and whimsy that can only make you laugh and the colors used are bold and bright. Be prepared for interesting lamps, wall sconces, and artwork carefully selected to be part of the integrated scheme; be prepared for bathrooms with heated tile floors, for brilliantly colored wall tile, for interesting accessories, and for top-of-the-line amenities. The restaurant, Thomas Henkelmann, softly lit with candles and its tables set with silver and fine china, provides cuisine of extraordinary caliber. There's nothing here that has been left to chance—absolutely every detail has been well thought out. This is a real winner: one of those treasures that must be experienced. *Directions:* From I-95, take exit 3, go left at the end of the ramp to the second light, and turn left onto Horseneck Lane. At the light turn left onto Field Point Road. The inn and restaurant are on the right.

HOMESTEAD INN–THOMAS HENKELMANN
Owners: Thomas & Theresa Henkelmann
420 Field Point Road
Greenwich, CT 06830, USA
Tel: (203) 869-7500, Fax: (203) 869-7502
18 rooms, Double: $250–$495*
 *Breakfast not included: $12–$18
Service charge: 20%
Closed: 2 weeks in Mar, Credit cards: all major
Relais & Châteaux
karenbrown.com/ne/homestead.html

Places to Stay–Connecticut

Ivoryton (Essex) — Copper Beech Inn — Map: 1

Originally constructed in the 1880s as the home of an ivory comb and keyboard manufacturer, this inn has lovely gardens and a fountain within a native woodland in Ivoryton, one of three villages that make up the town of Essex. The magnificent Copper Beech tree in front of the inn gives it its name. In the main house are four beautifully restored guestrooms, each air-conditioned, two with fireplaces; and in the renovated Carriage House there are nine rooms with whirlpool baths, TVs, and lovely decks. I especially loved the feeling of these Carriage House rooms with their soaring ceilings and exposed original beams. Bathrooms have been remodeled with extensive use of marble, heated floors and European accessories. The bedrooms are beautifully appointed and with their large size are particularly gracious with sitting areas and writing desks. The decor in this inn may be traditional but the guest has all the amenities that guarantee a restful stay and a return visit. The inn's award-winning restaurant features sophisticated French food served at tables set with linens, fresh flowers, and sparkling silver. It's warm and inviting and there's a plant-filled, Victorian-style conservatory offering a perfect spot for a glass of wine before dinner or an after-dinner drink. *Directions:* From New Haven drive east on I-95 to exit 69, travel north on Route 9 to exit 3, then west for 1¾ miles to the inn.

COPPER BEECH INN
Owner: Ian Phillips
46 Main Street
Ivoryton (Essex), CT 06442, USA
Tel: (860) 767-0330, (888) 809-2056
Fax: (860) 767-7840
13 rooms
Double: $135–$350
Credit cards: all major
Select Registry
karenbrown.com/ne/copperbeechinn.html

Places to Stay–Connecticut

Ledyard   Stonecroft Country Inn   Map: 1

The Stonecroft Country Inn is located on a winding country road adjoining a nature preserve and provides the visitor with a true escape from the pace of busy times. The inn has ten bedrooms, some in the historic 19th-century house and the rest in The Grange, which houses the inn's restaurant. Fireplaces abound and there are whirlpool tubs for your enjoyment. There's a wonderful blend of luxury and simplicity, where everything that the guest could want is anticipated and always right at hand. Rooms in the main house bear their historical heritage, and they do it well. They are comfortable and attractive, with French country fabrics and warm, cozy charm. Every amenity is available. In the newer building there are four rooms on the first floor and two suites on the second; these are extra spacious, with cathedral ceilings and oversized bathrooms. When you add a first-class restaurant with a European-trained chef, this inn makes for a great getaway retreat. The restaurant is particularly charming in its décor and its views. Tables are nicely set apart from one another. It is just a few minutes to drive to the nearby attractions, but the inn is so inviting that you might just stay put and enjoy the peacefulness of that which surrounds you. The restaurant is open by reservation only so be sure to call if you plan to dine there. *Directions:* Take I-95 to exit 89 and then turn left if coming from the south or right if coming from the north for 3¾ miles to the inn.

STONECROFT COUNTRY INN
Innkeeper: Joan Egy
515 Pumpkin Hill Road
Ledyard, CT 06339, USA
Tel: (860) 572-0771, (800) 772-0774
Fax: (860) 572-9161
8 rooms, 2 suites
Double: $150–$300
Open: all year, Credit cards: all major
Select Registry
karenbrown.com/ne/stonecroft.html

Places to Stay—Connecticut

Mystic Steamboat Inn Map: 1

The Steamboat Inn is an exceptional little hotel with an idyllic location right on the water with glorious views of the river. The entry, at the back, is small but handsome in a nautical theme of teaks, with an oar taking up the length of a side buffet and a gorgeous, large stained glass of a colorful steamboat hanging above the reception desk. The four first-floor bedrooms, all but one with river views, are large, with kitchenettes, spacious bathrooms, and double Jacuzzi tubs. Upstairs, six slightly smaller guestrooms enjoy wood-burning fireplaces and Jacuzzi tubs. All the rooms are sentimentally named for famous Mystic ships from the schooner days. We were able to see two bedrooms, both on the second floor: Mystic, which is very handsome with a mahogany four-poster queen bed, fabrics in reds and creams, and comfortable chairs set beside a corner fireplace, and Marie Gilbert, a very pretty room in rich blues and creams with a white-painted four-poster bed angled to maximize the view out of one long wall of windows, sofa, light-pine table, and lovely fireplace. Also on the second floor is an attractive common room where guests can help themselves to tea and coffee and where they enjoy evening sherry and a Continental breakfast of fresh juice, fruits, and baked goods. *Directions:* On the west side of the drawbridge overlooking the river and wharf.

STEAMBOAT INN
Owners: Paul Connor & John McGee
Innkeeper: Diana Stadtmiller
73 Steamboat Wharf
Mystic, CT 06355, USA
Tel: (860) 536-8300, Fax: (860) 536-9528
6 rooms, 4 suites
Double: $235–$300
Open: all year, Credit cards: all major
karenbrown.com/ne/steamboatinn.html

Places to Stay–Connecticut

Mystic — Whalers Inn

On the eastern approach to Mystic, just before the bridge over the Mystic River, sits a lovely, historic hotel that affords reasonably priced accommodation, a warm welcome, and comfortable rooms in four separate buildings. The reception is housed in the oldest building where guestrooms are found on three levels overlooking either the front street or back courtyard parking. We were impressed by the attention paid to decor and comfort in these nicely sized rooms, which enjoy reproduction period beds, writing desks, inviting armchairs with paired tables, and armoires concealing TVs. Each room is equipped with TV, telephone, and full bathroom. Our bathroom was simple but prettily wallpapered and stocked with soaps and hairdryer. Rooms are also found in the historic 1865 House next door, also fronting the main street. Behind it in two wings of rooms built about 20 years ago, The Stonington and the Noank Houses, which, in addition to standard double rooms, also have guestrooms that can accommodate two double beds—perfect for families. A Continental breakfast is set out in the lobby and guests are welcome to take it back to their rooms. Although there is no restaurant in the hotel itself, a corner restaurant in the same building, Bravo Bravo, is associated with it and serves wonderful Italian fare. *Directions:* From I-95 take exit 90 or exit 89 to Route 1 into downtown Mystic. The inn is located one block east of the drawbridge.

WHALERS INN
Owners: Paul Connor, Bill Griffin & John McGee
Manager: Richard Prisby
20 East Main Street
Mystic, CT 06355, USA
Tel: (860) 536-1506, (800) 243-2588
Fax: (860) 572-1250
40 rooms, 9 suites
Double: $135–$250
Open: all year, Credit cards: all major
karenbrown.com/ne/ctwhalersinn.html

Places to Stay—Connecticut

Norfolk   Manor House   Map: 1

To stay at Manor House is to visit a grand home built a century ago. As you approach the front door along the winding driveway, it's somehow easy to imagine that earlier life. When you walk through the door into the large hallway from which rises a grand staircase, you're sure that you are about to experience a romantic retreat. As the surroundings begin to come into focus, you're aware of incredible architectural details and then you notice the exquisite Tiffany stained-glass windows in the dining room and living room. I stopped, I stared, and I thought how wonderful it was to be a guest in this home. The comfortable guestrooms are all furnished with period antiques. I stayed in the room that was originally the master bedroom—its sitting area in front of the fireplace would have been a good place to linger longer than time permitted. Some rooms have fireplaces, some have private balconies, some have oversized Jacuzzis or soaking tubs. From the many windows views encompass lawns, gardens, and countryside. When I arrived I was welcomed by the smell of baking bread, an enticing prelude to the delicious breakfast which includes pure local maple syrup. *Directions:* Take I-84 to the exit for Route 8 north at Waterbury. At the end of Route 8 (Winsted) take Route 44 west to Norfolk.

MANOR HOUSE
Owner: Diane Tremblay
Innkeeper: Lisa Tomaselli
69 Maple Avenue
Norfolk, CT 06058, USA
Tel & fax: (860) 542-5690, (866) 542-5690
8 rooms, 1 suite
Double: $125–$250
Open: all year, Credit cards: all major
Select Registry
karenbrown.com/ne/manorhouse.html

Places to Stay–Connecticut

North Stonington   Antiques and Accommodations   Maps: 1, 2

Innkeepers Tom and Ann Gray have been antique dealers and their home is a treasure chest of antiques that they have collected over the years. They are delighted to share with you their many treasures and tell you how they came to be part of their lives. There are two buildings in this inn. The 1860 House has four bedrooms; one of which, Susan's room, has an adjoing single room making it ideal for families; and two of the bedrooms enjoy fireplaces. The House in the Garden, dating from 1820, set in the garden and tucked into the hillside, offers on the first level a family suite, known as Kerri's Cottage, which has three bedrooms, one bathroom, a huge country kitchen, living room, and a covered porch. On the second level, you find a country kitchen with fireplace, sitting room, two bedrooms, two large bathrooms, washer, and dryer. The House in the Garden is especially suited for self-catering, longer-term stays (call for rates). With the interest and background of the owners, naturally the bedrooms are decorated with antiques and accessories they have collected. Tom prepares special three-course breakfasts featuring scrumptious omelets and soufflés served in the candlelit dining room with silver and fine china. New this year is an antique shop in the barn with an emphasis on antique books.
Directions: Take I-95 to exit 92 to Route 2 west for 2-3/10 miles. Turn right at Main Street and go 2/10 mile to the inn on the right.

ANTIQUES AND ACCOMMODATIONS
Innkeepers: Tom & Ann Gray
32 Main Street
North Stonington, CT 06359, USA
Tel: (860) 535-1736, (800) 554-7829
Fax: (860) 535-2613
5 rooms, 3 suites, 1 house ($1200–$1500 weekly)
Double: $99–$378
Open: all year, Credit cards: all major
karenbrown.com/ne/antiques.html

Places to Stay–Connecticut

North Stonington — Randall's Ordinary

Maps: 1, 2

There is nothing ordinary about this wonderful inn and restaurant complex a few miles from the coast, so close to Mystic and Foxwoods Resort Casino yet seeming worlds away when you set foot on the 250 acres of unspoiled land. Randall's Ordinary is made up of multiple wood buildings encompassing a restaurant, guestrooms, and a cottage that doubles as a conference center, and fenced-off areas and huts that are home to all sorts of animals. In the main building, dating back to 1813, the decor is handsomely rustic—old slate and stone floors complement rough-hewn log banisters and an open stairwell. The guestrooms here range from nice-sized rooms with queen bed to a two-story mini-suite offering a sitting area with sofa bed and loft bedroom. The most dramatic rooms are those at the top set under high, beamed ceilings. All the rooms are lovely, with attractive stenciling, reproduction country furnishings set on old wooden floors, and a few well-placed antiques. The true romantic will adore the Silo Suite found in the turret round on two levels, the top one entirely devoted to a Jacuzzi tub. The restaurant is a step back in history, with wonderful old wooden tables and large open fireplaces. Above the restaurant are three more bedrooms, one of which is reputed to be the favorite haunt of the resident ghost. *Directions:* At exit 92 off I-95, take Route 2 west and travel approximately 1/8 mile to the inn. Randall's Ordinary is on the left side of the road.

RANDALL'S ORDINARY
Innkeeper: Tina Luzzi
Route 2
North Stonington, CT 06359, USA
Tel: (860) 599-4540, (877) 599-4540
Fax: (860) 599-3308
12 rooms, 4 suites, 1 cottage ($650)
Double: $99–$209*
 *Breakfast not included
Open: all year, Credit cards: all major
karenbrown.com/ne/randallsordinary.html

Old Lyme — Bee and Thistle Inn — Map: 1

One of the most charming villages in Connecticut must be Old Lyme where the Bee and Thistle Inn was built as a private home in 1756. Its second owners found its location too close to the road; so they moved it back from the wide main street of this village to its present gracious setting with a welcoming curved driveway, adding enhancements such as the lovely sunken garden which you should stroll around. In the late 1930s this home was transformed into an inn, now updated to offer 11 guestrooms. From the welcoming front hall there's a lovely carved staircase that takes you up to the tastefully decorated bedrooms on the upper floors, all decorated in Colonial style, with flowered wallpapers, quilts, and Oriental rugs. The rooms, with sitting areas and full bathrooms, have everything that a guest might want. The inn is noted for its award-winning restaurant and wine list, and the several dining rooms with their individual fireplaces are as attractive as the common areas where guests are invited to relax while staying at the inn. Readers of Connecticut Magazine voted this restaurant the most romantic in the state. I stayed here over 20 years ago and find everything about this inn to be as charming today as it was then. *Directions:* From I-95 traveling south take exit 70, turn right off the ramp to the third building on the left. Traveling north on I-95, turn left off the ramp and right at the second light, go to the end of the road, then turn left to the inn.

BEE AND THISTLE INN
Innkeepers: Marie & Philip Abraham
100 Lyme Street
Old Lyme, CT 06371, USA
Tel: (860) 434-1667, (800) 622-4946
Fax: (860) 434-3402
11 rooms, 1 cottage, Double: $110–$219*
 *Breakfast not included
Open: all year, Credit cards: all major
Select Registry
karenbrown.com/ne/beeandthistle.html

Places to Stay–Connecticut

Old Mystic   Old Mystic Inn   Map: 1

Not far from the Mystic Seaport is a small inn with eight guestrooms in two buildings: one a former bookstore where the keeping room, with its original fireplace and lovely old paneling, dates back to 1784. Behind this a carriage house built in 1988. This is a simply furnished inn where each guestroom has a queen bed (five have canopies), antique quilts, its own sitting area, and a private bathroom (one is across the hall from the bedroom). Three rooms have wood-burning fireplaces, two have whirlpool tubs, three have gas fireplaces, and several have stenciling on the walls. Since this was once the Old Mystic Bookstore, each of the rooms is sentimentally named after a New England author and contains the works of that author as well as a synopsis of the author's life, which the innkeeper has thoughtfully provided. Michael Cardillo was trained at the Culinary Institute of America and breakfasts are his special creation and a time to show off his talent in the pleasant breakfast room with its fireplace and bay window. In addition to the Seaport, nearby are the Aquarium, the USS Nautilus Submarine Museum, and the casinos, and an hour away lies Newport, Rhode Island with its famous mansions. Mystic and its neighboring towns offer many attractions, among them antique shops, restaurants, and many festivals. *Directions:* From I-95 take exit 90 to Route 27 north 1½ miles to the first intersection. Turn right. The inn is across from the Old Mystic Post Office.

OLD MYSTIC INN
Innkeeper: Michael Cardillo
52 Main Street
P.O. Box 733, Old Mystic, CT 06372, USA
Tel: (860) 572-9422, Fax: (860) 572-9954
8 rooms
Double: $145–$185
Open: all year, Credit cards: all major
karenbrown.com/ne/oldmystic.html

Places to Stay–Connecticut

Ridgefield — West Lane Inn — Map: 1

Ridgefield is one of those glorious country towns in the mid-western corner of Connecticut and the West Lane Inn is perfectly situated for explorations of the area. The inn is set graciously in an elegant 19th-century estate, surrounded by an expanse of lawn, garden, and blooming shrubbery. There's a grand porch spanning the front of the building—a great place to sit and read with a cup of tea. The air-conditioned guestrooms all have queen four-poster beds, private baths, and every amenity a guest might want. All rooms have cable TV, modem access, 24-hour telephone service, and voice mail. Some have fireplaces. Flowered wallpapers are used extensively, adding to the rooms' charm and comfort. Dining is available at Bernard's next door. There's much to do in this area: great antiquing, good museums and shopping, cross-country skiing, golf, tennis, hiking, ice-skating, and any other sport you'd like to try. The inn has two rooms with kitchens for extended stays—and who wouldn't want to linger in this inn and this area! *Directions:* From New York City take the West Side Hwy to Saw Mill River Parkway to exit 6 and turn right on Route 35 east for 12 miles to the inn.

WEST LANE INN
Innkeepers: Maureen Mayer & Deborah Prieger
22 West Lane (Route 35)
Ridgefield, CT 06877, USA
Tel: (203) 438-7323, Fax: (203) 438-7325
16 rooms, 2 cottages with kitchens
Double: $125–$195
Open: all year, Credit cards: all major
Select Registry
karenbrown.com/ne/westlaneinn.html

Places to Stay—Connecticut

Simsbury   Simsbury 1820 House   Map: 1

The Simsbury 1820 House is located in one of those wonderfully charming Connecticut towns with wide streets, sweeping green lawns, and homes that cluster along the main street near the post office, the general store, and other conveniences. The history of these towns dates back to the 17th and 18th centuries when life was indeed simpler. Inns like the Simsbury 1820 House provide today's traveler with a sense of "home away from home" and a place to relax while vacationing or working in the area. The guestrooms, with king or queen beds and private bathrooms, are all decorated in the same palette of soft blues and whites, but there is no "hotel" feeling in this property at all. The inn is unique in that it offers its guests a small dining room with a limited but excellent menu. Monday through Thursday nights, the chef prepares dinner—a wonderful option for those who would prefer at the end of the day to stay put rather than to go out to find a restaurant. My dinner was excellent and was topped off with a mocha pecan tart with whipped cream that was nothing short of decadent. The Simsbury 1820 House also has several beautifully furnished private function rooms for dinners, weddings, and other gatherings. *Directions:* From I-91 take exit 35B to Route 218 west. Follow Route 218 to 185 west. Turn right onto Route 10 north—the inn is about 1 mile along on the left.

SIMSBURY 1820 HOUSE
Innkeeper: Robin Taraskewich
Manager: Jan Losee
731 Hopmeadow Street
Simsbury, CT 06070, USA
Tel: (860) 658-7658, (800) TRY-1820
Fax: (860) 651-0724
34 rooms, Double: $99–$229
Restaurant open Mon to Thurs (for guests only)
Open: all year, Credit cards: all major
karenbrown.com/ne/simsbury1820house.html

Stonington   Inn at Stonington   Maps: 1, 2

The Inn at Stonington, overlooking the water in the picturesque village of Stonington, is a relative newcomer to the hospitality world but it exhibits all the features, amenities, and charm a traveler would expect in an inn with many years of experience. The living room, graciously decorated with seating areas and a fireplace has windows that capture the magic of the waterfront activity, a bar off one end, and an area where breakfast is served. On the top floor guests have the use of a sitting room overlooking the harbor. Downstairs, below the bedrooms, is an exercise room. While the bedrooms are individually decorated, most varying in style of bed, they have in common their comfortable furnishings, seating areas, nice linens, and up-to-the minute bathrooms with all the amenities. Rooms have fireplaces and some have Jacuzzis to add to the pleasure of your visit. The work of local artists is shown throughout the inn. Within a short walking distance you find restaurants, antique shops, boutiques, and several coffee houses. Boaters will appreciate the inn's 400-foot deepwater dock. *Directions:* Traveling north or south on I-95, take exit 91 to the end of the ramp—turn right if traveling north and left if traveling south. Continue for ½ mile to North Main Street where you turn left for 1-6/10 miles to Route 1. Cross Route 1 to the first stop sign, turn left then right at the next stop sign, driving 6/10 mile to the inn.

INN AT STONINGTON
Innkeeper: Bill Griffin
60 Water Street
Stonington, CT 06378, USA
Tel: (860) 535-2000, Fax: (860) 535-8193
18 rooms
Double: $195–$395
Open: all year, Credit cards: all major
karenbrown.com/ne/stonington.html

Places to Stay—Connecticut

Washington　　　　Mayflower Inn　　　　Map: 1

When we passed through the gates of the Mayflower Inn, we felt as if we had been transported from bucolic New England to a European country estate. While the mood is European, the inn and the town boast a strong American heritage. The village was settled by descendants of the original Mayflower party and in its early days the inn hosted such distinguished guests as Eleanor Roosevelt. The Mnuchins wanted to create the ambiance of the finest European auberge and traveled France and England to collect art and antiques that now enrich the decor. Set on 28 acres, the inn houses 25 luxurious guestrooms and suites and anticipates and provides for guests' every possible want and need. From the moment you enter you are embraced by the warmth, elegance, and richness of the ambiance. We arrived on a Saturday afternoon and found the setting and mood enviable: guests were reading, sleeping, writing, or enjoying hushed conversations in front of log fires crackling in intimate sitting areas, salons, and the library. A few guests were already studying the dinner menu over a drink in the cozy bar and the critically acclaimed restaurant was elegantly staged. Stay here and take advantage of the beautiful grounds, the fitness center, pool, cross-country trails, and the endless walks. Let yourself be transported to another world. *Directions:* Located off Rte 47 on the northern outskirts of the village of Washington, just south of the junction with Rte 109.

MAYFLOWER INN
Owners: Adriana & Robert Mnuchin
Manager: John Trevenen
Box 1288, 118 Woodbury Road
Washington, CT 06793, USA
Tel: (860) 868-9466, Fax: (860) 868-1497
25 rooms, Double: $430–$1400*
　*Breakfast not included
Open: all year, Credit cards: all major
Relais & Châteaux
karenbrown.com/ne/mayflowerinn.html

Places to Stay – Connecticut

Westport — Inn at National Hall — Map: 1

Every once in a while a really wonderful inn is created from an historic structure by a group of very talented artists. Such is the Inn at National Hall: where all imaginable comforts are augmented by a staff and level of service always present, yet unobtrusive. Every conceivable amenity is available and there are extra-special touches such as slippers at turn-down time, little readings to take to bed, the next day's weather forecast, and suggestions of things to. This is a great, fabulously decorated inn and you are tempted to cancel all plans just for the privilege of staying here—and that is exactly what I did. I stayed in a corner suite with mustard-painted walls, expansive river views, a king bed with a paisley corolla canopy, and a desk. Painted on the bathroom wall were whimsical trompe l'oeil monkeys, which reflected in the mirrors. This inn has polish, charm, wonderful furnishings and uses whimsy in its decor to create an enduring memory of a time spent in total comfort. Westport, just an hour from New York, is a very sophisticated community and this inn complements the town perfectly. *Directions:* From New York: take the I-95 to exit 17 and turn left to Route 33 for 1½ miles. Then after the traffic lights turn immediately right to the inn. From Merritt Parkway: leave at exit 41, drive south toward Westport, and in about 2 miles you find the inn on the left.

INN AT NATIONAL HALL
Innkeepers: Gene Gorab & Jim Cooper
Two Boston Post Road
Westport, CT 06880, USA
Tel: (203) 221-1351, (800) 628-4255
Fax: (203) 221-0276
8 rooms, 8 suites
Double: $295–$750
Open: all year, Credit cards: all major
karenbrown.com/ne/innatnationalhall.html

Devil's Hopyard

Maine
Places to Stay

Bar Harbor   Manor House Inn   Map: 4

Nestled in the shade of the pretty trees that line historic West Street, the Manor House Inn is an attractive, soft-yellow, three-story home with shuttered windows, steep pitches and angles to its roof, and lovely wide verandas. Built in 1887 as a lavish 22-room residence, Manor House has now been authentically restored to its original splendor and is listed on the National Register of Historic Places. The grounds are lovely and the common room on the first floor with its grand piano and ornate Victorian furnishings is inviting. Guestrooms, all with private bathrooms, are found in the original Manor House, the two Garden Cottages, the original Chauffeur's Cottage, and the Acadia Cottage, which was constructed in 2000 to provide an additional three luxurious rooms. Breakfast begins with freshly baked blueberry muffins and breads, fresh fruit, and cereals, followed by a hot dish such as ham-and-cheese baked omelet or baked blueberry-stuffed French toast. Manor House's in-town location is only moments from the water and just a few more moments away from all of Bar Harbor's restaurants and galleries. Access to Acadia National Park with its many attractions is less than a mile away. *Directions:* Take Route 3 south and just as you enter Bar Harbor turn left onto West Street (the first cross street). Manor House is three blocks down on the right.

MANOR HOUSE INN
Innkeepers: Stacey & Ken Smith
106 West Street
Bar Harbor, ME 04609, USA
Tel: (207) 288-3759, (800) 437-0088
Fax: (207) 288-2974
9 rooms, 7 suites, 2 cottages
Double: $135–$265
Open: mid-Apr to Nov, Credit cards: all major
Select Registry
karenbrown.com/ne/manorhouseinn.html

Places to Stay–Maine

Bar Harbor — The Inn at Bay Ledge — Map: 4

Picture yourself standing on the sweeping porch looking out over the swimming pool down to the water through the towering pine trees; imagine that morning cup of coffee or tea as you watch the activity on the sea and the changes in the water's reflections; conjure up your perfect bedroom with its lovely four-poster bed, one you have to climb into and from which you can gaze out through the windows to the sea. My room 7 had that bed plus a comfortable sitting area with a love seat, a good chair for reading, and a bathroom with all the amenities one could possibly want including a spa tub. Bedrooms in this inn are spacious, welcoming, and attractively decorated. There's a long living room with a grand piano for entertaining both yourself and other guests. Breakfasts are sumptuous, featuring Jeani's granola, fresh fruit, a morning pastry, and a special entree (on my visit I enjoyed a zucchini soufflé with pesto sauce and a piece of pumpernickel toast with ricotta cheese and herbs). Dinner at Thrumcap could not have been more enjoyable with its tasting menu and its host Tom, who guides you through the wine list with great knowledge. This inn is in the perfect location for a visit to the Acadia National Park where you can enjoy the splendor of nature at its best. *Directions:* Take Route 3 on Mount Desert Island for 5 miles. Opposite the Best Western turn onto Sand Point Road and drive for ¾ mile to the inn on your left.

THE INN AT BAY LEDGE
Owners: Jack & Jeani Ochtera
150 Sand Point Road
Bar Harbor, ME 04609, USA
Tel: (207) 288-4204, Fax: (207) 288-5573
10 rooms
Double: $150–$375
Open: May to Oct 19, Credit cards: MC, VS
Select Registry
karenbrown.com/ne/theinnatbayledge.html

Places to Stay—Maine

Bar Harbor — Ullikana — Map: 4

The Ullikana, built in 1885, is one of the few remaining original cottages in Bar Harbor. Though located within an easy walk of all the town's activities, it provides a quiet haven overlooking the water. The 16 rooms, all with king or queen beds, are situated in one of two adjoining buildings, one in Tudor style, the other painted a sunny yellow, both old-fashioned homes with big rooms and cross ventilation. The guestrooms I viewed were large and airy and painted in colors appropriate to an oceanside town in summer. I particularly liked Audrey's, tucked up under the eaves with its spacious feeling and down-home comfort. Some rooms have views of the water and the boating activity for which Bar Harbor is so well known. There's also a cottage where you can settle in with your entire family. The common rooms are of a dark wood—appropriate to the era in which the inn was built—and the furnishings of the period are an integral part of the inn's mood and setting. Breakfasts are served either in the dining room or in the garden, which is delightful during the summer months. If you like staying away from the bustle of Bar Harbor, but want to be able to walk within a minute or two to the shops and restaurants, then this inn is perfectly situated. *Directions:* Take Route 3 to Bar Harbor, turn left onto Cottage Street, right on Main Street, then left after the Trust Company building. Follow the gravel road towards the water.

ULLIKANA
Innkeepers: Helene Harton & Roy Kasindorf
16 The Field
Bar Harbor, ME 04609, USA
Tel: (207) 288-9552, Fax: (207) 288-3682
16 rooms
Double: $150–$295
Open: May through Oct, Credit cards: MC, VS
Select Registry
karenbrown.com/ne/ullikana.html

Blue Hill   Blue Hill Inn   Map: 4

What I love about the Blue Hill Inn (c.1840) is that it's right in the heart of a picture-perfect, historic little town, which has a history that stretches back before the town was chartered in 1789 to the time when it was first settled in 1762. Blue Hill is a charming coastal village and both the town and the inn offer the classic New England hospitality of yesteryear. The Blue Hill Inn has provided lodging since 1840 and it is exceptionally comfortable, with friendly and helpful innkeepers: Mary and Don will asssit you to find that out-of-the-way antique shop or point you in the direction of a good restaurant or a leisurely drive. There are eleven bedrooms and one luxury suite. I stayed in one of the front bedrooms and it just felt utterly comfortable, with a queen bed, a chair or two for reading, and a private bath. Each evening the inn serves wine, cocktails, and hors d'oeuvres and during May and October offers special "Wine Dinners." Breakfast offers a choice of five entrees. *Directions:* Take the Maine Turnpike (I-95) to Augusta, then Route 3 east to Belfast, continuing east through Bucksport. Take Route 15 south to Blue Hill. Bear right at the Blue Hill Inn sign on Route 177 east (4½ miles to the inn).

BLUE HILL INN
Innkeepers: Mary & Don Hartley
Union Street
P.O. Box 403, Blue Hill, ME 04614, USA
Tel: (207) 374-2844, (800) 826-7415
Fax: (207) 374-2829
8 rooms, 3 suites, 1 cottage, Double: $158–$345
Special dinners by arrangement
Closed: Dec to mid-May, Credit cards: all major
Select Registry
karenbrown.com/ne/thebluehillinn.html

Places to Stay–Maine

Boothbay Harbor — Five Gables Inn — Map: 4

Everyone should experience the pleasure of staying in an inn on the Maine coast where the casual life of a small village is imbued with the charm of the surrounding sea and the activities of those who make their living on that sea. When you're driving to Boothbay Harbor and then on to East Boothbay through winding country roads with glimpses here and there of the water, lush green trees, and windowboxes full of geraniums and petunias, you are aware that this is quintessential Maine. To enjoy this area to the fullest, you can do no better than to relax in a 19th-century retreat. The Five Gables Inn, one hundred plus years old, sits on a hill overlooking the sea with boats just waiting for a sail to be raised for a day of exploration along the craggy, rocky coast. This inn has a great common room with a wood-burning fireplace and several tables in front of big water-view windows. There are 16 bedrooms from which to choose, all but one with views of the water. Number 10, furnished with a queen pencil-post bed, is a corner room that catches the morning sun and has water views in two directions. Room 14, the inn's largest bedroom, is under a gable. It has a king bed, a bath with shower, a wood-burning fireplace, and a seating area from which there are great views of the harbor. *Directions:* Take Route 1 to Route 27 south to Route 96 through East Boothbay. Turn right at the yellow blinking light onto Murray Hill Road for ½ mile to the inn on the right.

FIVE GABLES INN
Owners: Mike & De Kennedy
107 Murray Hill Road
PO Box 335, Boothbay Harbor, ME 04544, USA
Tel: (207) 633-4551, (800) 451-5048
16 rooms
Double: $130–$195
Open: late May to late Oct, Credit cards: MC, VS
karenbrown.com/ne/fivegablesinn.html

Places to Stay–Maine

Camden — Camden Maine Stay — Map: 4

Listed in the National Registry, the Camden Maine Stay is a grand old New England home dating from 1802. Camden is one of those picturesque towns surrounded by hills from which you peer down onto a harbor of schooners and boating activity—for me as mesmerizing as staring into a star-filled evening sky. The Camden Maine Stay is delightfully decorated and shipshape in every respect, and you'll find any one of the rooms to be totally comfortable for as long as you can stay. There's a variety of accommodation both in the main house and the attached carriage house, from the two-bedroom Stitchery Suite with its own sitting room to my favorite, the cozy Carriage House with its private patio overlooking the spectacular gardens. There is no such thing here as a room that I would not love to stay in for nights on end. Two recently redecorated parlors provide guests with comfortable places to relax and chat with one another. There's also a sitting room with fireplace, TV, and DVD player and, of course, a porch—the kind that makes New England inns so very special. A huge Aga stove warms the kitchen and bakes all the wonderful food that you'll enjoy at breakfast. You can walk to everything in town and the innkeepers are happy to steer you in the right direction for all the interesting places to visit in the area. *Directions:* Take I-95 to Route 1 to Camden. The inn is three blocks north of the village.

CAMDEN MAINE STAY
Innkeepers: Juanita & Bob Topper
22 High Street
Camden, ME 04843, USA
Tel: (207) 236-9636, Fax: (207) 236-0621
6 rooms, 2 suites
Double: $100–$260
Open: all year, Credit cards: all major
Select Registry
karenbrown.com/ne/mainestay.html

Places to Stay—Maine

Camden   Hartstone Inn   Map: 4

When the love of innkeeping and fine cuisine come together in an inn located in one of the most charming of all seaside towns, you can be assured of a memorable visit. Mary Jo, with her passion for orchids, gives the inn its elegant and interesting decor, and Michael, with his incredible talent for preparing fine food, both combine to provide superb hospitality. The inn's twelve rooms, including six suites, are furnished lovingly and my stay in the Tea Cup Suite showcased Mary Jo's collection of tea cups. It was bright and cheerful and a skylight over the bed added to the enjoyment of early-morning reading while curled up under the sumptuous comforter. Other rooms are similarly furnished and include comfortable seating for those times when you want to relax. The dinner was a feast including a seared five-spice quail, Maine lobster ravioli with seared diver scallops and lobster tail, and a hot raspberry soufflé served with a chambord crème anglaise. After such a wonderful meal, relaxing in the living room in front of the fire was the frosting on top of a perfect evening. This is an in-town inn, so everything is close to hand, with the main street just outside the front door (triple glazing does much to subdue the sound). During the winter the inn runs cooking classes and its owner-chef has just published his own cookbook—it is spectacular, like everything these two do. *Directions:* Take I-95 to Route 1 to Camden. The inn is on the left at 41 Elm Street.

HARTSTONE INN
Innkeepers: Michael & Mary Jo Salmon
41 Elm Street
Camden, ME 04843, USA
Tel: (207) 236-4259, (800) 788-4823
Fax: (207) 236-9575
14 rooms
Double: $125–$235
Open: all year, Credit cards: MC, VS
Select Registry
karenbrown.com/ne/hartstone.html

Camden   The Camden Windward House   Map: 4

In one of the prettiest villages on the Maine coast, set high above the harbor, is The Camden Windward House. There are eight bedrooms, several with their own private entrances, all individually air-conditioned and comfortably decorated with nautical decor and period furnishings. Most of the rooms enjoy fireplaces, a few of the suites have private decks; and all of the rooms have cable TV and VCR, telephones with data ports, and a sitting room or area with chairs where you can read and relax. Allergy-free feather beds guarantee a great night's sleep and that's exactly what I had when I stayed in one of the rooms. Mine was on the second floor with its own separate entrance and had a separate sitting room with TV and fireplace. From its windows, I could look down High Street toward the village and the harbor with its fishing boats and sailing vessels. There's nothing like the fresh salt air to work up an appetite for a dinner featuring freshly caught seafood, and your hosts are happy to help you select a local restaurant. Breakfast usually includes a choice of several hot entrees. Camden is the host harbor for many seafaring schooners on which you can take a week's or few hours' cruise along the spectacular coast, either helping with the sailing or relaxing and soaking up the sun on deck. *Directions:* From Boston or Portland, take I-95 or I-295 north to exit 28 at Brunswick. Follow Route 1 to Camden. The inn is one block north of the village center on the left.

THE CAMDEN WINDWARD HOUSE
Owners: Lee & Philip Brookes
Six High Street
Camden, ME 04843, USA
Tel: (207) 236-9656, (877) 492-9656
Fax: (207) 230-0433
5 rooms, 3 suites
Double: $169–$250
Open: all year, Credit cards: all major
karenbrown.com/ne/camdenwindwardhouse.html

Places to Stay—Maine

Deer Isle — Pilgrim's Inn — Map: 4

Pilgrim's Inn, an historic 1793 Colonial building, overlooks Northwest Harbor and a picturesque millpond on Deer Isle in Penobscot Bay. The setting is magnificent and the views of the flowering gardens and the pond behind the inn are both enchanting and mesmerizing. Somehow this combination of flowers, water, and reflections always makes for immediate and total relaxation. The inn's decor is warm and inviting and furnishings respect the history and character of the island. There are pine floors, several large fireplaces, and antique furnishings. Warm Colonial colors enhance the cozy feeling of comfort. Twelve lovely guestrooms along with a couple with gas stoves are found in the main house. If you are traveling with children, consider one of the three complete cottages for a longer stay. Gourmet dinners featuring creative American cuisine are served in the barn dining room with its hand-hewn beams and vaulted ceiling. The inn is a good base for visiting Acadia National Park and Isle au Haut (40 minutes by ferry). At the inn's doorstep you can hike, bike, and go boating, while nearby are tennis and golf. The local library is just across the street and there's a great gallery just up on the corner. *Directions:* From Boston take I-95 north to Augusta and Rte 3 to Belfast, then follow Rte 1 north to Rte 15. Turn right onto Rte 15 (south), heading for Deer Isle through the Blue Hill Peninsula. In the village turn right onto Main St. (the 15A).

PILGRIM'S INN
Owners: Rob & Cathy DeGennaro
P.O. Box 69
Deer Isle, ME 04627, USA
Tel & fax: (207) 348-6615, (888) 778-7505
12 rooms, 3 cottages
Double: $99–$229
Open: mid-May to Nov, cottages open all year
Credit cards: all major
Select Registry
karenbrown.com/ne/pilgrimsinn.html

Places to Stay – Maine

Deer Isle–Sunset — Goose Cove Lodge — Map: 4

Overlooking the majestic beauty of Penobscot Bay at the end of a long dirt road on one of the fingers of land jutting out to sea is the Goose Cove Lodge. With its 22 cabins, rooms, and suites, this inn provides a rustic yet sophisticated setting for a wonderful stay on the Maine coast. The cabins are scattered about the grounds, some rather near one another and others tucked back in the woods where you have total privacy. All are rustic in character and furnishings, most having fireplaces and some having sundecks. This is a great place to bring children, with lots of activities organized for them and their own separate dinnertime. In season, the cabins are available only on a weekly basis. The drive to this inn takes a bit of time. It's my guess that once you arrive and settle in you'll be perfectly delighted not to move because right on site you'll find sailing, kayaking, hiking, biking, and nature trails. The lodge has a great restaurant with a fine menu featuring fresh local ingredients. Breakfast and dinner are served during the May to October season, and there are four cottages available year round where you can stay with either breakfast or breakfast and dinner. This is a special place to go for a relaxing break away from it all. *Directions:* Take Route 1 north through Bucksport, then Route 15 south to Deer Isle Village. Turn right on Main Street, travel 3 miles to Goose Cove Road, and turn right to the lodge.

GOOSE COVE LODGE
Innkeepers: Joanne & Dom Parisi
P.O. Box 40
Deer Isle–Sunset, ME 04683, USA
Tel: (207) 348-2508, (800) 728-1963
Fax: (207) 348-2624
3 rooms, 6 suites, 13 cabins, Double: $160–$550
Open: May to Oct (4 cabins all year)
Credit cards: all major
Select Registry
karenbrown.com/ne/goosecove.html

Durham   Bagley House Inn   Map: 4

The Bagley House Inn is just ten minutes from downtown Freeport, situated on 6 acres of countryside dotted with fields and woods. Nearby in Freeport is the internationally renowned L. L. Bean store, open 24 hours a day. Freeport is also home to many discount stores so you can shop here well beyond the point of dropping from exhaustion. The Bagley House, built as a public house in 1772, provides a quiet refuge from all this hustle and bustle. Its eight guestrooms, located in the main house and the recently built carriage house just a few steps away, are attractively and simply decorated with antiques and beautifully hand-crafted pieces and hand-sewn quilts on the beds. Each room has its own private bath. One room has a double bed plus a ¾ bed for a third person and the inn will provide porta-cribs for children. The rooms in the carriage house are somewhat larger than in the main house, but you give up the wide pine floors and the charm of staying in a building from the 18th century. Full breakfasts are served at the 8-foot antique baker's table in the magnificent country kitchen with its hand-hewn beams, vaulted ceiling with loft, and large fireplace with beehive oven. There are two parlors to relax in, each with a large, welcoming fireplace. *Directions:* Take I-295 to Freeport, exit 22. Turn right as you get off onto Route 136, then right to the inn after approximately 6 miles.

BAGLEY HOUSE INN
Innkeepers: Susan Backhouse & Suzanne O'Connor
1290 Royalsborough Road
Durham, ME 04222, USA
Tel: (207) 865-6566, (800) 765-1772
Fax: (207) 353-5878
7 rooms, 1 suite
Double: $120–$175
Open: all year, Credit cards: all major
karenbrown.com/ne/bagleyhouseinn.html

Greenville   Lodge at Moosehead Lake   Map: 4

Magic is everywhere in this northern part of Maine—particularly at the Lodge at Moosehead Lake. Bruce, one of the owners of this paradise, is the consummate innkeeper: it would be hard to imagine someone more devoted to seeing that his guests experience all that this part of Maine can offer. Here you can sit on a porch and overlook the broad waterscape and islands of the largest lake in Maine; go dogsledding, snowshoeing, snowmobiling, and cross-country and downhill skiing in the winter; enjoy mountain biking, whitewater rafting, touring by plane, hiking, canoeing, or fly fishing in some secret stream or lake in summer. And where else can you go on a moose safari? The other half of this team is Sonda, the visionary and creator of all the inn's decor. The five bedrooms and three suites are nothing short of fabulous. I stayed in the Bear Room in a hand-carved four-poster queen bed with bears carved into and perched on its posts. There was a hand-carved bear bench at the foot of the bed, two different sitting areas, and a gas corner fireplace with a chair nearby for gazing out at the lake. Twigs are used to create borders instead of moldings and to simulate picture hangings. *Directions:* Take I-95 to Newport, Route 7 north to Dexter, Route 23 north to Guilford then Route 15 north to Greenville. (1½ hours' drive from Bangor, 2½ hours from Portland, 4½ hours from Boston.)

LODGE AT MOOSEHEAD LAKE
Owners: Sonda & Bruce Hamilton
Upon Lily Bay Road
P.O. Box 1167, Greenville, ME 04441, USA
Tel: (207) 695-4400, Fax: (207) 695-2281
5 rooms, 3 suites
Double: $250–$475
Open: all year, Credit cards: MC, VS
Select Registry
karenbrown.com/ne/thelodgeatmooseheadlake.html

Hancock · Le Domaine · Map: 4

France in the middle of northern Maine? You can be sure that an overnight at this charming inn and dinner in its restaurant will transport you to Provence without any need for a passport. The warm colors of red and yellow are predominant in the common rooms and the dining room. The two suites, Les Baux and St. Remy, are particularly spacious with cathedral ceilings and sitting rooms; each has a bath with a clawfoot tub and shower. From each of the rooms, the suites and the other three rooms, you can walk out to a large deck where you can spend hours looking at the gardens and the towering pines in the back yard. Breakfast can be served on this deck or in the garden. There are beds of herbs growing for the foods of the kitchen, and perennial gardens providing continuous bloom. The lush green of the lawns and the white wicker furniture beckon one to take a book and be lulled to sleep while taking in the natural beauty. During my stay there were fabulous hanging baskets of flowers so full that one wondered if they were real—and they were. In the living room, there is a fireplace where you can await your table in the restaurant. There's also a very attractive small bar which was stocked with every libation that your heart could desire. The dinner menu is so enticing—all in the true French style of cooking—that a return visit will be high on your list of future plans. *Directions:* Route 1 northeast of Ellsworth to Hancock; the inn is on the right.

LE DOMAINE **New**
Owner: Nicole Purslow
HC 77, Box 496
Hancock, ME 04640, USA
Tel & fax: (207) 422-3916, (800) 554-8498
5 rooms
Double: $200–$370
Open: June to Nov, Credit cards: all major
Select Registry
karenbrown.com/ne/ledomaine.html

Hancock Point — Crocker House Country Inn — Map: 4

The Crocker House Country Inn is a lovely, three-story, gray-shingle home trimmed in white and dating back to 1884. The setting on Hancock Point is very picturesque and quiet, and if you arrive by boat, it's just a short stroll over the hill from the harbor at Frenchman Bay. The current owners, the Malabys, have restored the property and created a warm and inviting ambiance both in the decor and welcoming service. Each of the guestrooms is individually and simply decorated; each has a country flavor and beds are topped with old quilts. Two bedrooms are located in the former carriage house, which also provides an additional common room and a spa. Guests have a lovely living room and two sitting rooms, one of which boasts a piano and live music on weekends. The inn is probably best known for its food, which you can enjoy in either of two dining rooms. The restaurant, open to both resident and non-resident guests, offers breakfast and dinner. Always busy and quite popular, the inn hosts many weddings, family reunions, and small business retreats. Attractions include a croquet court, clay tennis courts, antiquing, golf, kayaking, biking, and the fabulous Acadia National Park about 20 minutes away. *Directions:* From Ellsworth travel 8 miles east on Route 1, turn right on Point Road and go 5 miles to the inn (on the right).

CROCKER HOUSE COUNTRY INN
Innkeepers: Elizabeth & Richard Malaby
967 Point Road
Hancock Point, ME 04640, USA
Tel: (207) 422-6806, Fax: (207) 422-3105
11 rooms
Double: $85–$165
Open: Apr through Dec 31, Credit cards: all major
Select Registry
karenbrown.com/ne/crockerhouse.html

Places to Stay–Maine

Kennebunk Beach — The Beach House — Map: 4

Being at the ocean's edge facing a wonderful sandy beach, a rarity in Maine, is just the beginning of the treats awaiting you at The Beach House. This 35-room inn is owned and managed by the proprietors of the spectacular White Barn Inn, located just a short distance away. The Beach House is elegant with its inviting living room with woven rattan chairs, oversized sofas, a large stone fireplace, and a large porch where you can spend hour-after-hour just people watching. The bedrooms—standard, superior, and deluxe—have all the amenities any guest could desire. They are beautifully furnished and exude that inviting welcome that comfortable chairs and sofas give. There are TVs, VCRs, and a selection of videos available. An extended Continental breakfast is served in what used to be one of the house's parlors with long windows facing the beach. In the afternoon, tea and cookies are set out and dinner is served in either of two restaurants at the White Barn. (There are also many good restaurants in Kennebunkport). The inn provides its guests with complimentary beach towels and chairs, bicycles, and canoes. During the winter holiday season, The Beach House offers packages that include dinner at the White Barn Inn. *Directions:* From Maine, take exit 3 to Kennebunk and follow Route 35 south for 6 miles to Kennebunkport. At the intersection of Routes 35 and 9, continue straight on Beach Avenue for 2 miles.

THE BEACH HOUSE
Owner: White Barn Inn
Manager: Roderick Anderson
211 Beach Avenue
Kennebunk Beach, ME 04043, USA
Tel: (207) 967-3850, Fax: (207) 967-4719
35 rooms
Double: $240–$490
Open: all year, Credit cards: all major
karenbrown.com/ne/thebeachhouse.html

Places to Stay—Maine

Kennebunkport — Bufflehead Cove — Map: 4

Just outside the village of Kennebunkport yet within an easy walk of the shops, galleries, and restaurants is Bufflehead Cove, an inn set at the edge of a saltwater inlet. The inn, formerly a private home, now has five guestrooms, a cozy living room, and a dining room. The Balcony Room has water views, a private balcony, gas fireplace, king bed, and whirlpool tub. The queen-bedded River Room, with its collections of folk art and its ceiling shimmering with sunlight reflected off the water, has a private balcony where you can sit and read or enjoy a glass of wine. The River Cottage has an upstairs bedroom with a downstairs living room and wood-burning fireplace, a deck with a water view, a kitchen, and a two-person spa. A delicious full breakfast is served either in the dining room, on the porch by the water, or on the open sunny deck. One breakfast menu included freshly squeezed orange juice, ginger-poached pears in an English custard sauce, apple-stuffed French toast, maple-glazed sausage, and either coffee or a selection of teas. The inn serves wine and cheese in the evening and the innkeepers will be glad to review restaurant options for dinner and then make reservations for you. The personable dog, Lili, adds to the enjoyment of your stay. *Directions:* Leave the Maine Turnpike (I-95) at exit 25 onto Route 35 south. At the intersection of Routes 1 and 35, continue on Route 35 for 3-1/10 miles to the inn's sign on the left. Follow the lane down to the water.

BUFFLEHEAD COVE
Innkeepers: Harriet & James Gott
P.O. Box 499
Kennebunkport, ME 04046, USA
Tel & fax: (207) 967-3879
3 rooms, 2 suites, 1 cottage ($2425 weekly)
Double: $145–$375
Open: May to Oct, Credit cards: MC, VS
karenbrown.com/ne/buffleheadcove.html

Kennebunkport — Captain Jefferds Inn — Map: 4

This 1804 Federal-style mansion was originally built by Daniel Walker as a wedding present for his daughter, Mary, and her husband, the seafaring Captain William Jefferds. The Bartholomew family has restored this home with great attention to detail and has created a 15-room inn that shows the love and care that come from the passion of being innkeepers and masters of the art of hospitality. Guestrooms, all furnished with period antiques or reproductions, have been redesigned to reflect favorite places where the owners have traveled. In addition to private baths, the rooms have air conditioning, remote-controlled CD players, and down-filled comforters. Some rooms have private porches, large showers, soaking tubs, and two-person whirlpool spas, and eight rooms have working fireplaces. The blue-and-white Monticello room has a queen, four-poster canopy bed, a fireplace, four large windows with Indian shutters, and a bath with shower. The Charleston room has a queen four-poster pineapple bed and a working fireplace, and is given its southern style by blue-and-gray wallpaper with magnolia blossoms. The inn is within a short walk of Kennebunkport with all its shops, restaurants, and historical sights, as well as the picturesque harbor and the activity of lobster boats. *Directions:* From the Maine Turnpike (I-95) take exit 19 to Wells. Drive east to Route 1, then take Route 9 to Kennebunkport to Pearl Street to the inn.

CAPTAIN JEFFERDS INN
Innkeeper: The Bartholomew Family
5 Pearl Street
P.O. Box 691, Kennebunkport, ME 04046, USA
Tel: (207) 967-2311, (800) 839-6844
Fax: (207) 967-0721
15 rooms
Double: $155–$350
Open: all year, Credit cards: all major
karenbrown.com/ne/captainjefferds.html

Kennebunkport — Captain Lord Mansion — Map: 4

The town green sloping down from the Captain Lord Mansion to the river gives this stylishly decorated inn a very prominent position that befits its splendid interior. The decor is lavish, from the lovely wallpapers that adorn the walls in the halls to those in the bedrooms, each of which is named after a ship built here in an earlier era. Paintings in ornate frames hang everywhere—an obvious love of the owners who have searched long and hard to find the touches that make this inn so special. I stayed in the Cactus room with a king four-poster bed, gas fireplace, and a bath with double vanity and shower. Other bedrooms have canopy beds and whirlpool tubs for two. A delicious complete breakfast with a hot entree is served in the kitchen most mornings at two long tables where you have a good opportunity to meet and talk to your fellow guests. The parlor has a large fireplace that was burning warmly on the occasion of my visit and comfortable chairs in which to sit, relax, and have a good conversation or a cup of afternoon tea. Captain Lord Mansion is a quiet haven just a few minutes' walk from the heart of Kennebunkport with its many shops, activities, and restaurants. *Directions:* Take the I-95 (Maine Turnpike) to exit 25, go left on Route 35 for 5½ miles, then east on Route 9. Turn left over the bridge and first right in the square to Ocean Avenue. Go 3/10 mile and turn left into Green Street. The inn is at the top of the hill on the left

CAPTAIN LORD MANSION
Innkeepers: Bev Davis & Rick Litchfield
P.O. Box 800
Kennebunkport, ME 04046, USA
Tel: (207) 967-3141, (800) 522-3141
Fax: (207) 967-3172
15 rooms, 1 suite
Double: $125–$499
Open: all year, Credit cards: all major
Select Registry
karenbrown.com/ne/captainlordmansion.html

Places to Stay—Maine

Kennebunkport — Maine Stay Inn at the Melville Walker House — Map: 4

As I walked through the doorway of my bedroom in sea captain Melville Walker's home, I saw the bed reflected in the antique dressing-table mirror and knew that my stay would be a comfortable one. The exterior of this beautiful 1860 Victorian with wraparound porches and an impressive cupola sets the tone for the style that you find inside, where a magnificent suspended spiral staircase winds its way up from the entrance hall. The ground floor has been redecorated and the original oak floors uncovered and refinished. Guestrooms are divided between the main house and cottages on the grounds. There are many variations of amenities so be sure to discuss your preference for a fireplace, whirlpool tub, sitting room, kitchen, or microwave when you make your reservation. If you are staying in one of the cottages, you have the option of either coming to the inn for a full breakfast or having a breakfast basket delivered to your door. The Maine Stay is located within a very short walk of Dock Square, the center of all the activity in this little seaside village. Antiques, clothing, and remembrances of your visit are all available in the many fine shops. There are several good restaurants that specialize in freshly caught local seafood. *Directions:* Take exit 25 from the Maine Turnpike (I-95), turning left on Route 35 south. Go 5½ miles to Route 9, turn left, then go over the bridge and through the village to the stop sign. Turn right on Maine Street. The inn is three blocks down.

MAINE STAY INN At The Melville Walker House
Innkeepers: George & Janice Yankowski
34 Maine Street
P.O. Box 500A, Kennebunkport, ME 04046, USA
Tel: (207) 967-2117, (800) 950-2117
Fax: (207) 967-8757
4 rooms, 3 suites, 10 cottages
Double: $109–$289
Open: all year, Credit cards: all major
Select Registry
karenbrown.com/ne/mainestayinn.html

Kennebunkport   Old Fort Inn   Map: 4

The Old Fort Inn is a beautiful 16-room inn offering elegance and tranquility. Surrounded by old estate cottages in one of Kennebunkport's most attractive residential neighborhoods, the inn has its own swimming pool and tennis court. The spacious and luxurious air-conditioned rooms—in the main building and in the circa-1880 converted carriage house—are stylishly decorated with antiques, fine fabrics, and attractive wall coverings. All guestrooms feature canopy or four-poster beds with down comforters and private baths. Some rooms have gas fireplaces and whirlpool baths. One room I visited had a fishnet canopy over the bed and was decorated in shades of gray and beige with black accents, an attractive color pallette echoed in the bedspread. The inn has a separate large living room with a fireplace, comfortable chairs, and a view out to the pool and gardens. A lavish gourmet breakfast is served daily in the Great Room. The inn, in its own private, peaceful grounds of 15 acres, is just one block from the ocean, yet only 1¼ miles from the bustle of Kennebunkport's shops, galleries, and restaurants. *Directions:* Take the Kennebunk Exit, exit 25 from the Maine Turnpike (I-95), then turn left on Route 35 for 5½ miles. Turn left at the light onto Route 9 for 3/10 mile, then right onto Ocean Ave for 9/10 mile to the Colony Hotel (Kings Hwy.), where you take a left. Turn right at the T-junction and follow signs for 3/10 mile to the inn.

OLD FORT INN
Innkeepers: Sheila & David Aldrich
8 Old Fort Avenue
P.O. Box M, Kennebunkport, ME 04046, USA
Tel: (207) 967-5353, (800) 828-3678
Fax: (207) 967-4547
16 rooms
Double: $160–$400
Open: mid-Apr to mid-Dec, Credit cards: all major
Select Registry
karenbrown.com/ne/oldfortinn.html

Kennebunkport — The Inn at Harbor Head — Map: 4

Four wonderful rooms in a seacoast village surrounding a working harbor on the coast of Maine: tranquil, casual, pretty, and very relaxing. This, and much more, can be said about The Inn at Harbor Head, which opens its doors to guests on the first of May and closes for the season on October 31. All the bedrooms are comfortably furnished. In the Summer Suite, the wicker king bed permits you to glance out the window toward the harbor or to the gas log fireplace. This room has a balcony with views of the harbor, a bathroom with a cathedral ceiling, a Jacuzzi, and another water view. Reflecting warm woods and chintz fabrics, the Ocean Room has a massive, mahogany plantation queen bed and a love seat on which to curl up. Early risers can find nothing more magic than to take a mug of coffee and watch the harbor come alive, or walk down the road enjoying the charm of this little village. Come back to the inn for a full breakfast; and then explore the surrounding countryside on foot, by car, or (ideally) by bicycle. There are art galleries, antique shops, and great little places to get a lobster roll, just minutes away. The inn's living room and dining room are there for your enjoyment—if you can find the time to do it all. *Directions:* Maine Turnpike Route 95 to Exit 25 Kennebunk, take Route 35/9A to Kennebunkport. L on Route 9 through Kennebunkport to Cape Porpoise. At Bradbury's Market go straight to inn at 41 Pier Road.

THE INN AT HARBOR HEAD *New*
Owners: Dick & Eve Roesler
41 Pier Road
Kennebunkport, ME 04046, USA
Tel: (207) 967-5564, Fax: (207) 967-1294
4 rooms
Double: $160–$325
Open: May 1 to Oct 31, Credit cards: MC, VS
karenbrown.com/ne/harborhead.html

Kennebunkport — White Barn Inn — Map: 4

Just beyond the historic town of Kennebunkport is the lovely White Barn Inn. Eighteen guestrooms and seven suites are found in the main building, the pool house, and the carriage house. Three cottages have recently been opened on a wharf by the river's edge. All the rooms have been meticulously restored and furnished with period pieces, with a great eye for detail. Plush amenities include fresh flowers, bathrooms with whirlpool tubs, thick robes, elegant toiletries and wood-burning fireplaces. My room had softly painted walls and two comfortable upholstered chairs with an ottoman on which to rest my feet after a long day of walking around Kennebunkport. The restaurant is one of only five AAA five-diamond restaurants in New England and the special focus on locally caught seafood makes the ever-changing menu a real treat. Complimentary bicycles are available for cycling the short distance to the village or for riding down to the ocean beach for a walk or a swim. If you prefer swimming in warmer water, try the inn's heated swimming pool. Golf, tennis, horseback riding, deep-sea fishing, whale watching, and sailing are all available close by. The nearby wildlife preserve is a great place to walk and to enjoy the special beauty of Maine's rugged coast. *Directions:* Leave the Maine Turnpike (I-95) at exit 3 for Kennebunk then take Route 35 south for 7 miles to Kennebunkport. Cross the light at Route 9 and the inn is on the right after ¼ mile.

WHITE BARN INN
Director: Roderick Anderson
Beach Avenue
P.O. Box 560 C, Kennebunkport, ME 04046, USA
Tel: (207) 967-2321, Fax: (207) 967-1100
25 rooms, 8 suites, 3 cottages, up to $1250
Double: $285–$750
Open: all year, Credit cards: all major
Relais & Châteaux
karenbrown.com/ne/whitebarn.html

Lincolnville Beach (Camden)   Inn at Sunrise Point   Map: 4

Just 4 miles north of Camden in the little village of Lincolnville Beach there's an inn sitting at the water's edge that provides an idyllic place for you to rest while listening to the water lapping at the shore and the wind sighing in the pines. The Inn at Sunrise Point, consisting of the main house with three bedrooms, four cottages, and two suites named after Maine's most famous writers and artists, offers comfortably decorated guestrooms of great charm, most containing a wood-burning fireplace. The newest suite is so complete (with a kitchen) that one could move in and never move out. Bedrooms have either queen or king beds and bathrooms with large tubs and plush robes. In the cottages there are two-person spa tubs, wet bars, and private decks. A full gourmet breakfast is served in the glass conservatory of the main house. This inn is nicely located for exploring all of the wonders of the Camden region, and at the end of a day of excursions, you can return to the inn to enjoy a glass of wine sitting by the fire in the cherry-paneled library. I can imagine nothing nicer than to rest in this setting for days on end, venturing out to the shops and the restaurants and yet taking full advantage of the spectacular setting at the water's edge. *Directions:* Take exit 28 from I-295 in Brunswick. Follow Route 1 north to Camden. Continue through Camden, 4 miles farther on turn right at fire road #9 and drive down to the inn.

INN AT SUNRISE POINT
Innkeepers: Deanna & Stephen Tallon
P.O. Box 1344
Lincolnville Beach (Camden), ME 04843, USA
Tel: (207) 236-7716, Fax: (207) 236-0820
3 rooms, 4 cottages, 2 suites
Double: $250–$495
Open: all year, Credit cards: all major
karenbrown.com/ne/innatsunrisepoint.html

Newcastle — Newcastle Inn — Map: 4

The Newcastle Inn, looking down sloping lawns with lovely gardens to the water's edge, commands an enviable position in the charming seacoast village of Newcastle with its many cute shops and wonderful bookstore. The inn is as lovely inside as out and not long ago received a fresh look with new wallpapers, carpeting, and reupholstered furniture. A very special touch is the living-room floor, which has been hand-painted in the most attractive of designs. Off the living room, an enclosed porch with beautiful views from its many windows is a great place to sit in the afternoon with a book and a glass of wine. The restaurant menu changes weekly and specializes in the best of the local foods—especially seafood. The breakfast I had when I stayed there was wonderful, with an omelet preceded by fresh fruit and juice. I stayed in a room on the third floor looking out to the water. While simply furnished, it was very comfortable with its floral wallpaper and upholstered chair where I enjoyed reading in the evening. The rooms do not have individual telephones, but off the dining room there is an anteroom with a desk where you can make a private telephone call. *Directions:* From Coastal Route 1 travel 6 miles north of Wiscasset Bridge. Turn right on River Road. The inn is on the right after half a mile.

NEWCASTLE INN
Innkeepers: Peter & Laura Barclay
60 River Road
Newcastle, ME 04553, USA
Tel: (207) 563-5685, (800) 832-8669
Fax: (207) 563-6877
12 rooms, 3 suites, 3 suites
Double: $155–$295
Closed: Jan, Credit cards: all major
Select Registry
karenbrown.com/ne/newcastle.html

Places to Stay–Maine

Northeast Harbor　　　　Grey Rock Inn　　　　Map: 4

The northern section of the Maine coast consists of fingers of land that run down to the ocean, creating long inlets and miles of rocky coastline settled with centuries-old little fishing villages. Northeast Harbor is a very popular community of summer homes with great ancestral lineage. Here Grey Rock Inn is situated on 7 acres overlooking the harbor, the lighthouse, and the outer islands off Mount Desert. Its seven rooms and one suite are decorated in the style of fashionable summer homes of an earlier era. The Sun guestroom has twelve double-hung windows and a set of French doors wrapping the room. Through the doors is a private porch and veranda with eight granite pillars. The room comfortably contains a king and single beds, a secretary, sofa, three stained-glass lamps, a pair of window seats, and a brick wood-burning fireplace. The Butterfly room is lovely, with views of Northeast Harbor, pretty silvery wallpaper that comes alive with hundreds of butterflies, a handsome white wrought-iron-and-brass antique double bed, white wicker chairs, and a painted bureau. The inn provides a full breakfast and there are restaurants nearby for dinner. The village is charming with its old-fashioned shops and galleries and many sports can be enjoyed in the area. Acadia National Park is a just short drive away. *Directions:* From Ellsworth follow Route 3/198 on Mount Desert Island. Just before Northeast Harbor the inn is on the right bordering the Acadia National Park.

GREY ROCK INN
Innkeepers: Janet, Karl & Adam Millett
Harborside Road
Northeast Harbor, ME 04662, USA
Tel: (207) 276-9360 (summer), (207) 244-4437 (winter)
Fax: (207) 276-9894
7 rooms, 1 suite
Double: $155–$375
Open: mid-May through Oct, Credit cards: all major
Select Registry
karenbrown.com/ne/greyrockinn.html

Ogunquit   Hartwell House   Maps: 3, 4

Hartwell House is located just outside Perkins Cove, one of those scenic Maine lobster-fishing villages. There are many inns in the region and yet Hartwell House, a lovely, traditional New England home, is always described as the most elegant and very beautiful. The inn consists of two buildings that face each other across a street going down to the harbor. Set on an acre-and-a-half of lush green lawn and gardens, the elegant main building houses the common rooms: the sun porch, the dining room, and a lovely sitting room. Attached to the main house, where there are also seven guestrooms, are two studio bedrooms that step up to their own outside entrance. New spa tubs for two have been added in some rooms. Across the street all the bedrooms have a terrace or balcony and there are three suites. The inn serves a full gourmet breakfast and afternoon tea. Conference and wedding facilities are available. Close to the inn is the Marginal Way footpath, one of the most picturesque spots on the coast of lower Maine. There is much to do here—fishing, golf, tennis, sailing, galleries to visit, antiquing, and summer theater. *Directions:* Take exit 4 from the Maine Turnpike (I-95) north, turning left on Route 1 (north) for 4-4/10 miles. Turn right on Pine Hill, left on Shore, and go 2/10 mile to the inn on the left. From the Maine Turnpike south, take exit 2, go left on Route 109, right on Route 1 for 6 miles, then left on Shore Road for 6/10 mile to the inn on the right.

HARTWELL HOUSE
Owners: Trisha & James Hartwell
Innkeepers: Gail & Paul Koehler
312 Shore Road, Ogunquit, ME 03907, USA
Tel: (207) 646-7210, (800) 235-8883
Fax: (207) 646-6032
11 rooms, 3 suites, 2 garden apartments
Double: $110–$265
Open: all year, Credit cards: all major
Select Registry
karenbrown.com/ne/hartwell.html

Portland   Pomegranate Inn   Map: 4

A small city like Portland needs to have a great inn so that you can settle in to explore all that there is to do here for a day or two or three. The Pomegranate Inn is just the place, located in the historic district and within an easy walk of all the sights. Its totally conforming, external historical appearance belies the eclectic decorating that you'll find inside. The artwork—pictures and sculpture—demands your attention and your involvement. Whether you understand it or not doesn't matter—but you will love it just the same. The inn's eight rooms, including one suite and a garden room, are all beautifully decorated with antiques and show more of that eclectic touch with walls sporting hand-painted flowers. It would be hard to beat the carriage house with its own private terrace for real seclusion. Every room has a private bath, telephone, television, and some have fireplaces. This inn provides a different visual experience in a traditional setting and I think you'll like it as much as I did. There's wine to greet your arrival and a full breakfast is served in the dining room. *Directions:* From northbound I-95 take I-295, leaving at exit 4 for Route 1A. Turn immediately left onto Danforth Street, first left onto Vaughan, then right on Carroll for 1 block. From the north, take I-295 to exit 6A to Route 77, which is also State Street, turn right on Pine, then left on Neal.

POMEGRANATE INN
Innkeeper: Isabel Smiles
49 Neal Street
Portland, ME 04102, USA
Tel: (207) 772-1006, (800) 356-0408
Fax: (207) 773-4426
8 rooms, 1 suite
Double: $175–$245
Open: all year, Credit cards: all major
Select Registry
karenbrown.com/ne/pomegranateinn.html

Rockland   Berry Manor Inn   Map: 4

On a quiet residential street in Rockland sits the Berry Manor Inn, built in 1898 as an elegant residence and now a twelve-bedroom inn. The bedrooms, all large and with queen and king beds lavishly piled with mountains of pillows, are located on three floors, with four spacious and interesting accommodations in and around the eaves on the third floor. Room 1, once the boudoir for the lady of the house, is decorated in shades of moss, sage, basil, and dark quartz. It has a mahogany half-tester canopy bed, a double chaise, a working fireplace, and an attached private bath with a large whirlpool tub and two shower heads. All bedrooms are equipped with individually controlled thermostats, air conditioning, fireplaces, telephones, high-speed internet access, and private luxury baths. The adjoining carriage house has been newly refurbished and provides four guest suites with spectacular bathrooms featuring whirlpool tubs and walk-in showers with body jets. Guests enjoy morning coffee in the library, a full gourmet breakfast in the large dining room at individual tables, and evening sweets (usually one of Mom's homemade pies) are provided in the well-stocked guest pantry area. *Directions:* Take I-95 to Route 295 North (Exit 44). Follow Route 195 to Exit 28, Coastal Route 1 Bath/Brunswick until Rockland. At the first traffic light, turn left onto Broadway. After next traffic light, proceed to the fourth road and turn right onto Talbot Avenue.

BERRY MANOR INN
Innkeepers: Cheryl Michaelsen & Michael LaPosta
81 Talbot Ave
P.O. Box 1117, Rockland, ME 04841, USA
Tel: (207) 596-7696, (800) 774-5692
Fax: (207) 596-9958
12 rooms
Double: $135–$255
Open: all year, Credit cards: all major
karenbrown.com/ne/berrymanor.html

Waterford   Waterford Inne   Maps: 3, 4

I first learned of Waterford when my dear friend Helen decided to return to her family ties in Maine. When I think of Waterford I think of an idyllic, classic New England town with its white steepled church on a grassy knoll. The Waterford Inne, a bed and breakfast with seven bedrooms and one suite, provides a terrific place to stay. The inn is a 19th-century farmhouse on a country lane amidst 25 acres of fields and woods—just viewing it tells you that this is another of those homes that now serves guests as it once did the original family. The guestrooms are uniquely decorated, mixing the warmth of antique furnishings with contemporary comforts in their modern bathrooms. The simple but elegant common rooms echo the decor of the bedrooms, with antiques and art, barn-board, brass, pewter, and primitives. With advance notice the innkeepers will provide a special dinner but there are also numerous restaurants nearby. Skiing and other winter sports are available in the area and in the summer there are many musical events, while antiquing is fun year round. *Directions:* Leave the Maine Turnpike (I-95) at exit 63, following Route 26 north for about 28 miles to Norway where you pick up Route 118 west. Drive 9 miles to Route 37, turn left, and travel half a mile to Chadbourne Road. Turn right and the inn is half-a-mile up the hill.

WATERFORD INNE
Innkeeper: Barbara Vanderzanden
P.O. Box 149
Waterford, ME 04088, USA
Tel & fax: (207) 583-4037
7 rooms, 1 suite
Double: $100–$175
Open: all year, Credit cards: AX
Select Registry
karenbrown.com/ne/thewaterfordinne.html

Wiscasset Squire Tarbox Inn Map: 4

At the end of a long country road, the Squire Tarbox Inn, a farmhouse dating from 1763 to 1825, listed on the National Register of Historic Places, exudes the peace and quiet of the countryside surrounding it. This rambling colonial farm affords a lovely spot to settle and to enjoy the splendor of being in the country. Sure, you can walk the path that leads to the water's edge and do some boating, but I'd settle in with a good book in front of a wood-burning fire and let time slide by. The common rooms and the cozy dining rooms all have fireplaces. Guests can enjoy the mouthwatering meals created by the Swiss owner and chef. The dinner menu, with an emphasis on local produce, is an exciting culinary adventure. Bedrooms, generally king, are made up with featherbeds and most have fireplaces. For those who do want to venture out, there are harbors and beaches nearby, plenty of antiquing, shopping at discount stores, countryside excursions, and several fascinating museums with a variety of different themes. The inn's 11 bedrooms are simply, but very comfortably, decorated. *Directions:* From the south, take I-95 to I-295 to Rte 1, traveling north through Brunswick. Seven miles north of Bath Bridge, turn right on Rte 144. From the north, take south on Rte 1 through Wiscasset to Rte 144. Once on Rte 144 travel for 8½ miles—the inn is on the right.

SQUIRE TARBOX INN
Innkeepers: Mario & Veronica De Pietro
1181 Main Road
Westport Island, Wiscasset, ME 04578, USA
Tel: (207) 882-7693, (800) 818-0626
Fax: (207) 882-7107
11 rooms
Double: $125–$190
Open: Apr through Dec, Credit cards: all major
Select Registry
karenbrown.com/ne/squiretarbox.html

York Dockside Guest Quarters Maps: 3, 4

Once you cross into Maine life seems different: first there's the smell of the sea air; then there are views down picturesque inlets of open water and the rise and fall of the ocean tides. Next you see the signs for lobster and the lobster boats—and you realize that you are in a place where the people, the food, and the scenery are unique. At the Dockside Guest Quarters, whose lawns and gardens sweep down to the water's edge, you are immediately captured by the setting on the water and the fishing boats bobbing up and down. The bedrooms and suites, which are located in several buildings, are comfortably decorated, but it's the views that capture your eye and demand your attention. I stayed in one of the suites with a nicely furnished living room, bedroom, and a full bath. Your visit will be enhanced by your hosts, the Lustys, who encourage you to take advantage of all the coast-oriented activities such as boating, fishing, beach walking, and biking. Nearby you find whale watching, lobstering, golf, tennis, summer theater, lots of antiquing, lighthouses, and outlet stores for the avid shopper. Lunch and dinner are served in the inn's restaurant where you can dine on the porch overlooking the harbor and all of its activities, while breakfast is served in the Maine House. *Directions:* From I-95 heading north, take exit 7 and head south on Route 1. Turn left at the first light to Route 1A, go through York Village, then turn right on Route 103 and follow signs to the inn.

DOCKSIDE GUEST QUARTERS
Innkeeper: The Lusty Family
Harris Island Road
P.O. Box 205, York, ME 03909, USA
Tel: (207) 363-2868, (888) 860-7428
Fax: (207) 363-1977
13 rooms, 6 suites, Double: $110–$250*
 *Breakfast not included: $5
Open: all year, weekends only Nov to May
Credit cards: MC, VS, Select Registry
karenbrown.com/ne/docksideguestquarters.html

Places to Stay–Maine

Massachusetts
Places to Stay

Barnstable — Ashley Manor — Map: 2

Barnstable is one of those wonderfully quaint villages found on the north shore of Cape Cod and Ashley Manor is an inn worthy of a night's visit. Dating back to 1699, the inn sits back from the road in 2 acres of landscaped gardens surrounded by high hedges. Ashley Manor reveals its age with its wide-board flooring, large open-hearth fireplaces, and hand-glazed wainscoting. This inn is both elegant and warm, with beautiful decor and furnishings that include Oriental rugs, antiques, and handsome country furniture. Relax in the comfortable parlor and library or enjoy the privacy of your lovely room, which is equipped with everything you need for a pampered stay—imported chocolates and the finest soaps, shampoos, and lotions. All but one has a cozy fireplace and the suites offer the additional luxury of large whirlpool tubs. Breakfast is served in the parlor, the formal dining room, or in good weather on the terrace. If you have any spare time, you can play tennis. *Directions:* From Boston take Route 3 south to Sagamore Bridge onto Cape Cod, then follow Route 6 to exit 6. Turn immediately left onto Route 132 north to Route 6A and go about 3 miles through Barnstable Village to the traffic light. The inn is 6/10 mile down on the left.

ASHLEY MANOR
Innkeeper: Kathy Callahan
3660 Olde Kings Hwy
P.O. Box 856, Barnstable, MA 02630, USA
Tel: (508) 362-8044, (888) 535-2246
Fax: (508) 362-9927
2 rooms, 4 suites
Double: $150–$225
Open: all year, Credit cards: all major
karenbrown.com/ne/maashleymanor.html

Barnstable   Cobb's Cove Inn   Map: 2

This 1643 inn sits high on a hill with views of the village of Barnstable, the harbor, and the ocean. The simple rustic quality of this six-bedroom inn (each of whose air-conditioned rooms has a snug bathroom with whirlpool tub) provides the visitor with an alternative to the more formal and highly decorated inns found elsewhere on the Cape. The inn was built of 12-by-12-inch rough-cut timbers and many of the walls are covered in rough burlap. The innkeepers are charming and determined to make your visit to their inn and to the Cape a special memory. The third-floor suites, my first choice, have comfortable seating in front of a view to the ocean that you can hardly tear yourself away from—Cape Cod Bay, Sandy Neck, and all the way to Provincetown Light. The keeping room (living room) has a large Count Rumford fireplace (an efficient, shallow fireplace designed by a master craftsman). The dining room is furnished with a long table where scrumptious breakfasts are served. Outside, Henri's pretty gardens are full of color, attracting numbers of birds and butterflies. *Directions:* From Boston follow Route 3 to the Sagamore Bridge to Route 6 then take exit 6 to Route 132 north to Route 6A. Turn right on Route 6A to Barnstable Village, going through the only traffic light and past the church. Turn left onto Powder Hill Road and into the first driveway on left.

COBB'S COVE INN
Innkeepers: Evelyn Chester & Henri-Jean Studley
Powder Hill Road
P.O. Box 208, Barnstable, MA 02630, USA
Tel & fax: (508) 362-9356, (877) 378-5172
6 rooms
Double: $149–$189
Open: all year, Credit cards: all major
karenbrown.com/ne/cobbscoveinn.html

Places to Stay–Massachusetts

Boston   Beacon Hill Hotel & Bistro   Map: 2

In a perfect location just off Boston Common on Charles Street, site of many antique shops, restaurants, and boutiques, you find the new Beacon Hill Hotel & Bistro, a very sophisticated small hotel with the feel of a bed and breakfast. The bedrooms, reached via an elevator are small, but have all the amenities that a traveler might expect including a flat-screen TV mounted on the wall. Nine of the rooms have queen beds, two have doubles, one has twin beds, and on the top floor there is an in-room suite. The color palette of the bedrooms' decor is soft and soothing, with tones of taupe accented by off-white trim and black accessories. Satellite TV is available, including the movie channels, and there are telephones with dual lines and a data port for Internet access. Most of the rooms do not have seating areas but there is a small and comfortable sitting area for guests on the second floor. The hotel is air-conditioned and there is parking available for guests—a very nice feature in downtown Boston. The trendy but comfortable adjoining bistro-restaurant, which has received much acclaim, provides room service and the hotel offers all the concierge services one could want for maximizing a stay in the Boston area.

Directions: From Storrow Drive take the Government Center exit. At the end of the off ramp proceed through two stoplights, leaving the CVS Pharmacy on your left, onto Charles Street. The hotel is on the left on the corner of Chestnut and Charles Streets.

BEACON HILL HOTEL & BISTRO
Owners: Peter & Cecilia Rait
25 Charles Street
Boston, MA 02114, USA
Tel: (617) 723-7575, (888) 959-2442
Fax: (617) 723-7525
13 rooms
Double: $245–$365
Open: all year, Credit cards: all major
karenbrown.com/ne/beaconhill.html

Places to Stay–Massachusetts

Boston Charles Street Inn Map: 2

The Charles Street Inn is beautifully located at the foot of Beacon Hill, that historic district where colonial merchants first built their homes, within walking distance of all that you may want to explore in downtown Boston. The inn's guestrooms—two per floor—offer 21st-century comforts while retaining a 19th-century elegance. Each one is uniquely decorated in period colors, fabrics, and furnishings and named for a famous Boston Victorian. Front rooms with queen beds offer views of Charles Street, with its tempting restaurants and unique shops, while rooms at the back are larger and quieter, overlooking the very private area of Mount Vernon Square, and most feature king beds. Each room has a sitting area where you may enjoy your deluxe Continental breakfast and relax in style. The rooms' superb amenities include working marble fireplaces, air conditioning, extra-large whirlpool spa tubs, in-room mini fridge, coffee pots and tea kettles, complete set of dishes, high-speed internet access, cable TVs and VCRs, and Bose AM/FM/CD systems. Baths have granite counters, white tile finishes, and cherry-wood cabinets. *Directions:* From I-90 (Mass Pike) take the Cambridge Storrow Drive exit, following Storrow Drive to the Government Center/Kendall Square exit, then turn right off the exit onto Charles Street.

CHARLES STREET INN
Innkeepers: Louise Venden & Sally Deane
94 Charles Street
Boston, MA 02114-4643, USA
Tel: (617) 314-8900, (877) 772-8900
Fax: (617) 371-0009
9 rooms
Double: $225–$500
Open: all year, Credit cards: all major
Select Registry
karenbrown.com/ne/charlesstreetinn.html

Places to Stay–Massachusetts

Boston   Clarendon Square Inn   Map: 2

One of the many pleasures of visiting Boston is that you can walk to almost everything you'd like to see. The best location is the Clarendon Square Inn, as its doors open onto all of Boston's restaurants, galleries, and shopping. This historic property, with its traditional exterior, has been transformed into an elegant urban retreat. Guest suites are spacious with wood-burning fireplaces and limestone bathrooms. High-count cotton sheets, down pillows, and European bath amenities will pamper you. There is a sundeck on the roof, complete with a hot-tub overlooking Boston's skyline. The inn's parlor has 11-foot high ceilings with period detail and a grand piano. The garden suite's modern furniture, subtle textures, and calming colors stimulate, but also relax. The window seat in the bay room, furnished in Empire style and decorated in deep sensuous colors, invites you to curl up with a book, or perhaps a glass of wine, while the fireplace crackles in the background. Such is the style and experience you will have at an inn whose owners have traveled widely, capturing and translating the finest elements to make your stay memorable and your return guaranteed. *Directions:* From Mass Pike Route 90, take exit 22 for Copley Square, keep right on the off-ramp to Copley. Take first right onto Dartmouth Street. At 2nd light take right onto Warren Avenue. West Brookline St is the 2nd right and the inn the 5th house.

CLARENDON SQUARE INN   *New*
Owner: Stephen Gross
Innkeeper: Jimmy Ward
198 West Brookline Street
Boston, MA 02118, USA
Tel: (617) 536-2229
3 rooms
Double: $129–$289
Open: all year, Credit cards: all major
karenbrown.com/ne/clarendon.html

Boston — Fifteen Beacon — Map: 2

Elegant is the word that sums up every aspect of one of Boston's newest hotels. In a great location next to the State House, within a few minutes' walk of all the historical buildings and the Freedom Trail, with Boston Common just across the way, and with every creature comfort offered by the hotel's staff, there is no better place to spend the night. Sophisticated in every sense, Fifteen Beacon welcomes you into its front lobby where the concierge and the reception desk staff make you instantly feel like a treasured returning guest. The muted palette of colors used throughout is warm and inviting, contemporary in feel, and totally relaxing. In your bedroom the sitting areas, the fireplace, the wall coverings, the carpet, the artwork, and the crispness of the bed and its linens all contribute to the ambiance of this special experience. In one room, a spotlight focused attention on the simple beauty of a tall glass cylinder filled with apples. The elegant bathrooms provide every amenity in a very contemporary setting. A delightful place to relax is the roof deck with herb garden, where you can drink in lovely views while nibbling on something delicious brought to you by room service. *Directions:* From Storrow Drive take the Government Center exit. Go straight through the traffic light on Cambridge Street for ¾ mile to Park Street, turn right and drive to the end. At the light turn right on Beacon Street for 1½ blocks to the inn on the left.

FIFTEEN BEACON
Manager: William J. Sander III
15 Beacon Street
Boston, MA 02108, USA
Tel: (617) 670-1500, (877) 982-3226
Fax: (617) 670-2525
60 rooms
Double: $395–$2500*
 *Breakfast not included: $20
Open: all year, Credit cards: all major
karenbrown.com/ne/fifteenbeacon.html

Places to Stay–Massachusetts

Boston　　　　　　　　　　　The Lenox　　　　　　　　　　　Map: 2

In the heart of Boston's Back Bay on Exeter Street stands The Lenox, recently renovated by the Saunders family into a very chic place for you to stay while you are visiting the many attractions of Boston. It is located in the heart of Boylston and Newbury Streets' shopping and art galleries, which could keep you busy for days. Copley Place and the Prudential Center are a few steps from the hotel. The hotel features 212 guestrooms, each with private bathroom. Since the hotel was recently refurbished, the rooms are especially attractive. One of the rooms I visited had a corner fireplace, wonderfully comfortable seating, and two queen beds. It was decorated in tones of taupe and had flowered drapes, which pulled across the windows in the evening. This is a full-service hotel offering amenities such as concierge and valet, voice mail, in-room fax machines, wireless internet, phones with modem ports, laundry service, and conference facilities. Azure is the formal dining room (where breakfast is also served) but there is also a pub, Solas, serving lighter food in a casual setting and the City Bar, serving food and drink in an engaging ambiance. Room service is also available. The hotel has the bonus of an on-site exercise room. *Directions:* Take I-93 into Boston, exiting at the signs to Copley Square. Turn right at Beacon Street for four blocks and then take a left on Exeter Street. The Lenox is four blocks down on the right.

THE LENOX
Owner: Saunders Hotel Group
61 Exetor Street
Boston, MA 02116, USA
Tel: (617) 536-5300, (800) 225-7676
Fax: (617) 236-0351
212 rooms
Double: $199–$499*
 *Breakfast not included
Open: all year, Credit cards: all major
karenbrown.com/ne/thelenox.html

Brewster By The Sea, A European B&B

Brewster — Map: 2

As you drive along Cape Cod's north shore route you're instantly attracted to the Brewster By The Sea B&B with its neat and tidy appearance. Brewster is but one of several villages along Route 6A that make for great places to stop overnight. These little villages are all charming with their historical homes, an antique store or two, a shop here and there, maybe a restaurant next to the post office. You enter into the inn's large gathering room with a fireplace at one end and a lovely sitting area at the other end of this expansive space with its cathedral ceiling. A full gourmet breakfast is served in this area during cooler months and in the summer on the deck, which leads out to the heated pool and spa. While the beach is just a short distance away, the pool area is so attractive it might be tempting to stay right at the inn. Hydrangeas surround the pool and provide a floral background during much of the summer. In the afternoon the owners serve tea to guests returning from a day of exploring. The guestrooms are all attractively decorated. The Audubon Suite has one bathroom and two bedrooms, each of which has a queen canopy bed. The Garden Room is furnished with a king rice-carved canopy bed and a private deck—right near the pool. *Directions:* From Boston, take Rte 3 south to Bourne Bridge to Rte 6 to exit 9b (Rte 134). Turn right onto Rte 134 for about 3 miles to Rte 6A, then turn right onto 6A for about 2 miles. The inn is on the right.

BREWSTER BY THE SEA, A EUROPEAN B&B
Innkeepers: Donna & Byron Cain
716 Main Street
Brewster, MA 02631, USA
Tel: (508) 896-3910, (800) 892-3910
Fax: (508) 896-4232
8 rooms
Double: $125–$245
Open: all year, Credit cards: all major
karenbrown.com/ne/brewsterfarmhouse.html

Places to Stay–Massachusetts

Brewster   Captain Freeman Inn   Map: 2

Sea captains' homes fill the landscape in this lovely Cape Cod town. The Captain Freeman Inn was home to one of those merchants whose wealth came from the rich clipper trade in the late 1800s and a picture of his ship, the Kingfisher, hangs in the entry hall. Elegant architectural details are everywhere in this building—ornate plaster moldings, wood floors in intricate patterns, a commanding center staircase, and a parlor with marble fireplace and floor-to-ceiling windows. There are traditional and luxury guestrooms, all wonderful and all air-conditioned. The luxury rooms have queen canopy beds, fireplaces, and spa tubs in the bathrooms. Among the traditional rooms it is hard to choose a favorite between the cozy bedroom with dark paneling, queen bed, and hand-sewn canopy and the queen bedroom with the pine four-poster and lace canopy. Some rooms can accommodate an extra person. An elegant wraparound porch is a perfect spot to rock away the hours with iced tea or lemonade. The inn has its own swimming pool. A short walk from the inn will bring you to the local beach. The Captain Freeman Inn has winter weekend cooking classes. *Directions:* Leave Route 6 at exit 10, taking Route 124 towards Brewster. At the end of Route 124, go right on Route 6A, then left on Breakwater to the first driveway on the left.

CAPTAIN FREEMAN INN
Innkeepers: Donna & Peter Amadeo
15 Breakwater Road
Brewster, MA 02631, USA
Tel: (508) 896-7481, (800) 843-4664
Fax: (508) 896-5618
12 rooms
Double: $150–$250
Open: all year, Credit cards: MC, VS
Select Registry
karenbrown.com/ne/captainfreeman.html

Brewster — Isaiah Clark House — Map: 2

Like so many of the homes along the north shore of Cape Cod, this 1780s home once belonged to a sea captain. It has now been restored to become an inn offering seven bedrooms, all with private bathrooms, four of which are across the hall from the room—plan to use one of the inn's robes and you'll be all set. The bedrooms are attractively decorated in simple Cape-Cod style with comfortable, homelike furnishings. Whether you choose to relax in your bedroom or in the inn's living room, this is an inn that has the ambiance of home, a sentiment reinforced by the innkeeper, whose gracious welcome will make you feel like a friend rather than a guest. In the morning a full breakfast is served either in the keeping room or outside on the deck with its surrounding gardens. The inn is air-conditioned for comfort in the warm summer months. Brewster has good restaurants, antique shops, and places to browse around, and is a pleasant town for walking. Here you are within an easy drive of the Cape Cod National Seashore where Atlantic Ocean beaches beckon you to stroll along their edge. Using the inn as the place for a good night's rest, you can enjoy bird watching, nature walks, wildlife preserves, boating, swimming, bicycling, golf, tennis, and horseback riding. *Directions:* From Boston, take Route 3 south to Sagamore Bridge to Route 6 to exit 9B. Follow Route 134 north then at Route 6A turn right for 3 miles to the inn on the left.

ISAIAH CLARK HOUSE
Innkeepers: Dale & Jan Melikan
1187 Main Street
Brewster, MA 02631, USA
Tel: (508) 896-2223, (800) 822-4001
Fax: (508) 896-2138
7 rooms
Double: $140–$150
Open: Mar to Jan 1, Credit cards: MC, VS
karenbrown.com/ne/isaiahclark.html

Places to Stay–Massachusetts

Cambridge   A Cambridge House   Map: 2

Situated on the outskirts of Cambridge and Boston, A Cambridge House has 15 bedrooms, each with private bath and all elegantly furnished with premier fabrics and charming decor. While the rooms are not large, they provide everything the visitor might want, and most especially that cozy feeling of home. The four-poster beds have down comforters and an assortment of pillows and each room has comfortable seating, a telephone, voice mail, data port, and color TV. Many of the rooms have fireplaces. The flowered or patterned wallpapers are exquisite and in some rooms the matching fabric has been used on the bed canopy. A full buffet breakfast is served in either of the two equally beautiful living rooms and in the evening, hors d'oeuvres and beverages are offered to guests returning from the day's activities. The inn provides complimentary parking, although it's not on the inn property. Public transportation is the key to getting around Boston and Cambridge: it's easy and convenient and you'll be glad to leave your car while you explore the endless array of things to do in the Boston area. Logan Airport is about 20 minutes from the inn. *Directions:* The inn may be reached by car, taxi, or bus and has very detailed directions, which are given to every guest. Please contact the hotel directly for written directions.

A CAMBRIDGE HOUSE
Innkeeper: Ellen Riley
2218 Massachusetts Avenue
Cambridge, MA 02140-1846, USA
Tel: (617) 491-6300, (800) 232-9989
Fax: (617) 868-2848
15 rooms
Double: $149–$290
Open: all year, Credit cards: all major
karenbrown.com/ne/acambridgehouse.html

Places to Stay–Massachusetts

Chatham — Captain's House Inn — Map: 2

Captain Hiram Harding, a packet skipper in the 1800s, built this home in 1839, and the inn's very individual rooms are named after his family and the ships he sailed. This inn is an elegant compound with its guestrooms clustered around a handsome Greek Revival home. The common areas are attractively furnished with antiques and the dining-room sun porch is surrounded by floor-to-ceiling windows giving views into the delightful gardens. Breakfast is served here with sterling silver and fine china on linen-covered tables. Each bedroom is individually decorated and many will remind you of the cozy feeling of colonial times with their beamed ceilings, fireplaces, and queen or king beds with antique bedposts. Many rooms have original random-width pine floors, adding to the decor's charm. All rooms have private baths, a few have spa tubs, and several have private decks. I loved my room with its dark paneling, massive king bed, and a fireplace with two comfortable wing chairs. The Clarissa and Lady Hope rooms are examples of the owners' passion to offer the best of accommodations. Among the many amenites you'll find a new fitness center with exercise room; spa or in-room massages, body treatments and facials; and outdoor heated pool. *Directions:* Leave Rte 6 at exit 11 south, taking Rte 137 to Rte 28. Turn left; drive about 3 miles to the rotary. Follow the rotary around to the left (still on Rte 28) toward Orleans. The inn is ½ mile along on the left.

CAPTAIN'S HOUSE INN
Innkeepers: Jan & Dave McMaster
369-377 Old Harbor Road
Chatham, MA 02633, USA
Tel: (508) 945-0127, (800) 315-0728
Fax: (508) 945-0866
12 rooms, 4 suites
Double: $235–$450
Open: all year, Credit cards: all major
Select Registry
karenbrown.com/ne/thecaptainshouseinn.html

Concord

Concord's Colonial Inn

Map: 2

The historic town of Concord is one of those very special New England towns that draw the visitor in to share their past and to experience their welcoming charm. Here you find a quaint village with interesting shops, lovely old homes lining the streets, a magnificent white Unitarian church set back on the green, and on the far edge of the green a landmark inn—Concord's Colonial Inn, built in 1716 as a family residence. It became an inn in 1889, providing cozy bars with fireplaces, a choice of dining rooms, and comfortably decorated bedrooms. Several wings have been added to the original structure, giving 56 bedrooms in the various buildings, including the Cottage and Rebecca's Guest House. The inn reflects all the busyness of a hotel that can accommodate up to 80 for a meeting or six private room functions, but there are many places where the guest can find a quiet place to sit and enjoy the very special warmth that comes from a house that has lived so long. The bedrooms have all the amenities expected by the business traveler: concierge, voice mail, fax, wireless high speed internet access, cable TV/DVD, and laundry service. Suites with kitchenettes are perfect for extended stays. *Directions:* Concord is easily reached by taking Route 2 from downtown Boston or from the I-95/Route 128. Signs on Route 2 lead you into Concord and the inn sits at the far end of the village green.

CONCORD'S COLONIAL INN
Innkeeper: Jurgen Demisch
48 Monument Square
Concord, MA 01742, USA
Tel: (978) 369-9200, (800) 370-9200
Fax: (978) 371-1533
45 rooms, 7 suites, 4 guesthouse suites
Double: $99–$225*
 *Breakfast not included: $10
Open: all year, Credit cards: all major
karenbrown.com/ne/concordscolonial.html

Concord   Hawthorne Inn   Map: 2

The town of Concord is steeped in the history of the founding of the American Colonies and in the battles with Britain that led to independence. Set amongst trees and gardens, the Hawthorne Inn, built in 1870 and situated on land that once belonged to Ralph Waldo Emerson, the Alcotts, and Nathaniel Hawthorne, is within easy walking distance of many of the town's points of historical interest. The bedrooms are named after famous people or places associated with this area—for example, Emerson, Alcott, Walden, and Sleepy Hollow—and the books in the rooms continue the theme. Flowered wallpapers, queen canopy beds, and hand-sewn quilts make the bedrooms very comfortable. They are not large but they provide all you'll want after a day of touring the history-filled countryside. Children are welcomed and if yours are interested in history, it would be hard to think of a better place to stay. The owners are art aficionados and have hung the walls with an eclectic collection of contemporary art. Continental breakfast, the only meal served, offers fresh fruit, juice, home-baked breads, and either a selection of teas or the inn's own blend of coffee. The innkeepers have prepared a week's program of things for you to do while visiting the area—follow their suggestions for a memorable and educational vacation. *Directions:* Take exit 30 (Route 2A west) from Routes 128 and 95. Bear right at the fork toward Concord for 1-2/10 miles. The inn is across from Hawthorne's home.

HAWTHORNE INN
Innkeepers: Gregory Burch & Marilyn Mudry
462 Lexington Road
Concord, MA 01742, USA
Tel: (978) 369-5610, Fax: (978) 287-4949
7 rooms
Double: $155–$315
Open: all year, Credit cards: all major
Select Registry
karenbrown.com/ne/hawthorneinn.html

Deerfield   Deerfield Inn   Map: 1

Visiting historic Deerfield is dropping into the heart of a 330-year-old New England village, with historic homes lining its wide Main Street. Fourteen of the village's old houses hold more than 20,000 objects—furniture, silver, glass, ceramics, and textiles—made or used in America between 1650 and 1850. The classic 1884 Deerfield Inn is the centerpiece of this village and its 23 guestrooms are all named after people associated with the village's history. Horatio Alger, room 141, has pastel window draperies inspired by a book on period valances. The wallpaper picks up the floral, romantic theme and the mahogany king-sized sleigh bed has an inviting patchwork quilt across the foot. Many of the bedrooms have the vibrant paintwork typical of the Federal period in New England, while others are reminiscent of the English settlers that first made Deerfield their home. The Everett House room has a delicate English window treatment and sunny wallpaper in greens and warm yellows, with cheerful throw pillows on the cannonball bed. All rooms have private baths, telephones, TVs, and individual climate controls and many have faux testers and antique four-posters. The award-winning restaurant serves American cuisine, the terrace café provides light meals, and the tavern offers local and international brews and a supper menu. *Directions:* Going north on I-91 take exit 24, exit 25 going south. Deerfield Village is just off Routes 5 and 10 north.

DEERFIELD INN
Innkeepers: Jane & Karl Sabo
81 Old Main Street
Deerfield, MA 01342-0305, USA
Tel: (413) 774-5587, (800) 926-3865
Fax: (413) 775-7221
23 rooms
Double: $188–$255
Open: all year, Credit cards: all major
Select Registry
karenbrown.com/ne/deerfieldinn.html

Dennis — Isaiah Hall Bed & Breakfast Inn — Map: 2

The Isaiah Hall Bed & Breakfast Inn sits on a street running parallel to Route 6A, which gives it the simple advantage of being away from the hustle and bustle of the principal tourist route along the north shore of Cape Cod. This farmhouse was built in 1857 by Isaiah Hall, whose grandfather cultivated the first cranberry bogs for which the Cape is so deservedly famous. There are twelve guestrooms in the main house and the adjoining carriage house. The attractively furnished, air-conditioned rooms, with double, queen, and king beds, are equipped with TV/VCRs, telephones, clock-radios, hairdryers, and bathrobes. One suite has a king four-poster pine bed, a sitting room with a pullout sofa, a refrigerator, and a balcony overlooking the gardens at the rear of the inn. The inn serves an expanded Continental breakfast in the dining room at one of two tables (the 12-foot cherry table is wonderful and gives you the chance to meet fellow guests) as well as tea and something delicious in the late afternoon. For relaxing, there's a porch with rockers and a comfortable parlor. It's only a short stroll to the sandy beach, and the street on which the inn is located just begs for you to walk along its length and admire the neighboring homes. *Directions:* From Boston, take I-93 to Route 3 to Route 6 (Bourne Bridge) to exit 8. Turn left for 1-2/10 miles to Route 6A, right for 3-4/10 miles to Hope Lane, and left onto Hope Lane. Turn right on Whig Street and the inn is on the left.

ISAIAH HALL BED & BREAKFAST INN
Innkeepers: Jerry & Judy Neal
152 Whig Street
P.O. Box 1007, Dennis, MA 02638, USA
Tel: (508) 385-9928, (800) 736-0160
Fax: (508) 385-5879
10 rooms
Double: $105–$255
Open: all year, Credit cards: all major
karenbrown.com/ne/isaiahhall.html

Duxbury   Powder Point Bed & Breakfast   Map: 2

Founded in 1620, Duxbury is a quaint New England town and the Powder Point Bed & Breakfast is located in an exclusive residential district that populates a peninsula with easy access to bike trails and beaches. After converting a wing of their home to accommodate their children, Richard and Linda decided to offer their charming guestrooms to more than just their extended family. With its own separate entrance, guests enjoy a lovely living room, back sun porch and expanse of lawn and garden. Just off the living room, the Rose Room has a queen four poster bed, fireplace, and a sitting area vestibule with a desk for writing postcards. There's a cozy floral comforter inviting you to take an afternoon nap and a full bathroom. Climb the stair to the Blue and Green rooms that share a bath—ideal for family or friends traveling together. The Blue Room has a queen bed, a bureaued closet and the bath with a tub/shower combination. The Green Room has dark walnut twin beds which may be converted into a king, a fireplace and two wing chairs. Refreshments are offered afternoons and breakfast is an elegant buffet-described by the innkeepers as "an expanded continental with an European flair." Richard and Linda encourage guests to settle in and use the accommodation as their home, to come and go as they like. *Directions:* From Boston, take Rte 93 south to Rte 3 to exit 11, take Rte 14 east to the town of Duxbury. Turn left on Powder Point Ave.

POWER POINT BED & BREAKFAST   *New*
Innkeepers: Richard & Linda Quigley
182 Powder Point Avenue
Duxbury, MA 02332, USA
Tel: (781) 934-7727, (866) 934-7727
3 rooms
Double: $140–$320
Open: all year, Credit cards: all major
karenbrown.com/ne/powderpoint.html

Eastham   Whalewalk Inn   Map: 2

Halfway along the length of Cape Cod an "elbow" marks the start of the unspoiled, unhurried, and absolutely beautiful Outer Cape. With 40 miles of National Seashore, this is a very special place, with none of the tourist activities usually associated with the Cape. Equally special is The Whalewalk Inn, an 1830s whaling master's home that has been meticulously restored to provide 16 beautifully decorated and spacious guestrooms, each with private bath, in the main house and the recently built carriage house. The rooms are just wonderful with their charm, sophisticated country decor, and individual palettes of colors. It would be hard to find a favorite here; but I loved the king-sized bedroom with its own private entrance and a fireplace and the bathroom with whirlpool tub and steam shower. Elaine and Kevin are innkeepers who are always on a quest to find a new Waterford crystal piece, the right painting, or art object to go in each room. The Whalewalk Inn sits on a street of colonial homes that beckons you to walk down to the beach. When the sun goes down the inn glows with the lights and candles in its windows. A lot of love has gone into the creation of the Whalewalk and the owners are also passionate about the preparation of food: the breakfasts served here are ones that you'll remember for a long time. *Directions:* Take Route 6 to the Orleans rotary, then the Rock Harbor exit off the rotary. Turn left on Rock Harbor Road and right on Bridge Road.

WHALEWALK INN
Innkeepers: Elaine & Kevin Conlin
220 Bridge Road
Eastham, MA 02642, USA
Tel: (508) 255-0617, (800) 440-1281
Fax: (508) 240-0017
16 rooms, 5 suites
Double: $190–$325
Open: all year, Credit cards: all major
Select Registry
karenbrown.com/ne/thewhalewalkinn.html

Places to Stay–Massachusetts

Falmouth — La Maison Cappellari at Mostly Hall — Map: 2

Mostly Hall, an Italianate Villa, was built in 1849 by Captain Albert Nye as a wedding present for his southern bride to equal the charm of her New Orleans home; and it's the only plantation-style home on Cape Cod. Its name came from a visiting child who, upon entering the building, exclaimed, "Why mama—it's mostly hall!" And so it is. It also provides the grand feeling found only in homes that have exceptionally high ceilings. The walls in the common rooms and in many bedrooms are faux painted with grand scenes and skies, giving this inn a distinctive European feeling and providing the guests with the illusion of a romantic escape. Bedrooms also enjoy high ceilings and each has its own private bath. Furniture is of a grand scale, making the rooms seem very special—as they are. There's a wonderful enclosed widow's walk on top of the inn where you can relax and look out in every direction. Mostly Hall is situated on the village green in the appealing coastside town of Falmouth on the lower Cape and makes a perfect stopover for travelers en route to or from the islands of Martha's Vineyard and Nantucket. *Directions:* From Boston take Route 3 south to the Bourne Bridge onto Cape Cod, then Route 28 south to Falmouth. The inn is just off the village green, with the driveway between granite posts.

LA MAISON CAPPELLARI AT MOSTLY HALL
Innkeepers: Charlene & René Poirier
27 West Main Street
Falmouth, MA 02540, USA
Tel: (508) 548-3786, (800) 682-0565
Fax: (508) 548-5778
6 rooms
Double: $195–$275
Open: all year, Credit cards: all major
karenbrown.com/ne/lamaison.html

Harwich Port — Dunscroft by the Sea — Map: 2

Just down from the white steepled church in the quaint, enchanting port town of Harwich sits the delightful Dunscroft by the Sea. This two-story, wood-shingled, shuttered house is charming and beautifully decorated. To the left of the entry is a gorgeous living room with cream-colored sofas in front of a cozy brick fire and an enclosed garden porch leading off it. In the elegant dining room guests enjoy a bountiful breakfast around one large table. The inn offers eight bedrooms in the main house and one in the garden cottage, which also has a living room with fireplace and a kitchen. We saw the rooms in the main house and they were all lovely. I especially loved the personalized welcome note in each room, addressed to Scarlett and Rhett in room 1, a lovely front corner room; to Helen and Paris in room 2, one of the larger rooms with a king canopy bed, Jacuzzi tub, and views over the back garden; to Steve and Edie in room 3, a pretty front corner room; to Mark and Cleo in number 4, one of the smaller rooms; and to Edward and Wallis in room 5 with its handsome king canopy bed and corner windows overlooking the back garden. A theme of roses pervades the inn, from the mailbox to the handsome wallpapers decorating many of the rooms. *Directions:* From Boston follow Route 3 to Cape Cod then Route 6 in the direction of "Hyannis to Provincetown." Take exit 10, 124 south to Route 28. Turn left on 28 and then go ¾ mile to Pilgrim Road.

DUNSCROFT BY THE SEA - COVER PAINTING
Owner: Alyce R. Mundy
24 Pilgrim Road
Harwich Port, MA 02646, USA
Tel: (508) 432-0810, (800) 432-4345
Fax: (508) 432-5134
8 rooms, 1 cottage suite
Double: $195–$355
Open: all year, Credit cards: all major
karenbrown.com/ne/madunscroftbythesea.html

Places to Stay–Massachusetts

Ipswich   Inn at Castle Hill   Maps: 2, 3

Nestled on the vast protected acreage of the Crane Estate, this handsome inn looks out over salt marshes and sand dunes to the distant Atlantic. The inn enjoys a lovely entry off a wraparound porch, warmed by a welcoming fire. Off the entry to one side is the guest parlor and in the oldest part of the house is the inn's beautiful dining room whose bright, fresh decor of blues, creams, and whites is a perfect complement at breakfast to the morning light. With the exception of one room off the lobby, guestrooms, all unique in decor, are found at the top of the handsome staircase. On the first floor are two of the inn's most dramatic rooms with stunning views of the marsh and ocean. Cornelius, whose subtle decor of soft beiges and whites was selected so as not to compete with the view out of one entire wall of windows, and the very pretty and inviting Miné with its wood-burning fireplace, sweet floral decor, and windows that look up to the wooded hillside. *Directions:* On Route 128 North, exit 15 and turn left on School St. Follow it for three miles. Bear right onto Route 133 west until crossing the Ipswich town line. Turn right at the sign for Castle Hill onto Northgate Rd. At the road's end, bear right onto Argilla and travel 1.9 miles to the inn.

INN AT CASTLE HILL
Innkeeper: Benson Willis
280 Argilla Road
Ipswich, MA 01938, USA
Tel: (978) 412-2555, Fax: (978) 412-2556
10 rooms
Double: $175–$385
Open: all year, Credit cards: all major
karenbrown.com/ne/mainnatcastlehill.html

Lee   Applegate Inn   Map: 1

Built in the 1920s as a summer home for a New York physician, Applegate is now a commanding country inn with a four-column façade set among perennial gardens, towering pine trees, and rolling lawns. A particularly gracious front hall has a lovely carved staircase leading up to the second floor. In addition to the living room, there is a TV room with a VCR and a video library for the use of guests. The bedrooms and cottage are furnished with reproduction antiques and provide all the amenities one would expect as a guest in a gracious home of this period. Room 1 has a four-poster king bed and a sofa in the sitting area, which has a fireplace; the bathroom contains a large steam shower. Room 3 has a French-style sleigh bed, a fireplace, and views out to the lawns and pine trees. Two new luxury suites with balconies and fireplaces offer a choice of a soaking tub or whirlpool tub for two. The Carriage House Cottage, with two bedrooms sharing one bath, a full kitchen, living room, dining room, and deck, would be ideal for a family or for two couples traveling together. The Carriage House also contains two luxury suites with large Jacuzzis and gas fireplaces. Amenities include a pool, bicycles, and 6 acres of grounds. A full gourmet breakfast is served in the candlelit dining room and wine and cheese are served in the evening. *Directions:* Take the Massachusetts Turnpike to exit 2 to Route 20 to the first stop sign. Continue on to the inn on the left.

APPLEGATE INN
Innkeepers: Len & Gloria Friedman
279 West Park Street
Lee, MA 01238, USA
Tel: (413) 243-4451, (800) 691-9012
Fax: (413) 243-9832
5 rooms, 5 suites, 1 cottage
Double: $125–$350
Open: all year, Credit cards: all major
Select Registry
karenbrown.com/ne/applegate.html

Places to Stay–Massachusetts

Lee   Devonfield   Map: 1

Devonfield is a gracious, large country home just outside the village of Lee. Its meadows, fields, and birch trees grace its setting and welcome you to its front door and the hospitality within. There are six guestrooms, three suites, and a guest cottage, each beautifully appointed with furniture and amenities chosen for your comfort. This Federal style of architecture lends itself to a graciousness not often found in inns of other architectural construction, and here you really feel like a guest in a country home. Stay several nights here in the coziness of your own bedroom with wood-burning fireplace or in the large living room and enjoy all that this area has to offer, or make use of the heated pool, the tennis court, and the bicycles available to guests. In winter bring along your cross-country skis and cross the meadows in the brisk country air. This inn is known for its breakfasts, which are as luxurious as the inn itself. In the afternoon there's a cup of tea to be enjoyed in front of the fire or outdoors on the patio. Rooms are all air-conditioned and have queen, king, or twin beds. There are Jacuzzis and TVs and in the Penthouse Suite and the Wilhelmina Cottage there are kitchenettes. Guests are treated to brandy, chocolates, and a special brand of hospitality from Devonfield's innkeepers. *Directions:* From Stockbridge, drive north from Main Street on Rte 7 for 8/10 mile to Lee Rd, which becomes Stockbridge Rd. After almost 2 miles the inn is on the right.

DEVONFIELD
Innkeepers: Jim & Pam Loring
85 Stockbridge Road
Lee, MA 01238, USA
Tel: (413) 243-3298, (800) 664-0880
Fax: (413) 243-1360
6 rooms, 3 suites, 1 guesthouse
Double: $110–$325
Open: all year, Credit cards: all major
Select Registry
karenbrown.com/ne/madevonfield.html

Places to Stay–Massachusetts

Lenox Blantyre Map: 1

Blantyre, a Tudor-style mansion built in 1902, is set on a hill on 100 acres of spectacular Berkshire countryside. Replicating a grand Scottish manor, Blantyre is indeed a step back into a place and time of elegance and gracious living, bringing to the visitor a world of serene European ambiance, calm, courtesy, charm, and cuisine. From the main hall with its immense fireplace and massive, ornate furniture, a sweeping oak staircase leads you up to eight of the bedrooms. I fell in love with the grandeur of The Paterson Suite with its king mahogany four-poster bed sitting beneath exquisite flower prints, large sitting area with fireplace, and two bathrooms. Additional guestrooms are found in the carriage house and cottages. In the carriage house Wyndhurst has a queen four-poster bed and French windows opening onto the expansive lawns. One of the cottages, The Ice House, has been converted to house a magnificent suite of rooms and a separate guestroom on the lower level. Several rooms have fireplaces and all provide every luxurious amenity. The conservatory, originally used for plants brought in from the greenhouse, is now the setting for breakfast and lunch. Dinner is served in the dining room of the main house (jacket and tie are required). There's also a covered terrace overlooking the south lawn where you can have lunch or an informal meeting. *Directions:* Leave I-90 at exit 2 in Lee and take Route 20 west 3 miles to the entrance.

BLANTYRE
Manager: Katja Henke
Blantyre Road
P.O. Box 995, Lenox, MA 01240, USA
Tel: (413) 637-3556, Fax: (413) 637-4282
12 suites
Double: $425–$1500
Open: May 7 to Nov 7, Credit cards: all major
Relais & Châteaux
karenbrown.com/ne/blantyre.html

Places to Stay–Massachusetts

Lenox Brook Farm Inn Map: 1

The Brook Farm Inn in the village of Lenox, born as a Victorian home, is today a bed and breakfast inn with 14 bedrooms and a suite with sitting room and bedroom, all air-conditioned. It's situated down the hill from Lenox itself, yet close enough to walk up to the village. The living room has a corner with a partially completed jigsaw puzzle. Bedrooms, either of standard or large size, are located on three floors of the inn, some tucked under the eaves, and in a new carriage house. On the inn's first floor, room M, in blue and white, is large and has a king/twin option. It has wicker furniture, a fireplace, and a bathroom with tub and shower. On the second floor, Room 1, with a queen canopy bed and a fireplace, is decorated in blue and pink and has lace accessories. The bathroom has both a tub and a shower. Room 8 on the third floor is smaller but still accommodates your choice of a king or twin beds. The two first-floor bedrooms in the carriage house are wheelchair-accessible and offer fireplaces, refrigerators, and whirlpool baths. The inn serves a full breakfast each morning in the dining room and in the afternoon an English tea is available. Outside you find a swimming pool and nearby a hammock begging you to climb in and relax. *Directions:* Take the Massachusetts Turnpike east or west to exit 2 to Route 20 west and turn left on Route 183. At the monument in the center of Lenox go left downhill on old Stockbridge Road. Make the first right on Hawthorne Street.

BROOK FARM INN
Innkeepers: Phil & Linda Halpern
15 Hawthorne Street
Lenox, MA 01240, USA
Tel: (413) 637-3013, (800) 285-7638
Fax: (413) 637-4751
14 rooms, 1 suite
Double: $160–$350
Open: all year, Credit cards: all major
Select Registry
karenbrown.com/ne/brookfarminn.html

Places to Stay–Massachusetts

Lenox — Gateways Inn & Restaurant — Map: 1

Gateways, a majestic inn that fronts Walker Street at the heart of Lenox, was once the summer mansion of Harry Procter of Procter and Gamble. Today, guests bask in the present owners' warmth of welcome and sense of humor (Fabrizio brings his own touch of Italian charm), which create a comfortable balance of elegance and hospitality. Just off the entry you find a lovely bedroom, The Berkshire, converted from what was once Mr. Procter's study, and the dining room, a very elegant room with a dark-rust wall and gorgeous high moldings contrasting in white. The menu is considered one of the best in Lenox and the wine list is marvelous. Climb the absolutely gorgeous wide staircase as its wide platform and gorgeous banister wind up to guestrooms. We selected what was Mr. Procter's own bedroom, a large front-corner room whose bath enjoys a claw-foot tub designed especially to accommodate his exceptional height. The next-door room is bright and sunny and decorated in cheery yellows. Room 4, formerly Mrs. Procter's apartment, is the only suite—a large living room was once her bedchamber and her porch is now the bedroom, enclosed by a bounty of windows framed in yards of rich, gorgeous fabric. *Directions:* Traveling Route 7 north, turn left at the first traffic light in Lenox onto Route 7A (Kemble Street). Continue to the stop sign and turn left—Gateways is immediately on your right.

GATEWAYS INN & RESTAURANT
Owners: Fabrizio & Rosemary Chiariello
51 Walker Street
Lenox, MA 01240, USA
Tel: (413) 637-2532, (888) 492-9466
Fax: (413) 637-1432
11 rooms, 1 suite
Double: $210–$450
Open: all year, Credit cards: all major
Select Registry
karenbrown.com/ne/magateways.html

Lenox   Wheatleigh   Map: 1

Wheatleigh offers a dreamlike escape from reality amid comfort and understated elegance. Set on 22 acres overlooking the Berkshire mountains and lake, Wheatleigh is described as a 16th-century Florentine palazzo. Renovations sport a handsome, modern look and contrast attractively with the columns and old details. The smallest guestroom is a studio unit with built-in bed and small but convenient bath, perfect for a teenager. By contrast, the Terrace Suite is segmented in three parts and flows dramatically from one room to the next—the bedroom flows into an enclosed glass patio sitting area and onto its own terrace where dramatic Italian columns frame the garden terrace and view. Another striking room on the second floor, a junior suite, has been renovated to continue the circular design incorporated into the entry—the bed is set center stage looking towards the fireplace, while a sofa whose back cleverly serves as the headboard looks out at the view. For dining you can choose a fixed-price meal in the elegant, internationally acclaimed Fine Dining Room with its magnificent glass-enclosed portico or lighter fare in the more informal Library. *Directions:* At the junction of Rtes 7 and 183 on the outskirts of Lenox, turn onto 183 south, Walker St. After almost 3 miles the road forks soon after Tanglewood's main gate—take the left fork (a continuation of 183 south). After 1/10 mile turn left on Hawthorne Rd—Wheatleigh is 1 mile down on the left.

WHEATLEIGH
Owners: Linfield & Susan Simon
Manager: Francois Thomas
Hawthorne Road
P.O. Box 824, Lenox, MA 01240, USA
Tel: (413) 637-0610, Fax: (413) 637-4507
19 rooms
Double: $475–$1550*
 *Breakfast not included: $29 average
Open: all year, Credit cards: all major
karenbrown.com/ne/wheatleigh.html

Places to Stay–Massachusetts

Marblehead — Harbor Light Inn — Map: 2

Marblehead is one of the great sailing capitals of the world today as it was in centuries past when tall-masted schooners carried the products of a new nation to and from Europe and the Far East. 17th- and 18th-century homes crowd the narrow, winding streets of one of the most popular places to visit on the New England coast. Within this historic district is an elegantly decorated inn that will make you feel as though you have stepped back in time while enjoying all the amenities of the 21st century. I loved the flowered wallpapers used in the front hallway, in the dining room, and in the parlors. Guestrooms have king and queen beds, some with canopies, some have fireplaces, some have decks or patios, some have Jacuzzis, but all provide a cozy ambiance and fine furnishings. Enjoy the stunning view from the rooftop walk from which you can see the famous Marblehead light. Surprisingly in a town where houses crowd the streets, there is a lovely garden and a heated swimming pool, which offers a refreshing respite after a day of exploring the town's shops, galleries, and restaurants. This is a formal inn but one of such comfort that you will instantly feel the warm welcome of the inn's staff and become yet another of its centuries of houseguests. Breakfast is served in the large dining room at a lovely long mahogany table. *Directions:* From Boston take Rte 1A north to Rte 129 east to Marblehead. Take the first right after the Mobil station: the inn is 1/8 mile on the right.

HARBOR LIGHT INN
Innkeepers: Suzanne & Peter Conway
58 Washington Street
Marblehead, MA 01945, USA
Tel: (781) 631-2186, Fax: (781) 631-2216
17 rooms, 3 suites
Double: $145–$295
Open: all year, Credit cards: all major
Select Registry
karenbrown.com/ne/harborlightinn.html

Places to Stay—Massachusetts

Martha's Vineyard—Edgartown Charlotte Inn Map: 2

The Charlotte Inn in Edgartown is a formal and beautifully decorated inn with lovely antiques and much original art. As with many of the inns on Martha's Vineyard, this historic home was built in the last half of the 19th century and once belonged to a whaling merchant. Brick paths lead you to lovely gardens and cozy places to relax: there's an especially beautiful rose garden with a lattice, which can be seen from several of the inn's rooms. Next door in the carriage house you find two of the inn's twenty-three bedrooms and one suite, all of which are luxurious and have every possible amenity. Each has that quality and feeling of a room you've been away from and to which you have just come home. The inn's restaurant, L'Etoile, celebrates the best of French style cuisine while making use of local ingredients. Dining is available in the glass-paned conservatory or outdoors on a terrace where you are surrounded by plants. This is not an inn where you wander through with sandy feet from the beach, but rather an inn where you celebrate a special occasion in a meticulously orchestrated setting.
Directions: You reach the island of Martha's Vineyard by plane from New York or Boston or seasonally by car ferry from Woods Hole or passenger ferry from Hyannis or New Bedford.

CHARLOTTE INN
Innkeepers: Paula & Gery Conover
Managers: Carol Read & Christie Knoff
27 South Summer Street
Martha's Vineyard—Edgartown, MA 02539, USA
Tel: (508) 627-4751, Fax: (508) 627-4652
23 rooms, 2 suites
Double: $295–$895
Open: all year, Credit cards: all major
Relais & Châteaux
karenbrown.com/ne/thecharlotteinn.html

Places to Stay–Massachusetts

Martha's Vineyard—Edgartown Hob Knob Inn Map: 2

Take an interesting Greek Revival home within walking distance of everything in town; add major refurbishments; mix traditional decor with modern; hire an artist to faux paint; plan cozy common rooms, a living room with views of the garden, and lovely dining rooms; throw in a fitness center and a conference facility; add an eclectic collection of art—and you have created a fabulous sanctuary on Martha's Vineyard: the Hob Knob Inn. Of course, the guestrooms provide every amenity you could possibly wish for. One of my favorite rooms is tucked up under the eaves with a painted four-poster bed, painted bedside tables and bureau, and chairs with English chintz fabrics. Enjoy a wonderful breakfast, afternoon tea with freshly baked goodies, and a frosty pitcher of lemonade on the beautiful wraparound porch, and then, if you've caught that bass on the inn's charter boat, the kitchen will grill it for you and friends at a private dinner party. The inn's staff suggest activities to keep you busy—fishing, walking the beaches, visiting galleries, kayaking—or will direct you to a chair by the fire in the living room. *Directions:* You reach the island of Martha's Vineyard by plane from New York or Boston or by car ferry from Woods Hole or seasonally by passenger ferry from Hyannis or New Bedford.

HOB KNOB INN
Innkeeper: Erin Mansell
128 Main Street, P.O. Box 239
Martha's Vineyard—Edgartown, MA 02539, USA
Tel: (508) 627-9510, (800) 696-2723
Fax: (508) 627-4560
20 rooms
Double: $245–$550
Open: all year, Credit cards: all major
karenbrown.com/ne/hobknob.html

Martha's Vineyard—Edgartown   Point Way Inn   Map: 2

The architecture of this inn is an interesting combination of Colonial and Greek Revival styles but it's what the owners have done to this property that makes it so very special. Built in the 1840s as a sea captain's home, it has been transformed into an inn with a blend of traditional and contemporary elegance, which makes your stay a memorable one. Decor in the public rooms is informal and comfortable, and has been designed by an owner with an artist's eye. I was especially interested in the artwork, a mix of old and new, of paintings, prints, and photography. I particularly liked the photos of beach, sea grass, and dunes. There's a lovely sunny room for breakfast and a warm and cozy common room for the evening. Plantings of sea grass in the garden and artfully placed sculpture make for an interesting twist on the conventional garden. The front porch gives you a place from which to watch the ebb and flow of Edgartown. Guestrooms are freshly decorated, many have fireplaces, and several have porches or decks that look over the delightful garden. Showers, beach towels, and luggage storage are available so that after you've checked out you can go to the beach till ferry time. A courtesy car is available on a shared-use basis for exploring the more distant parts of the island. *Directions:* You reach the island of Martha's Vineyard by plane from New York or Boston or by car ferry from Woods Hole or seasonally by passenger ferry from Hyannis or New Bedford.

POINT WAY INN
Innkeepers: Claudia Miller & John Glendon
P.O. Box 275
Martha's Vineyard—Edgartown, MA 02539, USA
Tel: (888) 711-6633, (508) 627-8633
Fax: (508) 627-3338
13 rooms
Double: $225–$600
Open: all year, Credit cards: all major
Select Registry
karenbrown.com/ne/pointwayinn.html

Martha's Vineyard—Menemsha   Beach Plum Inn and Restaurant   Map: 2

Up island away from the bustling towns on Martha's Vineyard is a charming inn and restaurant on its own secluded 6-acres—the Beach Plum Inn. Sitting on top of a hill with views of the sea and down to the harbor where fishermen come and go, it has a special charm all of its own. The inn exudes a traditional feel in its island architecture and comfortable furnishings and yet its dining room, with windows to the lawns, gardens, and the sea and mirror to reflect all that's happening, is very contemporary. The restaurant, specializing in fresh fish and prime meats accompanied by local produce, has the reputation as one of the best places to eat on the island. Bring your own wine, though, as the town is "dry" and you cannot buy alcohol here. The greeting is warm and welcoming at the Beach Plum Inn and the rooms are very comfortable. Mine had a queen bed, a bureau, a writing desk, and windows all around so that the freshness of the countryside was mine to enjoy. The bathroom was large and had a two-person spa tub (and shower). There are also cottages with their own decks. For recreation you'll find beaches for walking and swimming, golf, fishing, croquet, horseback riding, hiking, and more. *Directions:* Travel by plane or ferry to the island of Martha's Vineyard, then by taxi or rental car on the Edgartown-Vineyard Haven Road to Beetlebung Corner. Follow signs to Menemsha to a triangle then bear left to the inn on right.

BEACH PLUM INN AND RESTAURANT
Owner: The Arnold Family
50 Beach Plum Lane
Martha's Vineyard—Menemsha, MA 02552, USA
Tel: (877) 645-7398 or (508) 645-9454
Fax: (508) 645-2801
11 rooms, Double: $250–$400
Open: May 1 to Nov 30, Credit cards: all major
karenbrown.com/ne/beachpluminn.html

Places to Stay–Massachusetts

Martha's Vineyard—Vineyard Haven   Mansion House   Map: 2

The Mansion House was newly created in 2003. After a fire, the opportunities for building anew have been handsomely captured, providing many rewards for the lucky traveller as guest. Conveniences and amenities are top priority. Among the new rooms are suites with sitting rooms and separate bedrooms, some with private balconies. All are wonderful for those coming to enjoy this property, especially for its extensive spa services. There's so much within the new walls that leaving will require a fair amount of effort. The restaurant Zephrus, highly rated by Zagat, is now reawakening in former diners its awesome reputation, Guests who forget that this is a dry town (no alcohol sales) may have deliveries made from a neighboring town. A gourmet buffet breakfast, included in the rate, features fresh-baked goods and made-to-order omelets—served in the restaurant or outside. There is a spectacular roof deck where you can look down onto the harbor or gaze at the neighboring houses and church steeples. Under the building, there is a 75-foot indoor pool, mineral spring pool, and adjoining spa facility. A health club, with sauna and steambath, has trainers to guide you through exercise programs including yoga, aerobics, and body conditioning. This inn is almost a town unto itself, with all that it offers, including boutiques to tantalize its browsers. *Directions:* Take the ferry to Vineyard Haven and just walk up the street to the Mansion House.

MANSION HOUSE   *New*
Owners: Sherman & Susan Goldstein
Main Street
P.O. Box 428
Martha's Vineyard—Vineyard Haven, MA 02568, USA
Tel: (508) 693-2200, (800) 332-4112
Fax: (508) 693-4095
32 rooms, Double: $159–$269
Open: all year, Credit cards: AX, MC, VS
karenbrown.com/ne/themansionhouse.html

Places to Stay–Massachusetts

Martha's Vineyard—Vineyard Haven   Thorncroft Inn   Map: 2

The owners of the Thorncroft Inn have devoted 24 years to caring for guests here and have created an environment and a service level that are hard to beat. However, rather than resting on their laurels, they have continued to refine their service and to create new ways to make the guest experience even better. Thought has been given to every detail in the guestrooms, which are wonderful. The twelve rooms and one suite are in two restored buildings furnished with antiques and there's also a separate cottage. Ten of the bedrooms have wood-burning fireplaces and canopied beds. I stayed in a second-floor room that provided me with every comfort in the world, including turn-down service in the evening and coffee and the paper outside my door in the morning. In the inn itself there are family-type common rooms and two dining areas for breakfast and afternoon tea. On the morning I was there, the breakfast of quiche and an array of fresh fruits was so well presented and so colorful that it reminded me of a Gaugin painting. There are lovely paths through the woods and I felt that somehow they too had been designed to add to my relaxation. *Directions:* Take the Steamship Authority ferry from Woods Hole. Turn right at the first stop sign and next right onto Main Street. The inn is 1 mile along on the left.

THORNCROFT INN
Innkeepers: Lynn & Karl Buder
460 Main Street
P.O. Box 1022
Martha's Vineyard—Vineyard Haven, MA 02568, USA
Tel: (508) 693-3333, (800) 332-1236
Fax: (508) 693-5419
12 rooms, 1 suite, 1 cottage, Double: $200–$550
Open: all year, Credit cards: all major
Select Registry
karenbrown.com/ne/thorncroftinn.html

Nantucket Island—Nantucket   Pineapple Inn   Map: 2

The stately 1838 Greek Revival family home of whaling-ship captain Uriah Russell has been transformed into a very elegant inn in the town of Nantucket on the very charming island of Nantucket. Common rooms and bedrooms are furnished with a mix of authentic and reproduction antiques that give the inn a great deal of charm and warmth. Bedrooms have handmade four-poster beds with canopies, goose-down comforters with flower-print covers, Oriental carpets, and marble bathrooms. Each of the very attractively and elegantly furnished rooms has a private bath, air conditioning, TV, and telephone with data port. I particularly loved room 7 at the back of the building, which overlooks the garden. Breakfast, consisting of freshly squeezed orange juice, fresh fruit, hot and cold cereals, and homemade baked goods, is served in the dining room or on that lovely garden terrace where you can enjoy the bubbling fountain. I loved the commercial espresso machine from which you can choose a cappuccino, café latte, or an espresso. One of the many wonderful things about Nantucket is that it is an easy walk from the ferry docks to almost everything there is to do and every place there is to stay. *Directions:* From the steamship ferry landing walk up Broad Street, turn left on Center Street, then second right onto Hussey Street. From the Hy-Line landing walk up Main Street, turn right on Center Street, then third left onto Hussey Street.

PINEAPPLE INN
Innkeeper: Christopher Karlson
10 Hussey Street
Nantucket Island—Nantucket, MA 02554, USA
Tel: (508) 228-9992, Fax: (508) 325-6051
12 rooms
Double: $195–$325
Open: late Apr to early Dec, Credit cards: all major
karenbrown.com/ne/thepineappleinn.html

Nantucket Island—Nantucket   Seven Sea Street   Map: 2

There is a magic to being on the island of Nantucket and in the heart of its principal town. Stay here in a warm and cozy post-and-beam guesthouse with innkeepers who make you feel like family and it's difficult to imagine life much better. Seven Sea Street, newly built in traditional style, is appointed with early-American furnishings combined with all the modern conveniences. The guestrooms have queen beds with fishnet canopies, TVs, telephones, small refrigerators, and all those other amenities including air conditioning that make your stay so pleasant. I stayed in a simply but comfortably furnished small suite with a separate living room. Puddy, the inn cat, made it quite evident that he intended to spend the night in my room—cats do know cat people! There's a relaxing common room with a pot-bellied stove and a dining room with a long table on which breakfast is served. A Continental breakfast is available in your room if you don't feel like socializing in the morning. There's a hot tub for which you can sign up for that extra bit of relaxation. It's just a few blocks' walk from the inn to the ferry and to Main Street with all its fabulous architecture—don't miss the Three Bricks mansions built by a merchant for his three sons, and the upscale shops and galleries. *Directions:* By air from Boston, New York, and Providence. By ferry from Woods Hole, New Bedford, and Hyannis—the inn is three minutes from the dock.

SEVEN SEA STREET
Innkeepers: Mary & Matthew Parker
7 Sea Street
Nantucket Island—Nantucket, MA 02554, USA
Tel: (508) 228-3577, (800) 651-9262
Fax: (508) 228-3578
9 rooms, 2 suites
Double: $205–$325
Open: all year, Credit cards: all major
Select Registry
karenbrown.com/ne/sevenseastreet.html

Nantucket Island—Nantucket   Union Street Inn   Map: 2

Set just off Main Street in the charming town of Nantucket is the Union Street Inn, dating back to about 1770. From there you can walk to all the town's historic homes, shops, and galleries, so you'll only need transportation to visit the more distant villages like Siasconset and Wauwinet (bikers might welcome the challenge). This is an exceptional, attractively decorated inn whose bedrooms have queen and king beds, often four-posters, and fireplaces. Room 3 on the first floor could well be my favorite with its red curtains and bed drapes and the two wing chairs in front of the fireplace. Across the hall, room 1 has a queen bed and green and white toile decorating the walls and bed. Upstairs, room 14 with its soft patterned wallpaper has a queen pencil-post bed and views out of its windows to neighboring trees and an ivy-covered hillside. Rooms have cable TV, Frette linens, duvets, bathrobes, and air conditioning. A full, cooked breakfast is served either in the dining room, on the terrace, or in your own room, and "goodies" are offered in the afternoon. The inn provides a walking tour through some of the old cobblestone streets to many of the town's charming homes, churches, and scenic sights. Numerous restaurants are close by: menus and suggestions are available from the innkeepers. *Directions:* Take the ferry to the island, walk five minutes to the inn from the ferry dock, or fly to the island and take a cab or rent a car.

UNION STREET INN
Owners: Ken & Deborah Withrow
7 Union Street
Nantucket Island—Nantucket, MA 02554, USA
Tel: (508) 228-9222, (800) 225-5116
Fax: (508) 325-0848
12 rooms
Double: $195–$475
Open: Apr through mid-Dec, Credit cards: all major
karenbrown.com/ne/unionstreet.html

Places to Stay–Massachusetts

Nantucket Island—Nantucket White Elephant Map: 2

The White Elephant is simply a special place. It stretches beside a harbor on the charming island of Nantucket and offers a high level of accommodation and attentive personal service in a relaxed atmosphere. Almost everything you could want is available to you. This is what the White Elephant is all about, and it meets and exceeds its goals of ensuring the guest a treasured visit that will be remembered only as being too short. From the greeting by the doormen to that of the front desk staff, your visit here will be one of a series of highlights as the staff effortlessly anticipates your desires. Rooms are extraordinarily comfortable—mine had a sitting room with a fireplace and doors opening to a small deck overlooking that magnetic view of a working harbor. The White Elephant is only a few blocks from all of Nantucket Town's shops, galleries, and restaurants. When you tire of all this charm, you can return to the inn and stretch out in the sun with the libation of your choice and a good book, and let the world go by. The Brant Point Grill will provide you with breakfast and at the end of the day, after a cocktail or a glass of wine in the attractive bar, a dinner where you will enjoy every taste. Amenities at the inn include an exercise room, a library, jitney service to the beaches, transportation to the ferry back to reality, and a business center. *Directions:* There is a complimentary shuttle service from the ferry dock, just a few minutes away.

WHITE ELEPHANT
Owner: The Karp Family
Manager: Dennis Barquinero
50 Easton Street
P.O. Box 1139
Nantucket Island—Nantucket, MA 02554, USA
Tel: (508) 228-2500, (800) 445-6574
Fax: (508) 325-1195
66 rooms, Double: $350–$800
Open: May to Dec, Credit cards: all major
karenbrown.com/ne/whiteelephant.html

Places to Stay—Massachusetts

Nantucket Island—Siasconset Summer House Map: 2

This delightful inn sits on a bluff overlooking the ocean in the island's most charming and quaint village away from all the hustle and bustle of the town of Nantucket. Climbing roses, often growing up and over the roof, festoon the weathered shingled cottages that line the streets of Siasconset, creating an old-fashioned look. The Summer House accommodations consist of a group of cottages with a common lawn and Adirondack chairs fronting a path to the inn's attractive restaurant. The cottages are decorated with hand-painted floral designs echoing the charm of the gardens surrounding the inn. English country pine antiques, white eyelet sheets, comforters, terry bathrobes, and comfortable seating are some of the amenities of the cottages. Some also have fireplaces and spa tubs. The inn serves a Continental breakfast each morning on the wide veranda of the building in which dinner is served in the evenings. This restaurant has the feel of island charm—it has a cozy bar at one end, with tall stools for intimate conversation, and then an expansive room with tables where guests enjoy dinner with flickering candles, fresh flowers, and music from the piano bar. Down the bluff there is a pool surrounded by loungers for sunning, a Beachside Bistro for lunches and dinners—and the sandy beach just begging for your visit. *Directions:* By road or bike path, 8 miles from the town of Nantucket to Siasconset to Ocean Avenue to the inn.

SUMMER HOUSE
Owner: Danielle de Benedictis
Manager: Susan Manolis
17 Ocean Avenue
Box 880, Nantucket Island—Siasconset, MA 02564, USA
Tel: (508) 257-4577, Fax: (508) 257-4590
10 cottages
Double: $525–$650
Open: late Apr through Oct, Credit cards: all major
karenbrown.com/ne/summerhouse.html

Nantucket Island—Wauwinet   The Wauwinet   Map: 2

"It takes a bit of extra effort to get yourself to most very special places." So says the brochure for The Wauwinet, and it's true. This inn is located on a spit of land jutting into the sea, a ten-minute drive from the town of Nantucket, with a wildlife refuge north of the inn providing many more miles of wonderfully wild isolation. Comprised of a cluster of cottages and the main house with 26 bedrooms, the inn is furnished with tasteful and comfortable seating areas, queen or king beds, and full bathrooms. I found it almost impossible to choose a favorite because the rooms are cozy and individually decorated with original country antiques, and have very attractive artwork and views to the bay or the garden. The ambiance is most definitely sophisticated and yet very comfortable. The Wauwinet's restaurant, Topper's, is fabulous in its setting, décor, food and service—and its 20,000 bottles of wine. Seafood is always a specialty but there's a full menu for your enjoyment. Paths lead to beaches on either the Atlantic or Nantucket Bay and the grounds have flower gardens, green lawn for sports like croquet, climbing roses, and water views—all enclosed by sand dunes and yet opened by paths leading to sparkling waters. Keep busy with sailing, tennis, biking, walking, sea fishing, and bird watching—there is more to do than you can possibly fit into a day! *Directions:* Travel by ferry from Hyannis or by air from major northeast coast cities and from Hyannis and Providence.

THE WAUWINET
Innkeepers: Eric & Bettina Landt
Wauwinet Road, P.O. Box 2580
Nantucket Island—Wauwinet, MA 02584, USA
Tel: (508) 228-0145, (800) 426-8718
Fax: (508) 228-6712
24 rooms, 2 suites, 5 cottages
Double: $230–$2000
Open: May through Oct, Credit cards: all major
Relais & Châteaux
karenbrown.com/ne/wauwinet.html

Places to Stay—Massachusetts

New Marlborough — Old Inn on the Green & Gedney Farm — Map: 1

Winding country roads hold the anticipation and promise that when you arrive at your destination you are in for a memorable time. The Old Inn on the Green and Gedney Farm is actually made up of the Old Inn, the Farm, the Manor, the Thayer House, and the Hannah Stebbins House, all buildings that have been expertly restored. While each provides the traveler with attractive and comfortable accommodations, there's a choice of location and amenities in suites, rooms with fireplaces, rooms with spa tubs, rooms with soaring ceilings and old beams, and centuries-old rooms that are intimate and cozy. Gedney Manor offers 12 bedrooms in what appears to be a stone fortress set in the seclusion and privacy of the countryside. It has a great manor hall with a central fireplace and a large terrace—perfect for relaxation or your private event. Back in the village itself you find the Old Inn; the Thayer House with its six bedrooms, library, and sitting rooms; and the four-bedroom Hannah Stebbins House, rented only as a private home; and just down the country road there's Gedney Farm. Dining in one of several small rooms lit totally by candlelight is particularly special at the Old Inn on the Green, with the chef using locally grown products to enhance his creations. A spa will soon be added at the Manor. *Directions:* From New York, take the Taconic Parkway north to the exit at Hillsdale and then Route 23 east to Route 57 to the inn.

OLD INN ON THE GREEN & GEDNEY FARM
Innkeepers: Brad Wagstaff & Leslie Miller
Route 57, Village Green
New Marlborough, MA 01230, USA
Tel: (413) 229-3131, (800) 286-3139
Fax: (413) 229-8236
42 rooms
Double: $175–$385
Open: all year, Credit cards: all major
karenbrown.com/ne/green.html

North Adams — Porches Inn — Maps: 1, 3

Six 1890s row houses, once the homes of mill workers in North Adams, have been renovated into a new hotel with 50 rooms and suites. Uniquely conceived and executed, these buildings have been combined and now have two long porches (with rocking chairs of course)—hence the name of the hotel. In the building where the reception and office are located there are two common rooms, one a living room with a fireplace and the other a den and a dining room where the expanded Continental breakfast is served. The rooms are individually decorated in a contemporary style, yet use lamps and other accessories from the 1940s and 1950s. The feeling of the rooms is definitely contemporary, with amenities presented in elegant but minimally designed containers—tissue, for example, is housed in a stainless-steel box. Behind the row houses is a building with an exercise room and a sauna and guests have the use of an outdoor heated pool. Two adjacent properties are now being renovated as part of the Porches property: one will provide longer-term accommodations including kitchenettes. There are two meeting rooms that can accommodate up to 20 people. The Porches Inn is located across the street from the Massachusetts Museum of Contemporary Art, the largest contemporary art museum in the country. *Directions:* Take Route 7 to Williamstown to Route 2 east. Go left onto Brown Street to River Street, and right at River Street.

PORCHES INN
Innkeeper: Olivier Glattfelder
231 River Street
North Adams, MA 01247, USA
Tel: (413) 664-0400, Fax: (413) 664-0401
50 rooms
Double: $230–$395
Open: all year, Credit cards: all major
karenbrown.com/ne/porches.html

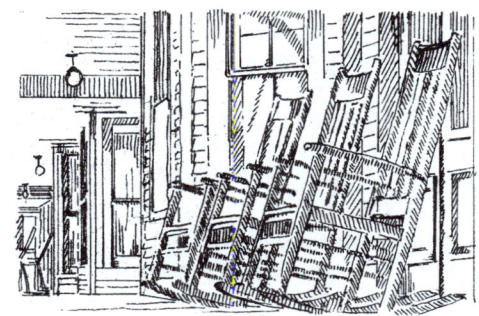

Places to Stay–Massachusetts

Orleans Morgan's Way Bed & Breakfast Map: 2

Between the towns of Orleans and Chatham there is a delightful two-room bed and breakfast inn set high on a hill overlooking a wooded ravine. Within its 5 acres Morgan's Way provides a tranquil setting for those who want to truly be away from it all. This architect-designed contemporary Cape-style house is the home of your hosts while also providing private guest accommodations including a spacious second-floor living area with a wood-burning stove, TV/VCR, library, and small refrigerator. Tall windows look onto the beauty of the surrounding woodlands and many gardens. Sliding doors open to a small deck and spiral stairs leading down to a heated pool (available in summer). The two large air-conditioned bedrooms are attractively furnished with queen beds and comfortable reading chairs and each room has its own bathroom (one is two steps down the hall). A full gourmet breakfast is provided each morning in the owner's dining room where you will feel like a member of the family. Beside the pool is an especially delightful self-catering house for two people, which is available on a weekly basis. If you plan to be in this area for a week or so, do look into the availability of this charming cottage, which is just about as perfect a spot as you can imagine. *Directions:* Take Route 6 from Sagamore Bridge to exit 12 then turn right onto Route 6A. At the first light turn right and then right again at the next light onto Route 28. Drive 1 mile to Morgan's Way.

MORGAN'S WAY BED & BREAKFAST
Innkeepers: Page McMahan & Will Joy
9 Morgan's Way
Orleans, MA 02653, USA
Tel & fax: (508) 255-0831
2 rooms, 1 cottage ($1300 weekly)
Double: $150–$170
Minimum nights required: 2 (3 on holidays)
Open: all year, Credit cards: none
karenbrown.com/ne/morgansway.html

Places to Stay–Massachusetts

Plymouth   By the Sea B & B   Map: 2

One couldn't ask for a more idyllic setting. The soft yellow, shuttered, two-story house on the corner, opposite the waterfront walk of Plymouth, will catch your eye. I couldn't help but think that from the vanatage point of the wrap-around porch, this would be the place to plant oneself to watch the town's patriotic fourth of July parade. Lucky for the traveler, Roger and Brenda have converted the charming home to offer overnight accommodation. There are three guestrooms, all priced the same but with very different offerings. The coziest in size, but with spectacular water views, is the Mayflower Suite in the front of the home at the top of the entry stairs. The four-poster, queen-sized bed is positioned to enjoy unobstructed views through the front corner windows, with a sofa tucked in the narrow passage set opposite an expanse of window. Choose the Govenor Bradford Suite and you will enjoy three rooms: a back bedroom with angled water views, a cozy living room with water views, and a kitchen that opens onto an expanse of back deck with a separate outside entrance off the deck's stairway. Entered from off the front porch is another queen-bedded room that enjoys its own private sun porch. In summer months, breakfast is offered on the front porch. The rest of the year a bountiful continental breakfast is delivered to the privacy of your guestroom. *Directions:* Located next to the village on Rte 20. Take I-84 to exit 3B, or Mass Pke 90 to exit 9.

BY THE SEA B & B   **New**
Owners: Roger & Brenda Silvieus
22 Winslow Street
Plymouth, MA 02360, USA
Tel: (508) 830-9643, (800) 593-9688
3 rooms
Double: $125–$150
Open: all year, Credit cards: none
karenbrown.com/ne/bythesea.html

Princeton The Fernside Inn Map: 2

Neighboring the Wachusett Reservation, Princeton was developed as a weekend escape from Boston. The Fernside Inn, handsome with its soft mustard-yellow façade, sits on a hillside above the heart of the village. It is a beautiful inn, uncluttered and elegant in its décor with traditional furnishings and oriental carpets set on wide plank floors. Unusual for a house built in 1830, the home has an abundance of windows that frame the surrounding setting and bathe the inn in light. For guests who settle here for a romantic escape, they will appreciate the intimate salons and the expansive back deck where one can appreciate the morning sunrise and evening stars. There are eight guestrooms, six of which enjoy woodburning fireplaces. Suite 1, on the entry level, is bright and cheerful in fabrics of reds and whites with front garden views. The other seven rooms are found at the top of one of the house's three stairways. All are lovely but I especially liked Suite 5, rich in warm colors, a four poster bed and views overlooking the backgrounds. From 1890 to 1989, the inn was a retreat for "women wage earners over 17" who worked the factories in Boston. The terms of stay has changed dramatically as first "guests" were "expected to share in the care of room and table work!" By contrast, today, you will be pampered and offered a bountiful breakfast. *Directions:* Located at the blinking light at the intersection of Rtes 31 and 62, take Mountain Rd north 1.5 miles to Fernside.

THE FERNSIDE INN   New
Owners: Richard & Jocelyn Morrison
162 Mountain Road
P.O. Box 303, Princeton, MA 01541, USA
Tel: (978) 464-2741, (800) 545-2741
8 rooms
Double: $150–$230
Closed: 2 weeks in Mar, Credit cards: all major
Select Registry
karenbrown.com/ne/fernside.html

Provincetown — Crowne Pointe Historic Inn — Map: 2

Crowne Pointe, within walking distance of the heart of Provincetown, offers 40 lovely guestrooms in a complex of neighboring buildings. Enter into the office and your first impression is one of elegance, which pervades the inn, then your hearts are won by the smells wafting from the open kitchen. A lavish, hot breakfast buffet is set in the charming small dining room and in the evenings guests gather in the public areas for wine and hors d'oeuvres. Bedrooms are handsome, with walls painted in rich colors of rusts, greens, maroons, and golds to complement the elegance of furnishings, fabrics, art, and rugs. Many rooms have fireplaces, intimate decks, Jacuzzis, and kitchenettes, and all rooms enjoy TVs, VCRs, telephones with voice mail, wet bars, and nightly turn-down service. My favorite guestrooms were those in the main house, which are decorated with the owners' personal furniture. The Crowne Pointe room, with its beautiful clock and gorgeous hand-carved headboard dating from 1830, is a favorite. Luxury apartments and efficiencies are also available. Guests delight in the full-service Shui Spa with full steam room and sauna, meditation garden, and mineral bath. *Directions:* From Route 6, take the third Provincetown exit, turning left on Shank Painer Road. Continue to Bradford Street and turn right—the inn is on the left. Or leave your car behind and take the owners up on their offer of complimentary transportation from the airport or ferry.

CROWNE POINTE HISTORIC INN
Owners: Tom Walter, David Sanford & Mom
82 Bradford Street
Provincetown, MA 02657, USA
Tel: (508) 487-6767, (877) 276-9631
Fax: (508) 487-5554
34 rooms, 6 suites
Double: $100–$550
Open: all year, Credit cards: MC, VS
Select Registry
karenbrown.com/ne/crownepointhistoricinn.html

Richmond   The Inn at Richmond   Map: 1

The Inn at Richmond is set in the countryside just to the west of Lenox and Tanglewood in 27 lovely acres of gardens, lawns, and fields with cottages and barns (and a wonderful "allee" of maples leading to the barn). Staying here is like being a guest on a sophisticated farm, with horses grazing in paddocks surrounded by white fences, which contrast sharply with the bright-green grass. The innkeepers have passion for what they do and it shows—there is nothing they would not do to make your stay more enjoyable. Each queen or king bedroom is air-conditioned and has a private bathroom, telephone, and cable TV. The Chanticleer Suite, in colors of yellow, cranberry, and hunter green, has a cherry pencil-post queen bed. The Federal Suite has a mahogany king four-poster bed, fireplace, bath with shower and claw-foot tub, and a sitting room with a sofa bed and cable TV/VCR. The cottages are special, with their own entrances and private decks, fireplaces, and whirlpool tubs. I'd stay in one of these if I could linger for more than one night—a necessity if you are going to be able to enjoy all that there is to do. Breakfasts are delectable—I enjoyed a medley of fresh fruits, cheese, a smoked-salmon frittata with asparagus, potatoes, onions, and dill, and buckets of great coffee. *Directions:* From Boston take the Mass. Turnpike (I-90) to exit 1 to Route 102/41 through West Stockbridge and continue on Route 41 for 6 miles to the inn on the left.

THE INN AT RICHMOND
Owners: Dan & Jerri Buehler
802 State Road
Richmond, MA 01254, USA
Tel: (413) 698-2566, (888) 968-4748
Fax: (413) 698-2100
9 rooms, 3 cottages ($1400–$1600 weekly)
Double: $135–$350
Open: all year (weekends only in winter)
Credit cards: MC, VS, Select Registry
karenbrown.com/ne/innatrichmond.html

Places to Stay–Massachusetts

Rockport — Emerson Inn By The Sea — Maps: 2, 3

This handsome white clapboard inn (which once welcomed Ralph Waldo Emerson into its peace and comfort) enjoys a wonderful location looking out to sea on the outskirts of picturesque Rockport. The lovely entry hallway leads to a spacious grand salon painted in a soft yellow, which beautifully complements the handsome, rich, wide-plank floors. The dining room (which also hosts wedding receptions), dressed in striking reds and blues, leads through French doors into a porch set with more tables—the blue-water views are magnificent. We saw rooms ranging from the small Emerson Room at the top of the stairs with its white iron bed and small bath with tub shower to room 305 with its inviting iron king bed with views, Jacuzzi built into the old closet, and separate toilet and shower. Room 303 is small and pretty in a rose and cream print and has views of the water. Some of the top-floor rooms have low ceilings but the bonus of small balconies and all rooms have cable TV. A large pool is set dramatically in the back garden, looking out to the sea. *Directions:* In Gloucester follow Route 128 through two traffic circles and turn left onto Route 127 north at the traffic light. Continue about 4 miles. Stay on Route 127 (it takes a sharp left at Rockport's Five Corners), follow signs to Pigeon Cove, and continue for 2 miles, turning right onto Phillips Avenue at the Emerson Inn sign.

EMERSON INN BY THE SEA
Owners: Bruce & Michele Coates
1 Cathedral Avenue
Rockport, MA 01966, USA
Tel: (978) 546-6321, (800) 964-5550
Fax: (978) 546-7043
33 rooms, 3 suites, 2 cottages
Double: $95–$339
Open: all year, Credit cards: all major
Select Registry
karenbrown.com/ne/maemersoninn.html

Places to Stay–Massachusetts

Rockport   Seacrest Manor   Maps: 2, 3

Seacrest's brochure says it all: "Overlooking Woods and Sea" and "Decidedly Small and Intentionally Quiet." Easy to reach and away from the town busyness of Rockport on Marmion Way, Seacrest Manor is located in an area where the residents are your neighbors-next-door. There are seven rooms (one is a two-bedroom suite) and they have all been decorated with loving care. Many have floral wallpapers, comfortable sitting areas, and views of the sea or the inn's surrounding garden. Room 1, on the first floor, is warm and cozy with pine paneling. A desk below a window is positioned to look out to the gardens and to the sea. On the second floor, Room 6 has floral wallpaper, a king (or twins) bed and a view onto a lovely, old-fashioned New England garden with a lyrical fountain. Also on the second floor, Rooms 7 and 8 (twin or king) have adjoining decks with lounge chairs where you can enjoy the sun and views to the adjoining ocean. All the rooms are large, have private bathrooms, and are extremely comfortable. From the inn, you can walk to the village of Rockport or along the shore. A drive will provide endless miles of scenic vistas and charming towns. The inn serves a full breakfast in its dining room overlooking the adjoining gardens and afternoon tea in the living room. *Directions:* Take Route 128 to Gloucester to Route 127. Go four miles to Rockport to Route 127A. At the harbor, turn right up the hill for 5 blocks to Marmion Way and the inn.

SEACREST MANOR   *New*
Owner: Dwight McCormick
99 Marmion Way
Rockport, MA 01966, USA
Tel: (978) 546-2211
7 rooms
Double: $98–$215
Open: Apr to Nov, Credit cards: none
karenbrown.com/ne/seacrest.html

Places to Stay–Massachusetts

Rockport   Yankee Clipper Inn   Maps: 2, 3

Perched on the ledges above the ocean about an hour north of Boston airport sits the Yankee Clipper Inn, its two buildings housing the guest accommodations (which include three suites), nicely separated from one another by landscaping and by the rolling terrain. Most of the rooms have views of the ocean through large picture windows, with comfortable chairs positioned for watching the ever-changing scenery of the seashore. Bedrooms are comfortably furnished with queen, king, or full beds, and all have private baths; several have been recently updated with marble tile. Seven rooms have jetted tubs. The owners have been updating the decor of the rooms, making them even more desirable as places to unwind for several days. In the Quarterdeck house new bathrooms have been installed in four rooms, some with jetted tubs. A swimming pool is available on the property and nearby you find tennis, golf, hiking, fishing, biking, and summer theater. Rockport is a charming village with galleries, antique shops, and restaurants as well as a large community of artists who spend the summer there. This would be a great stopover for anyone headed for Maine and the upper New England coast. *Directions:* Take Route 128 north to Cape Ann through Gloucester. Turn left on Route 127 for about 3 miles to Rockport's Five Corners and a sign for Pigeon Cove, where the road makes a sharp left. Turn left and continue for 1-2/10 miles to the inn.

YANKEE CLIPPER INN
Innkeepers: Randy & Cathy Marks
127 Granite Street
P.O. Box 2399, Rockport, MA 01966, USA
Tel: (978) 546-3407, (800) 545-3699
Fax: (978) 546-9730
13 rooms, 3 suites
Double: $129–$379
Open: all year, Credit cards: all major
karenbrown.com/ne/yankeeclipper.html

Places to Stay–Massachusetts

Salem — Hawthorne Hotel — Map: 2

Many travelers are drawn to Salem for its haunting tales of witches, the House of Seven Gables made famous in the writings of Nathaniel Hawthorne, the incredible Peabody Essex Museum, the Maritime National Historic Site, the Pickering Wharf, and the seasonal whale watch. The Hawthorne Hotel, just across from Salem Common and within walking distance of all historic sites, is a handsome brick building with some very attractive public areas and services. Just off the entry is the Nathaniel Bar and Restaurant and a most grand and spacious lobby decorated in attractive rusts and greens with comfortable, intimate seating arrangements. Off the lobby is the charming Tavern, which serves continuously from 11 am to 11 pm and is intimate with tables set in front of a log fire. Guestrooms are all similar, with reproduction furniture in style with the period of the hotel, but vary in size and amenities. The six suites are all corner rooms with a separate bedroom and a sitting room equipped with sofa bed. A National Historic building, this is a nice hotel with a good location. *Directions:* From I-95 or US1 to Route 28 north, take exit 26 east, Lowell Street, to Peabody. Proceed through Peabody center, turn onto Bridge Street (Route 107 north), then drive just over a mile to Winter Street (Route 1A south). Turn right and follow Route 1A around Salem Common. From Logan Airport, follow Route 1A north for 15 miles—the Hawthorne is on the right.

HAWTHORNE HOTEL
Manager: Juli Lederhaus
On the Common
Salem, MA 01970, USA
Tel: (978) 744-4080, (800) 729-7829
Fax: (978) 745-9842
89 rooms
Double: $130–$315*
 *Breakfast not included: $10
Open: all year, Credit cards: all major
karenbrown.com/ne/hawthornehotel.html

Sandwich — Belfry Inn & Bistro — Map: 2

Take an old abbey, its next-door parish house, and an adjoining home, add them together, and what you have is a wonderfully innovative inn and restaurant. Name the eight bedrooms in the Drew House after members of the family, the six bedrooms in The Abbey after the days of the week, Monday through Saturday, and add on the eight rooms in the Village Inn and you have a delightful complex for your individual enjoyment or for a family wedding, a reunion, or a gathering of friends. The restaurant setting is the old abbey church and the owner has cleverly preserved its old structure while making the restaurant and bar (the old confessional, obviously) into something fun and different. During the summer, wine tastings are held weekly. The rooms in each of the three buildings include queen and king beds. On the third floor of the Village Inn there are perfect family accommodations with a queen bed and a separate room with twin beds. Both the Drew House and the Village Inn have common rooms where you can relax or meet up with friends. Recently renovated, the former Meeting House and Doll Museum now offers luxurious guestrooms (sentimentally named for historic dolls) and public areas. A Continental breakfast buffet is served to all guests in The Abbey. *Directions:* From Boston take I-93 south to the Sagamore Bridge, to Rte 6 east, to exit 2 to Sandwich, then take Rte 6A to Jarves St. Turn left to the inn.

BELFRY INN & BISTRO
Owner: Christopher Wilson
8 Jarves Street
PO Box 2211, Sandwich, MA 02563, USA
Tel: (508) 888-8550, Fax: (508) 888-3922
25 rooms
Double: $95–$235
Open: all year, Credit cards: all major
karenbrown.com/ne/belfryinn.html

Sandwich — Daniel Webster Inn — Map: 2

In the center of the lovely town of Sandwich, one of the gateways to Cape Cod, sits the Daniel Webster Inn. The inn, the oldest in the country, occupies the site of a tavern built before the American Revolution and named for its most famous resident. This is a full-service inn with a cozy tavern, an informal dining room with a large fireplace, and a formal dining room with a glass wall looking onto an enclosed courtyard and garden. These are especially attractive spots where you can enjoy both the ambiance and the food. In the tavern the food focuses on tasty appetizers, a variety of salads, burgers, sandwiches, and, in the evening, a number of entrees. If you prefer a more gourmet meal, head for the restaurant where the emphasis is on fresh seafood, with plenty of additional choices for meat lovers. All guestrooms are most attractively appointed with period furniture including canopy or four-poster beds, highboy dressers, desks, and overstuffed chairs. I enjoyed a lovely, newer room with a fireplace, canopy bed, luxurious spa tub, and heated marble floor in the bathroom. In the low season there is an expanded Continental breakfast, while breakfast in the high season is à la carte. In addition to the inn's outdoor swimming pool, guests also have access to local private health and golf clubs. *Directions:* From Boston take Route 3 south to Route 6 then leave at exit 2. Turn left on Route 130 for 2 miles, going right at the fork—the inn is on the left.

DANIEL WEBSTER INN
Innkeeper: The Catania Family
149 Main Street
Sandwich, MA 02563, USA
Tel: (508) 888-3622, (800) 444-3566
Fax: (508) 888-5156
38 rooms, 16 suites, Double: $109–$379*
 *Breakfast not included
Open: all year, Credit cards: all major
Select Registry
karenbrown.com/ne/danielwebsterinn.html

Sandwich — Isaiah Jones Homestead — Map: 2

The Isaiah Jones Homestead, built in 1849, has many wonderful antiques of the sort that you would love to have in your own home. However, my envy of those antiques extends beyond the furniture, for I would love to install the graceful curved staircase leading from the front hall to the bedrooms in my home in California. The gathering room has an 11-foot ceiling and crown molding reminiscent of the Victorian era in which the home was built. Toast your toes by the fireplace and relax with a cup of tea nestled by the window. Breakfasts, served by candlelight at the mahogany dining table, are welcoming with the early-morning aroma of freshly baked breads and delicious entrees. All the bedrooms have queen-size beds, five have fireplaces, and four have whirlpool tubs. The Weeks room has a queen iron bed, sitting room, and a bathroom with a two-person spa. The inn has a living room that welcomes you and a breakfast room with two large tables—great for sharing the day's plans. There's a small porch where you can sit and rock while reading a good book. The location is ideal for walking into the center of the village of Sandwich, to the Glass Museum, the antique shops, and to the restaurants. Being just 3 miles east of the Sagamore Bridge, Sandwich is a great spot for an extended stay at the start or the end of your trip to Cape Cod. *Directions:* Leave Route 6 at exit 2, going left on Route 130. Bear right at the fork for 2/10 mile and the inn is on the left.

ISAIAH JONES HOMESTEAD
Innkeepers: Cecily Denson & Richard Pratt
165 Main Street
Sandwich, MA 02563, USA
Tel: (508) 888-9115, (800) 526-1625
Fax: (508) 888-9648
5 rooms, 2 suites
Double: $145–$185
Open: all year, Credit cards: all major
Select Registry
karenbrown.com/ne/isaiahjoneshomestead.html

South Egremont   Weathervane Inn   Map: 1

Opening the door of this 1835 Greek Revival inn with its 1785 origins, I was enveloped by the smell of cookies baking in the kitchen. This made it hard to concentrate on looking at the living and dining rooms but among the features that did stand out were the beehive oven fireplace and the spectacular moldings found throughout the inn. The common rooms are attractively decorated and there's a great fireplace in the New England tradition. There are ten guestrooms with a combination of kings, queens, and twins, each with its own bath. One room has a pencil-post king bed, hardwood floors, blue-flowered wallpaper, and comfortable chairs. A room under the eaves with dormers also has hardwood floors, braided oval rugs, and a red, white, and blue quilt on the queen bed. At the end of a day of enjoying the many activities in this area (antiquing, music, shopping, the Norman Rockwell Museum, and all the sports you can name), you can return to the inn for a cup of tea and a sweet. Afterwards you can dine in one of the many wonderful nearby restaurants. (The innkeepers will prepare dinner for parties of ten or more guests.) A scrumptious breakfast is served in the dining room, with its tables set for four and Hitchcock-style chairs. *Directions:* From New York take the Taconic Parkway to Rte 23 east and drive 13 miles to the inn on the right. From the Massachusetts Turnpike take exit 2 to Rte 202 to Rte 7 south, then Rte 23 west to the inn on the left.

WEATHERVANE INN
Innkeepers: Maxine & Jeffrey Lome
Route 23, Box 388
South Egremont, MA 01258, USA
Tel: (413) 528-9580, (800) 528-9580
Fax: (413) 528-1713
8 rooms, 2 suites
Double: $115–$275
Open: all year, Credit cards: all major
Select Registry
karenbrown.com/ne/weathervaneinn.html

Places to Stay—Massachusetts

South Orleans — A Little Inn on Pleasant Bay — Map: 2

As you are meandering along the coast of the "elbow" of Cape Cod, you find yourself enjoying the beauty and the scenery of Pleasant Bay. Here on a high hill overlooking the bay is A Little Inn with its nine bedrooms and private baths. The history of the inn dates back to 1798 and some believe that it was a stop for slaves traveling along the "underground railroad." Four of the inn's guestrooms are located in the Main House and three in the Paddocks. The Carriage House has two newly renovated king bedrooms, one with fireplace. In the Main House the Mercury Room has a king bed, a sitting area, bathroom with shower, a private entrance, and a garden patio. The Knockabout Room has a king bed, bay views, and a bathroom with shower. The other two rooms have queen beds, showers, and either bay views or a deck overlooking the back garden. A European Continental breakfast is served. Next door to the inn is a cranberry bog, the scene of much activity as the berries ripen and are gathered for harvest. The village of Chatham is close by with all its shops, galleries, and activities. Nauset and Skaket beaches are within easy reach and the inn has a dock that guests may use. *Directions:* From Boston take I-93 to Route 3 south to Sagamore Bridge to exit 11 (Brewster and Chatham). Turn left on Route 137 then left again onto Pleasant Bay Road. Continue straight at the stop sign at Route 39 then go left on Route 28 for ¾ mile to the inn on the left.

A LITTLE INN ON PLEASANT BAY
Owners: Sandra & Bernd Zeller, Pamela Adam
654 South Orleans Road
PO Box 190, South Orleans, MA 02662, USA
Tel: (508) 255-0780, (888) 332-3351
Fax: (508) 632-2400
9 rooms
Double: $185–$225
Open: mid-Apr to Dec, Credit cards: all major
karenbrown.com/ne/alittleinnonpleasantbay.html

South Yarmouth — Captain Farris House — Map: 2

As you stand at the door of the Captain Farris House and see the National Historic Register plaque, you know somehow that you are in for a real treat and when you're inside you'll not be disappointed. The cozy parlor is perfect for relaxing after a day of sightseeing, the dining room is stunning with its long table, corner cabinet, and sideboard. The informal garden breakfast room with its large skylight brings the outdoors in to you. The bedrooms, located in the main house and in a small building next door, are wonderful, with crisp, white linens, cable TV, and VCR. All but one of the bathrooms have Jacuzzi tubs and showers. Some rooms have sundecks or private porches and most have private entrances. Suites have fireplaces in the living rooms and a large bedroom, and there is one two-bedroom suite with a spacious living room and a dining room equipped with microwave. The Phoebe White Suite was my favorite with its spacious living room, fireplace, and bedroom with a queen canopy bed. Its bathroom has a two-person Jacuzzi and there's a sundeck as well. Breakfast features a freshly baked pastry, fresh fruit, and a hot entree. *Directions:* From Boston take I-93 south to Route 3 south, crossing the Sagamore Bridge to Route 6 toward Hyannis. Leave at exit 8 onto Station Avenue for 2-1/10 miles to the yield sign. Continue straight to the intersection of Route 28, cross over, and the inn is about one block down on the right.

CAPTAIN FARRIS HOUSE
Innkeepers: Patricia & Stephen Bronstein
308 Old Main Street
South Yarmouth, MA 02664, USA
Tel: (508) 760-2818, (800) 350-9477
Fax: (508) 398-1262
2 rooms, 4 suites
Double: $110–$250
Open: all year, Credit cards: all major
karenbrown.com/ne/captainferrishouse.html

Stockbridge — Inn at Stockbridge — Map: 1

The Inn at Stockbridge is a large Georgian-style building, constructed in 1906, situated down a driveway winding through a 12-acre estate. You arrive at a columned porch and on the other side of the front door is a very large, welcoming hall flanked by the dining room on one side and the gracious living room on the other. The living room, where wine is served in the afternoon, is comfortably furnished and reading by the fire here is a real pleasure. The inn's guestrooms are in the main house, the cottage house, and the recently built barn. Always a favorite, Blagdon, the original master bedroom, decorated in soft shades of yellow, has a spacious sitting area in front of the fireplace and a lovely two-poster king bed. The four spacious new deluxe barn suites—Shakespeare, Wharton, Rockwell, and Shaker—all enjoy gas fireplaces, whirlpool tubs, and private decks, and each is decorated appropriately for its name. The inn prides itself on its breakfasts, formal affairs by candlelight, and Len loves to share his breakfast recipes with guests. The inn is close to so many things to do that you'll have trouble deciding between the antiquing, the music festivals, the Norman Rockwell Museum, and a variety of sports. *Directions:* Take the Massachusetts Turnpike to exit 2, drive west on Route 102 to Route 7 north, then go 1-2/10 miles to the inn on the right. From New York take the Taconic Parkway to Route 23 east and Route 7 north past Stockbridge for 1-2/10 miles.

INN AT STOCKBRIDGE
Innkeepers: Alice & Len Schiller
Route 7N
P.O. Box 618, Stockbridge, MA 01262, USA
Tel: (413) 298-3337, (888) 466-7865
Fax: (413) 298-3406
8 rooms, 8 suites
Double: $150–$350
Open: all year, Credit cards: all major
Select Registry
karenbrown.com/ne/innatstockbridge.html

Stockbridge — Red Lion Inn — Map: 1

The Red Lion Inn dates back to 1773 when it was a small tavern where coaches stopped on their journey between Boston and Albany. Today this inn is an institution: visitors come to experience the setting, the history, the collections, the food, and the ambiance established by generations of hospitality. The owners take pride in maintaining the antique charm and authenticity of the inn. The floors tilt, the walls are not square, and the furnishings look as if they have been there forever. There are 108 guestrooms, 95 with private baths, all offering the amenities of a quality hostelry. Rooms have antique beds (be sure to specify your choice of queen or twins when you make your reservation), flowered wallpapers, white bedspreads, comfortable seating, and good lighting. Some rooms in the main building, my favorites, look out to the Main Street, while others look out to the several buildings that also house guests. Stockbridge and the Berkshires are rich in festivals of the performing arts—Tanglewood is close by—and fine-art and antique galleries. There is easy access to a wealth of sports and the inn has a pool. Stockbridge is New England at its best, especially in the fall with its glorious foliage in full color. *Directions:* Take I-90 to exit 2 at Lee, then Route 102 west to Main Street, Stockbridge. The inn is on the left.

RED LION INN
Owner: The Fitzpatrick Family
Manager: Bruce Finn
30 Main Street
Stockbridge, MA 01262, USA
Tel: (413) 298-5545, Fax: (413) 298-5130
83 rooms, 25 suites
Double: $110–$435*
 *Breakfast not included
Open: all year, Credit cards: all major
karenbrown.com/ne/redlioninn.html

Sturbridge Lodges at Old Sturbridge Village Map: 1

Ideal in its close proximity to the living museum of Old Sturbridge Village and housed in buildings that replicate the era of the village, the Lodges of Old Sturbridge Village offer comfortable accommodations. Surrounding a central lawn, the single-story, pastel-washed clapboard and shuttered buildings of the complex are newly constructed, but were designed to resemble houses of old. There are forty-seven "village units" that are ideal for families; all similar in hotel-style with one or two bedrooms, a private bathroom, television, and telephone. One of the village units also has two family suites made up of two connecting rooms. One room has a queen-size bed and sitting area for mom and dad. The second room can easily sleep up to three children. In contrast to the new village units, the two-story Oliver Wight House stands on its original site, and has been offering food and lodging by a tavern keeper almost from the day it was built in 1789. It has ten guestrooms furnished in the regal style of the Federal period that are recommended for couples wanting more atmosphere and charm. A continental breakfast is offered for an additional charge, but for lunch and dinner journey back to the Tavern at the entrance to the village. When visiting the museum, take advantage of the free parking at both ends, as the museum village covers over 200 acres. *Directions:* Located next to the village on Rte 20. Take Interstate 84 to exit 3B, or Mass Pke 90 to exit 9.

LODGES AT OLD STURBRIDGE VILLAGE *New*
Director: Laura Coonan
One Old Sturbridge Village Road
Sturbridge, MA 01566, USA
Tel: (508) 347-3327, (800) SEE -1830
Fax: (508) 347-3018
47 rooms, Double: $80–$135*
 *Breakfast not included: $3.95
Credit cards: all major
karenbrown.com/ne/sturbridgelodge.html

Places to Stay–Massachusetts

Sturbridge Publick House Historic Inn Map: 1

Sturbridge's location at the intersection of the Massachusetts Turnpike (I-90) and I-84 (between Connecticut and Massachusetts) gives it a perfect position for travelers coming and going through New England. The Publick House Historic Inn offers a selection of places to stay: the Publick House, the Chamberlain House, and the Country Lodge. Rooms at inns are more our cup of tea but if you do stay at the lodge you'll find attractive motel-like rooms with private balconies. The Chamberlain House features six gracious suites. At the Publick House Historic Inn the simply but comfortably furnished rooms (all non-smoking) are part of a building dating back to 1771—this inn has served as a tavern and pub since pre-Revolutionary days. In this building you find two different dining rooms: The Tap Room and Ebenezer's Tavern. The Dining Room, where I can attest to the deliciousness of the fabulous lobster pie or the turkey dinner, is also where breakfast is served. For a different ambiance but with the same menu for lunch or dinner you might want to settle in Ebenezer's Tavern. Historic Sturbridge Village is just a few minutes' drive away. *Directions:* Located on the green and common in Sturbridge. After leaving I-84 or I-90, follow the signs to Route 131.

PUBLICK HOUSE HISTORIC INN
Innkeeper: William Clifford
Route 131
Sturbridge, MA 01566, USA
Tel: (508) 347-3313, (800) 782-5425
Fax: (508) 347-5073
118 rooms, 8 suites
Double: $65–$199*
 *Breakfast not included
Open: all year, Credit cards: all major
karenbrown.com/ne/publickhouse.html

Sudbury — Longfellow's Wayside Inn — Map: 2

Longfellow's Wayside Inn, located on 106 acres not far west of Boston, has been open since 1716 and consequently is one of America's oldest operating inns. Preserving its heritage is the successful result of the owner's love of this inn. The original old bar room with its large fireplace, beamed ceiling, and Windsor chairs offers a cozy and welcoming spot for relaxing. The inn is perhaps best known as a restaurant and there are several comfortable dining rooms in various parts of the building. The ten guestrooms are cozy, comfortably furnished, and large enough for a sitting area and private bathroom with tub and shower. A full breakfast is served. As a National Historic Site, the inn provides a self-guided walking tour which not only takes you through the rooms of the inn with their individual history but also to the various buildings on the grounds, which include a working grist mill where the whole-wheat flour and cornmeal used in the bakery is ground. The Redstone School house of *Mary Had a Little Lamb* fame was moved to this site years ago and can be toured in seasonable weather. Also on the grounds you find the Martha-Mary Chapel, built in 1940 by Henry Ford in memory of his mother and mother-in-law and now a popular venue for weddings. The inn is now completely handicap accessible. *Directions:* Just west of Boston, between Boston and Worcester off Route 20. 11 miles west of Route 128 and 7 miles east of Route 495. Follow signs to the inn.

LONGFELLOW'S WAYSIDE INN
Innkeeper: Robert Purrington
Wayside Inn Road
Sudbury, MA 01776, USA
Tel: (978) 443-1776, (800) 339-1776
Fax: (978) 440-9630
10 rooms, Double: $125–$155
Closed: Jul 4, Credit cards: all major
Select Registry
karenbrown.com/ne/longfellow.html

New Hampshire Places to Stay

Ashland   Glynn House Inn   Map: 3

On a quiet tree-lined street in a residential section of Ashland you find the Glynn House Inn, a Victorian home made into an inn and now beginning a new life with new owners. Already their skillful redecoration is taking this lovely inn onto a new plateau. The living room and the dining room are gracious places to relax or to enjoy the inn's full gourmet breakfast. The air-conditioned guestrooms, furnished with queen and king beds and period antiques, all have TV/VCRs, many have a combination tub and shower, and twelve rooms have fireplaces. Eight rooms enjoy double whirlpool baths. The decor in all is very attractive and features Victorian wallpapers. Of the thirteen guestrooms (seven deluxe suites, one junior suite and five bedrooms) my favorite was the first-floor room with its two-person spa tub and two wing chairs facing the gas fireplace in front of the queen bed, which was topped by a black-and-white toile comforter. The full breakfast served in the dining room is a real treat since the room is so graciously inviting, as is the adjoining sitting room where afternoon tea is served daily. There are many things to enjoy in this area but Squam Lake is one of the best. Skiing, tennis, golf, fishing, hiking, antiquing, and traveling back-country roads in the fall foliage season would be added reasons to make Glynn House a place to stay in. *Directions:* Take I-93 to exit 24 to Ashland. Turn left on Highland Street to the inn.

GLYNN HOUSE INN
Innkeepers: Jim & Gay Dunlop
59 Highland Street
Ashland, NH 03217, USA
Tel: (603) 968-3775, (800) 637-9599
Fax: (603) 968-9415
13 rooms
Double: $119–$259
Open: all year, Credit cards: all major
karenbrown.com/ne/glynn.html

Places to Stay–New Hampshire

Bedford   Bedford Village Inn   Maps: 2, 3

Just ten minutes from the southern outskirts of Manchester and conveniently located the same distance from the airport, the Bedford Village Inn is a complex of yellow buildings sitting above the main road to the city. Now surrounded by urban sprawl, the inn dates back to the time when Bedford was a farming community and the core of the complex is the original barn and Federal-style farmhouse built in 1810. Although the complex appears quite large, the inn has just 14 deluxe guest suites—eight luxury suites, four executive suites with separate sitting areas, and two two-bedroom annex suites. All the rooms are appointed with marble baths, Jacuzzi tubs, four-poster beds, good lighting, and lots of amenities such as fine towels and soaps. The former milking room is now a comfortable sitting room for guests, with sofas set in front of a large fireplace. The barn also boasts an enormous room that is host to weddings and large functions. The inn's acclaimed restaurant is actually eight individually decorated, intimate dining rooms. We chose to dine in the Tavern Bar, which offered simpler, reasonably priced but still excellent fare. *Directions:* Take Rte 93 to Rte 293 to Rte 101 west. Follow Rte 101 to the first set of lights (intersection of Rtes 101 and 114), make a left turn, continuing on Rte 101 west. Go through the next set of traffic lights. The next right-hand turn is Village Inn Lane.

BEDFORD VILLAGE INN
Owners: Jack & Andrea Carnevale
2 Olde Bedford Way
Bedford, NH 03110, USA
Tel: (603) 472-2001, (800) 852-1166
Fax: (603) 472-2379
14 rooms, 14 suites, 1 cottage
Double: $200–$350*
 *Breakfast not included: $10–$18
Open: all year, Credit cards: all major
karenbrown.com/ne/nhbedfordvillage.html

Bethlehem   Adair   Map: 3

Adair sits on top of a hill in a stunning, 200-acre country estate encompassing rock walls, ponds, and gardens, with lovely views of the White Mountains. Its main house, painted white, is a great example of the architecture of the 1920s and is furnished elegantly with period antiques, fine reproductions, and original art. The entrance hallway is large and the dining and living rooms flow from each side. The guestrooms are lovely and many have fireplaces. The Kinsman is a large suite with a king sleigh bed, floor-to-ceiling windows, and a door leading to a private balcony. It also has a fireplace with comfortable reading chairs and a large two-person whirlpool tub. The Waterford room offers a cherry-wood queen bed, a corner fireplace with sitting area, and a bathroom with a two-person soaking tub. On the lower level you can relax in the Tap Room with its regulation pool table and in several comfortable sitting areas. In the afternoon when you return from the day's activities, tea is served with scrumptious cakes or cookies and, in season, dinner is available Wednesday through Sunday in the lovely dining room. If you stay here you'll want to save some time for a stroll on the many trails surrounding the inn. *Directions:* Leave I-93 at exit 40 onto Route 302 east, turn sharp left at the Adair sign, and follow signs to the inn. From the east, take Route 302 west for about 3 miles past Bethlehem, and turn right at the sign to the inn.

ADAIR
Innkeepers: Judy & Bill Whitman
80 Guider Lane
Bethlehem, NH 03574, USA
Tel: (603) 444-2600, (888) 444-2600
Fax: (603) 444-4823
8 rooms, 1 suite, 1 cottage
Double: $180–$400
Closed: 1-week closures possible Apr & Nov
Credit cards: all major, Select Registry
karenbrown.com/ne/adair.html

Places to Stay–New Hampshire

Chesterfield — Chesterfield Inn — Map: 3

Originally a 1787 New Hampshire farm, Chesterfield Inn today offers 15 guest accommodations in a variety of rooms that boast fireplaces, balconies, and full bathrooms with whirlpool tubs. Guestrooms put privacy and comfort first: they are spacious and traditionally decorated, and have individually controlled heating and air conditioning, telephones, TVs, and refrigerators. I looked at a room with flowered wallpaper, two wing chairs, and a king bed on top of which was a cozy quilt for napping. There were views out onto the lawn and the gardens surrounding the inn. The dining room serves dinner six nights a week except in the foliage season and food preparation emphasizes fresh ingredients in unique flavor combinations. The seafood served at the inn comes from Boston, herbs from the garden, and other produce from local farms, all making for a delicious dinner. The parlor, dining room, and terrace are ideal settings for functions as intimate as a family gathering or as large as a wedding. This inn is located right off the major north-south interstate and is ideally situated for an extended stay in the area or a stopover when coming or going. *Directions:* Take I-91 to exit 3, following Route 9 east for 3 miles to the inn on the left.

CHESTERFIELD INN
Innkeepers: Judy & Phil Hueber
Route 9
P.O. Box 155, Chesterfield, NH 03443, USA
Tel: (603) 256-3211, (800) 365-5515
Fax: (603) 256-6131
13 rooms, 2 suites
Double: $150–$275
Open: all year, Credit cards: all major
karenbrown.com/ne/chesterfield.html

Durham — Three Chimneys Inn — Maps: 3, 4

The Three Chimneys Inn, constructed in 1649 with an addition about a hundred years later, is full of a rare New England historical charm. Beamed ceilings, dark and warmly inviting paneling, four-poster beds, and large armoires are found throughout and are just what you would expect in such a setting. Many of the beds have Edwardian canopies and there are a few rooms with spa tubs for two. Bedrooms have telephones, TVs, data ports, air conditioning, hairdryers, and makeup mirrors, and some have working fireplaces. Oriental carpets are used throughout the inn, giving it a warm and inviting appearance. Breakfast is served in one of the two dining rooms to guests only, but lunch and dinner are available to the public as well. The Frost Sawyer Tavern with its hand-hewn beams and granite walls surrounding the 1649 cooking-hearth fireplace is cozy, warm, and inviting. Windsor chairs provide comfortable seating at tables in several adjoining dining rooms where wide floorboards add to the charm. There is a more formal dining room on the first floor, and in the summer the Conservatory Terrace provides an outdoor dining venue for your enjoyment. This inn has the facilities to host conferences and is popular for weddings. *Directions:* Take I-95 north to exit 4 (Spaulding Turnpike/Route 16). Take exit 6W (Durham/Concord), turn left at the bottom of the ramp and travel 1 mile to the light. Go left at the light. The inn is on the hill above Durham Town Hall.

THREE CHIMNEYS INN
Innkeeper: Ron Petersen
17 Newmarket Road
Durham, NH 03824, USA
Tel: (603) 868-7800, (888) 399-9777
Fax: (603) 868-2964
23 rooms
Double: $159–$239
Open: all year, Credit cards: all major
karenbrown.com/ne/nhthreechimneys.html

| Enfield | Enfield Shaker Inn | Map: 3 |

Staying at an inn that's part of the Shaker Village in the Enfield, New Hampshire area makes for a truly different experience. As an added treat, the world-renowned Shaker Museum is just a minute's walk away from this great stone building, which is continually being restored by the owners in the Shaker tradition. There remain some of the simple built-in cupboards of this Shaker style and more are being added as the owners bring back the beauty of this building and its contents. Most of the unusually large bedrooms have two queen beds and private baths, and from them there are views out onto the surrounding grounds and the lake. Simple though the Shaker style is, it is this very simplicity that gives this type of furnishing its charm: adornment is not permitted— design to accomplish purpose is the Shaker way. One feature that is particularly charming is the hanging chairs on pegs along the exterior of a room's walls. On the second floor there is a large room where the brothers and the sisters would gather for their meetings and the dancing which was such an important part of their lives. The flooring in the restaurant (where some menu items are based on Shaker recipes) contains markers showing the beginning positions for Shaker dances. An adjacent granite, marble, and stained-glass chapel is often used for weddings. *Directions:* Take I-89 to exit 17, turning right onto Route 4 for 1 mile to Route 4A. The inn is 3½ miles along on the left.

ENFIELD SHAKER INN
Innkeepers: Janet Ellis & Clint Dickens
447 Route 4A
P. O. Box 479, Enfield, NH 03748, USA
Tel: (603) 632-4900, (866) 918-4900
Fax: (603) 632-4554
24 rooms
Double: $105–$155
Open: all year, Credit cards: all major
karenbrown.com/ne/shakerinn.html

Places to Stay–New Hampshire

Francestown   Inn at Crotched Mountain   Map: 3

The historic Inn at Crotched Mountain dates back 175 years and has lots of charm with warm paneling, big fireplaces, and comfortable furniture. From the inn the views look out to the swimming pool and tennis courts and then in the distance to the Piscatagoug Valley—one of those splendid vistas that varies as the light of the morning changes into brilliant sunshine and then late in the day as the shadows creep across the distant hills. Most of the cozy bedrooms have views over the distant mountain range, all have comfortable chairs or a loveseat for reading. The inn is a great place to stay if you enjoy walking and in the winter months you can get your exercise with cross-country or downhill skiing. From this location you have access to many local antique and craft shops. If you are as fond of English cocker spaniels as I am, then you can be sure that your welcome will be a friendly one as the family has three in residence: Winslow, Lucy, and Frances. The Inn at Crotched Mountain is open seasonally, so be sure to note their open dates when you plan your trip in this part of New Hampshire. Light fare is served in the Winslow Tavern on Saturday nights. *Directions:* Take I-93 north to Route 101, driving west to Route 114 then north to Goffstown. Take Route 13 southwest to New Boston, Route 136 west to Francestown, then Route 47 north for 2½ miles. Turn left onto Mountain Road after 1 mile.

INN AT CROTCHED MOUNTAIN
Innkeepers: Rose & John Perry
534 Mountain Road
Francestown, NH 03043, USA
Tel: (603) 588-6840, Fax: (603) 588-6623
13 rooms
Double: $80–$140
Closed: Apr & first 2 weeks Nov
Select Registry
karenbrown.com/ne/nhcrotchedmt.html

Places to Stay–New Hampshire

Hancock   Hancock Inn   Map: 3

The Hancock Inn has been around since 1789, the first year of George Washington's presidency, and stands on a quarter-mile stretch of Hancock's Main Street where every house is listed in the National Register of Historic Places. Wide pine floorboards, paneling on the walls, cozy fireplaces, an old tavern pub, and an excellent restaurant ensure you of a comfortable and pleasurable stay. Without any doubt, the bedroom with the most history in this guide is the one in this inn with walls beautifully hand-painted by the renowned itinerant painter, inventor, and writer, Rufus Porter. There are fourteen other guestrooms, all with private baths and eight with fireplaces. Handmade quilts, cable TV, telephone, and air conditioning are de rigueur. The tavern is a great place to meet other guests, have a drink, and play a game of checkers. The inn's restaurant, which has been awarded many honors, presents hearty American fare with a large serving of New England, like cranberry pot roast, Nantucket seafood chowder, and roasted duckling with rosemary-mint brown sauce. In the area you can go antiquing, pick apples, go for a hike, or cut your own Christmas tree. *Directions:* From New York take I-91 to Brattleboro then Route 9 to Keene to Route 123. Turn right to the inn.

HANCOCK INN
Innkeeper: Robert Short
33 Main Street
Hancock, NH 03449, USA
Tel: (603) 525-3318, (800) 525-1789
Fax: (603) 525-9301
15 rooms
Double: $140–$250
Open: all year, Credit cards: all major
Select Registry
karenbrown.com/ne/thehancockinn.html

Places to Stay–New Hampshire

| Hart's Location | Notchland Inn | Map: 3 |

The Notchland Inn gives you the chance to get away from it all and yet be within a few miles of lots of activities. Built in the 1860s, this granite mansion is located on 100 acres of the White Mountain National Forest, sitting atop a knoll at the base of one mountain and looking across at two others. The inn has the air of a wonderful old summer home, a feeling that permeates every room. There are seven rooms, six suites, and one cottage, each with a wood-burning fireplace. Carter is a large two-room suite with the fireplace in the bedroom, a queen bed made of cherry with an arched headboard, and handmade stained glass hanging in two windows. There are a sofa and a rocker in the sitting room and a two-person spa tub in the bathroom. Doors open to a large deck with great views. On the second floor of the former one-room schoolhouse is the Dixville Suite, another two-room suite where you can lie in the country-French queen bed and look across the sitting room to the fireplace or to the view from the window. In the bath there's a large corner soaking tub. The inn's living room is especially fine, designed by Gustav Stickley, a founder of the Arts and Craft movement, and has lovely furniture of that style. The inn serves a five-course dinner five days a week in a romantic dining room overlooking the gardens and the pond. *Directions:* Take I-93 north to exit 35 to Route 3 north for 10 miles to Route 302. Turn right on Route 302 for 17½ miles to the inn.

NOTCHLAND INN
Innkeepers: Les Schoof & Ed Butler
Route 302
Hart's Location, NH 03812, USA
Tel: (603) 374-6131, (800) 866-6131
Fax: (603) 374-6168
7 rooms, 6 suites, 1 cottage
Double: $255–$315
Open: all year, Credit cards: MC, VS
Select Registry
karenbrown.com/ne/thenotchlandinn.html

Henniker — Colby Hill Inn — Map: 3

This is a simple country inn whose new owners were taking advantage of a lull between guests to repaint and redecorate when we visited, and yet the innkeeper was there to greet us and kindly showed us around. The entry to this charming, white-clapboard, two-story New England inn is cozy and opposite the reception desk is a bar tucked into a hallway niche. At the back, overlooking the garden, you find a cheerful breakfast room, which in the evening doubles as the hotel's public restaurant. Across from this is an interior room, also used for dining when there is an overflow of guests. Beyond the dining room is a guest sitting room made cozy by a wood stove and equipped with television, books, and board games. Also located on the first floor are two guestrooms, one with a queen bed warmed by one of the inn's true working fireplaces. At the top of the stairs is one of the larger rooms, number three, decorated in blues and reds with a contrasting white iron bed. There are ten rooms in the main house, varying in price according to size and amenities, and five in the Carriage House, where rooms are smaller. Two luxury suites feature two-person Jacuzzi tubs and a fireplaces. Amenities offered include an outdoor swimming pool and conferencing facilities. *Directions:* 17 miles west of Concord off Routes 202/9. Take Route 114 south to the blinking light and village center. Turn right and the inn is ½ mile along on the right.

COLBY HILL INN
Owners: Cyndi & Mason Cobb
3 The Oaks
P.O. Box 779, Henniker, NH 03242, USA
Tel: (603) 428-3281, (800) 531-0330
Fax: (603) 428-9218
15 rooms
Double: $115–$265
Open: all year, Credit cards: all major
Select Registry
karenbrown.com/ne/colbyhillinn.html

Holderness — Manor on Golden Pond — Map: 3

Who hasn't heard of Golden Pond and who wouldn't be delighted to stay at this inn perched on Shepard Hill among ancient pines with a 65-mile panoramic view of Squam Lake and the surrounding mountains? Impressive and enchanting at the same time, with beamed ceilings, fireplaces, moldings, and large, gracious rooms, the house will delight you with its architectural details. The bedrooms are elegant and well appointed. The Buckingham Room's old-world charm made it the master bedroom, with a king four-poster with canopy, striking black-and-ivory decor, and double French doors leading to a private deck from which there are views of the lake and the foothills. The Stratford Room, decorated with a wall-mounted bearskin, deer antlers, snowshoes, and sled, is just plain fun. With Persian rugs on the hardwood floor, chintz-fabric walls in terracotta and cream, and barn-board bookcases, this room provides an enchanting blend of the primitive and the cozy. During the warmer months you can also stay in a delightful cottage at the inn's private beach. Dining in the elegant dining room with its acclaimed cuisine is another of the pleasures of staying here, while in the afternoon you can enjoy a formal English tea. Tennis, swimming, croquet, and badminton are available within the 14 acres of the estate. *Directions:* Take I-93 to exit 24, go south on Route 3 for 4-7/10 miles then turn right at the inn sign.

MANOR ON GOLDEN POND
Innkeepers: Mary Ellen & Brian Shields
Route 3
P.O. Box T, Holderness, NH 03245, USA
Tel: (603) 968-3348, (800) 545-2141
Fax: (603) 968-2116
25 rooms, carriage house & cottages (open seasonally)
Double: $225–$435
Open: all year, Credit cards: all major
Select Registry
karenbrown.com/ne/themanorongoldenpond.html

Places to Stay–New Hampshire

Intervale (North Conway) — New England Inn — Map: 3

Tucked away on a side loop of Route 16 between Jackson and North Conway, there are several inns where skiers love to stay. It's easy to understand why skiers and non-skiers alike would love the New England Inn for its variety of lodging choices: rooms in the inn, cottages, log cabins, cottage suites, and the new adults-only lodge across the street with its spectacular log-cabin construction. Many of the accommodations have Jacuzzi spa tubs for two, most have fireplaces, and many have an extra bed. Rooms in the inn are traditionally decorated; all are comfortable, but the cottages and the lodge are guests' favorites. The new lodge is quite special, with a natural wildlife decor achieved with beams, antler chandeliers, and mounted animal trophies in the grand, high-ceilinged entrance hall. The king-bedded Bear Room upstairs has a two-person Jacuzzi tub in one corner of the extra-comfortable living room along with a gas fireplace and TV/VCR set into a fieldstone surround. The Tuckerman Tavern has a full bar and serves an extensive dinner menu. There are several living rooms for relaxing before and after dinner, but it would probably be hard not to steal away to one's room. The inn has a seasonal outdoor swimming pool and children's wading pool. Children are welcome in the family cottage suites. *Directions:* Take Route 16 north to North Conway to Route 16A, Intervale Resort Loop. The inn is about a mile on the right.

NEW ENGLAND INN
Innkeepers: Chet & Chris Hooper
Route 16A
P.O. Box 100
Intervale (North Conway), NH 03845, USA
Tel: (603) 356-5541, (800) 826-3466
Fax: (603) 356-2191
15 rooms, 16 suites, 3 cottages, 6 cabins
Double: $75–$260
Open: all year, Credit cards: all major
karenbrown.com/ne/newengland.html

Jackson — Inn at Thorn Hill and Spa — Map: 3

The design concepts of Stanford White have inspired Jim and Ibby Cooper in their rebuilding of the Inn at Thorn Hill after a disastrous fire destroyed most of it in late 2002. They have taken the opportunity to maintain the essence and character of this marvelous inn while adding the facilities most desired by guests today. The inn has been enlarged to 25 rooms, including four suites. Each room has a gas fireplace, private bath, and DSL/TV/DVD, and some have spa tubs for two. Some rooms have steam showers or showers for two; some have views of the mountains with their ever-changing patterns of sun and shadow. The inn's award-winning dining room now offers fine dining in an enlarged room with French doors leading to a wraparound porch, a private dining room seating 20, a downstairs dining room for 40, and a lounge serving more casual meals. The lounge has been configured in a new turretlike space, which also creates a uniquely designed area on the second floor. An elevator has been installed, permitting handicap access to bedrooms on the second and third floors. The inn still has three cottages and a carriage house for guests, all decorated in French country style. Attractive packages for golfing, skiing, and other outdoor activities are offered. *Directions:* From Boston take I-95 north to the Spaulding Turnpike then Route 16 north to Jackson. Follow signs to the inn.

INN AT THORN HILL AND SPA
Innkeepers: Ibby & Jim Cooper
Thorn Hill Road
P.O. Box A, Jackson, NH 03846, USA
Tel: (603) 383-4242, (800) 289-8990
Fax: (603) 383-8062
21 rooms, 4 suites, 3 cottages
Double: $175–$340
Open: all year, Credit cards: all major
Select Registry
karenbrown.com/ne/theinnatthornhill.html

Places to Stay–New Hampshire

North Conway — Buttonwood Inn   Map: 3

Located away from the bustling commercial areas of North Conway, the acclaimed Buttonwood Inn sits on a hill amidst 6 acres of fields and forest—yet it's just minutes to the ski areas and to town. This inn was originally an 1820s farmhouse and the owners have retained that country atmosphere with antiques, quilts, and period stenciling. There are ten simply but comfortably decorated bedrooms, each with private bath. My favorite was a room painted in a shade of cream that had a pencil-post four-poster queen bed, wonderful wide-board floors, scattered area rugs, a sofa, gas fireplace, spa tub for two, TV, and telephone. Breakfasts are special here and entrees are cooked to order. Guests have no trouble finding a good restaurant for dinner in North Conway or Jackson. When you're not out exploring the surrounding area, you can swim in the inn's pool, enjoy the award-winning gardens, and hike or cross-country ski right in the back yard. North Conway offers seven major ski resorts, more than 200 tax-free shops and outlets, over 50 restaurants, golf, tubing, kayaking, canoeing, fishing, ice-skating, snowshoeing, and sleigh rides. *Directions:* From Boston take I-95 to the Spaulding Turnpike to Route 16 north to North Conway. In the village turn right on Kearsarge Street for 1½ miles to the stop sign. Cross the intersection and drive up the hill to the inn.

BUTTONWOOD INN
Innkeepers: Elizabeth & Jeffrey Richards
Mt. Surprise Road
P.O. Box 1817, North Conway, NH 03860, USA
Tel: (603) 356-2625, (800) 258-2625
Fax: (603) 356-3140
10 rooms
Double: $165–$245
Open: all year, Credit cards: all major
Select Registry
karenbrown.com/ne/thebuttonwoodinn.html

Places to Stay–New Hampshire

Plainfield — Home Hill Inn — Map: 3

The owners of Home Hill have brought a touch of France to a gorgeous country-house estate on the banks of the Connecticut River. We traveled up a beautiful tree-lined drive blanketed in snow and could only imagine how lovely it would be with autumn's brilliant foliage or with sunlight filtering through summer's thick greenery. Home Hill Inn is spectacular and I was captivated from the moment we stepped inside. Victoria and her French husband, Stephan, have created a wonderful European ambiance with warm Provençal colors washing the interior walls, walls dressed in gorgeous papers, beautiful fabrics selected for the bed spreads, and many pieces of lovely Moustiers pottery on display and used in the dining service. The faience was chosen partly for sentimental reasons as it comes from Stephan's hometown. The main house accommodates the intimate dining rooms and a few guestrooms. I loved all these rooms but most especially St. Gaudens, one of the coziest—a charming corner room with lots of light that filters over the beautiful rich rose and tans that decorate the rooms. The Carriage House offers six guestrooms, while the pool house provides guest quarters in summer only. Victoria brings her acclaimed brilliance as a chef to the restaurant, which, like the inn, boasts a four-diamond rating of excellence. *Directions:* From West Lebanon, head south on 12A, travel 3 miles, then turn right onto River Rd. The inn is 3-3/10 miles farther on the left.

HOME HILL INN
Innkeepers: Stephan & Victoria du Roure
703 River Road
Plainfield, NH 03781, USA
Tel: (603) 675-6165, Fax: (603) 675-5220
10 rooms, 1 pool house cottage
Double: $235–$425
Open: Jan 18 to Dec 31, Credit cards: all major
Relais & Châteaux
karenbrown.com/ne/homehillinn.html

Places to Stay–New Hampshire

Rhode Island Places to Stay

Block Island — The 1661 Inn & Hotel Manisses — Map: 2

Block Island, described by the Nature Conservancy as one of the last 12 great places in the Western Hemisphere, can be reached by ferry or plane from Connecticut, Rhode Island, or Long Island. There is nothing like an island with its magical feeling of being a place apart—in this unspoiled spot you really feel you have stepped back in time. The 1661 Inn and Hotel Manisses, with fifty-seven guestrooms in seven buildings, offers a range of delightful accommodations. Rooms are individually decorated, with various combinations of whirlpool tubs, decks, ocean views, and wood-burning fireplaces. Some rooms accommodate three or more persons, very convenient for families. There are wide porches for sitting and gazing at the ocean with its ever-changing activity and light. Breakfast (at The 1661 Inn) includes a hot entree. Dinner, showcasing local seafood, is enjoyed at the Hotel Manisses, where you find fine dining in a casual atmosphere. On this island there is much or little to do—strolling along wide sandy beaches, bicycling, hiking, horseback riding, shopping, boating, fishing, bird watching, kayaking, and visiting historical lighthouses—or relaxing at the hotel with a good book. Guests can take a tour of the island in the inn's van. *Directions:* By ferry: from Point Judith (year round) and Montauk, NY. By air: from Westerly and Providence or by charter. Contact the inn for schedules.

THE 1661 INN & HOTEL MANISSES
Innkeepers: Justin Abrams, Rita & Steve Draper
1 Spring Street
P.O. Box 1, Block Island, RI 02807, USA
Tel: (401) 466-2421, (800) 626-4773
Fax: (401) 466-3162
57 rooms
Double: $145–$399
Open: all year, Credit cards: MC, VS
Select Registry
karenbrown.com/ne/rithe1661inn.html

Newport   Abigail Stoneman Inn   Map: 2

Cliffside, Adele Turner, and the Abigail Stoneman Inn are all inns owned by Winthrop Baker. Each is a gem of décor and specializes in attention to guests' needs, comfort, and service. Rooms are sumptuously decorated with lush fabrics, beds are covered with exquisite comforters, and wallpapers tastefully chosen. All have individually controlled air conditioning. The Abigail Sherman Inn is unique, not for the number of rooms (only five), but in the number of amenities offered—including a choice of 20 different pillows. Guests choose from 30 complimentary premium soaps, gels, and bath oils; which are then delivered on a tray to their room. There is also a Bottled Water Menu of 24 international favorites from which to choose, in a room devoted to their display with information provided to assist in the selection. Each room or suite has a two-person spa tub, at least one fireplace, high ceilings, and tall windows. The two level suite at the top of the building has a circular staircase that leads you to a library sitting room with a fireplace and comfortable wing chairs. All three inns offer high English tea in the afternoons, 35 varieties in all (with all the pomp and substance one would expect to find in England), and upon your return from dinner, a selection of sweets. *Directions:* Route 95 to exit 38 to Route 138 E to Newport Bridges. Take Scenic Newport exit to right off ramp onto America Cup Blvd, to Bellevue Ave through light to Touro Street to inn.

ABIGAIL STONEMAN INN   **New**
Owner: Winthrop Baker
Innkeeper: Theodora Polluck
102 Touro Street
Newport, RI 02840, USA
Tel: (401) 847-1811, (800) 845-1811
Fax: (401) 848-5850
5 rooms, Double: $425–$700
Open: all year, Credit cards: all major
karenbrown.com/ne/stoneman.html

Places to Stay–Rhode Island

Newport Adele Turner Inn Map: 2

The Adele Turner, Cliffside, and Abigail Stoneman inns comprise the Legendary Inns of Newport. The Adele Turner Inn is the one located nearest to the heart of Newport's collection of shops, restaurants, and tourist activity. Its 13 rooms are luxuriously decorated; each is a pure pleasure to stay in for their attention to detail and the comfort. Each bed makes a statement with its high posts and formal presentation. There are fireplaces, spa tubs, beautifully appointed fabrics on the beds, striking wallpapers, and comfortable seating, including window seats to curl onto with a good book. Like its sister properties, the Adele Turner serves an elegant English tea in the afternoon, but the daily wine tasting events are an exclusive Adele delight. The staff sommelier pairs fine wines with artisan cheeses for a unique taste experience. Exceeding even the culinary delights, which include a full breakfast served in the dining room, is the sense of care that has gone into the preparation for your visit. This is Newport—the Newport that derives its reputation from the days of the Mansions and the Cliff Walk along the ocean. This is a place to visit, absorb and return to again-and-again. *Directions:* Take route 95 N to exit 3B, then Route 138 E over Newport Bridges to Scenic Newport. Exit to America Cup Blvd to end. L on Memorial Blvd, and then make a second left on Bellevue Ave. Take another left onto Pelham Street, the inn is on the left.

ADELE TURNER INN   **New**
Owner: Winthrop Baker
Innkeeper: Susan Mauro
93 Pelham Street
Newport, RI 02840, USA
Tel: (401) 847-1811, (800) 845-1811
Fax: (401) 848-5850
13 rooms, Double: $195–$600
Open: all year, Credit cards: all major
Select Registry
karenbrown.com/ne/adeleturner.html

Places to Stay–Rhode Island

Newport   Castle Hill Inn & Resort   Map: 2

With its superb oceanside location on 40 gorgeous acres at the west end of Newport's world-renowned Ocean Drive, the Castle Hill Inn & Resort offers guests romance, seclusion, and beauty. This Victorian mansion has been elegantly restored, with guestrooms in the main building, the private Harbor Houses, and a Swiss-style chalet. The renovated Beach House rooms with their breathtaking views, king beds, fireplaces, and beautifully equipped bathrooms are situated on a private white-sand beach. In the main house bedrooms are decorated with Victorian furniture, while the other guestrooms are decorated in an elegant seaside style. All are comfortable and inviting. Castle Hill's dining room has lovely views out to sea and the sunset; and any meal here, including a decadent afternoon tea at the top of the stairs in front of a fire, is an experience not to miss. The two-story Turret Suite, with 360-degree views, a sensational cupola, soaking tub, steam shower, fireplace, and every possible luxury, is extraordinary. Newport is such a small, intimate town and the mansions are so amazingly large that a visit here garners a near-perfect ten. *Directions:* From New York City take I-95 to Route 138 east. Take the first exit off the Newport Bridge and turn right at the second light. Turn right on Americas Cup then at the fifth light turn right on Thames to Wellington and then right on Ocean Drive for 3 miles. The inn is on the right.

CASTLE HILL INN & RESORT
Manager: Chuck Flanders
590 Ocean Drive
Newport, RI 02840, USA
Tel: (401) 849-3800, (888) 466-1355
Fax: (401) 849-3838
21 rooms, 2 suites
Double: $145–$650
Open: all year, Credit cards: all major
karenbrown.com/ne/castlehill.html

Places to Stay–Rhode Island

Newport Cliffside Inn Map: 2

For about 40 years the legendary artist Beatrice Turner lived a sheltered life in this fabulous Victorian manor house, and in that time created a vast number of paintings of herself—over 100 of her works are on display in the inn. There is a feeling of grandeur in all the 16 rooms and suites with their fireplaces, private baths, air conditioning, telephones, and cable TV. The unusual Tower Suite features a Victorian cupola tower and octagonal cathedral ceiling, Queen Eastlake bed, fireplace, and bay window with its own seat for gazing out at the world below. There's morning coffee room service, a full gourmet breakfast, and an afternoon Victorian tea that's way beyond sensational. The inn is decorated with fine period antiques and the fabrics used on the upholstered pieces are luxurious. Bathrooms are elegantly supplied with everything you desire. Add to all the above warm hospitality, good company, genial innkeepers, and fine food; and you will enjoy a stay you'll long remember. The inn is perfectly located a five-minute walk from the beach on a quiet, tree-lined street, a half block from the Cliff Walk, Newport's renowned seaside walking trail in front of its even more legendary mansions which are open for touring. This inn has it all. *Directions:* From New York City take I-95 north to exit 3 in Rhode Island for Route 138 east into Newport. From Boston take I-93 south to Route 24 south then Route 138 south. The inn is on the corner of Cliff and Seaview.

CLIFFSIDE INN
Innkeeper: Winthrop Baker
2 Seaview Avenue
Newport, RI 02840, USA
Tel: (401) 847-1811, (800) 845-1811
Fax: (401) 848-5850
8 rooms, 8 suites
Double: $250–$675
Open: all year, Credit cards: all major
Select Registry
karenbrown.com/ne/cliffsideinn.html

Newport — Hydrangea House Inn — Map: 2

You'll be totally enchanted by the best of accommodations, hospitality, and gorgeous decor in the inn owned by Dennis Blair and Grant Edmondson in the heart of Newport. Located on magical Bellevue Avenue, this inn has it all. It will capture your heart and demand a return visit. All nine guestrooms are decorated differently but in high style, great use of color, sumptuous fabrics, and a sense of drama—enhancing your experience in this city of lavish, extraordinary old homes. The two-room, two-level Chesterfield Suite, designed to pamper, is decorated in warm, lush tones of reds and gold, warm woods, a canopy four-poster king bed, fireplace, two-person spa tub, and marble walk-in steam shower. The "Carrie in Paris" suite with a magnificent French Regency bed, fireplace, spa tub and two-person "rain" shower is striking in its color palette of gold, yellows, periwinkle blues, and crimson reds. Silk curtains flow in the breeze overlooking the elegant Bellevue Avenue neighborhood. A formal dining room is the setting for a full "not to be missed" breakfast, fortifying you for the day's activities. In the afternoon, there's an English tea in winter and cooling refreshments in warmer seasons. *Directions:* From north, take Route 138 south to Newport beaches. Go through the second light and at the next major intersection turn right on Bellevue Ave. From west, follow route 138 east over Narragansett Bay to scenic 238 through the harbor front left on Bellevue Ave.

HYDRANGEA HOUSE INN
Owners: Dennis Blair & Grant Edmondson
16 Bellevue Avenue
Newport, RI 02840, USA
Tel: (800) 945-4667 or (401) 846-4435
Fax: (401) 846-6602
10 rooms, 8 suites
Double: $225–$360
Open: all year, Credit cards: all major
karenbrown.com/ne/hydrangeahouse.html

Providence   Christopher Dodge House   Map: 2

Home to Brown University, Providence is a charming city and it is quickly becoming one of Rhode Island's treasures. Three rivers weave a course through the heart of town and segment the key districts: the lovely residential and university quarter, the business, convention center and mall, and the seat of government. Tucked just on the other side of the 95 from the State House, the Christopher Dodge House is a convenient base from which to explore Providence and rooms are competively priced. One of three neighboring buildings converted to offer travelers lodging, referred to as the State House Inns, this is most definitely our favorite of the group, as the architecture of this three-story, brick, 1858 Italianate manor affords lofty, eleven-foot ceilings and spacious accommodation. A lovely banistered main stairway (as well as back stair) winds up to the guestrooms which are attractively decorated with early American reproductions. Each guest room enjoys a private, marble tiled bathroom, many boast a gas fireplace or stove and room furnishings include a comfortable reading chair, desk and comfortable bed. With exposed brick walls and tall windows that frame the backyard greenery, the dining room is a restful spot to enjoy the breakfast buffet. *Directions:* From 95 northbound, take exit 23. At light at end of ramp go straight onto State St. Take first right onto Smith St; pass the State House; take 3rd left onto Holden St to the corner of West Park St.

CHRISTOPHER DODGE HOUSE   *New*
Owners: Ken & Phyllis Parker
Innkeepers: Frank & Monica Hopton
11 West Park Street
Providence, RI 02908, USA
Tel: (401) 351-6111, Fax: (401) 351-4261
15 rooms
Double: $150–$200
Open: all year, Credit cards: all major
karenbrown.com/ne/dodge.html

Providence — Historic Jacob Hill Farm B & B Inn — Map: 2

Actually located on a winding country road in Seekonk, MA, yet just a ten-minute drive from Providence, the Jacob Hill Farm Bed and Breakfast Inn was built in 1722 and was once known as the Jacob Hill Hunt Club. Today this property has been transformed into an inn, with guestrooms providing every comfort. All the rooms are individually decorated and the private bathrooms have been updated, some with Jacuzzi tubs. A few of the rooms have fireplaces and many of the old wooden floors are covered with Oriental rugs. Four new, luxurious rooms have been added in the barn and as well as a Billiard room with Plasma Home Theater. The owners have decorated one room with a scenic mural and have innovatively made use of canopies as decor over some of the antique beds. There is air conditioning for the summer months if the usual breeze here on top of the hill isn't blowing. On the property you find a pool and tennis court and there are plenty of places to sit and look out over the valley below. The owners take great pride in every detail of this inn that they have created and their breakfasts are no exception—a great start to the day's activities. *Directions:* From Providence take I-195 east and leave at Massachusetts exit 1, turning left at the light (Route 114A). After about 1-7/10 miles turn right on Route 44 then 1½ miles left on Jacob Street. The inn is on the left at the top of the hill.

HISTORIC JACOB HILL FARM B & B INN
Innkeepers: Eleonora & Bill Rezek
P.O. Box 41326
Providence, RI 02940, USA
Tel: (508) 336-9165, (888) 336-9165
Fax: (508) 336-0951
8 rooms, 2 suites
Double: $179–$319
Open: all year, Credit cards: all major
Select Registry
karenbrown.com/ne/jacobhillfarm.html

| Westerly | The Villa | Maps: 1, 2 |

This part of Rhode Island is an overlooked stretch of coast with beautiful beaches just made for walking and squiggling your toes in the sand. On the shore road, just a short distance from these beaches, is The Villa, an inn of six guestrooms where you can enjoy the gardens and the pool as much as the inn's interiors. The inn's living room is comfortably furnished and there is an adjoining dining area where guests have breakfast if they do not want to eat poolside or in their rooms (a full breakfast is served on weekends, Continental during the week). Guests select from a varied and changing menu the night before. Two of the bedrooms are located in a separate building looking down at the gardens and the pool. I especially liked one with its own spa tub for two. A hot tub provides the perfect evening relaxation if you like to stare at the stars from a steaming, relaxing cauldron of bubbles. The Villa is located in an area close to the quaint historic village of Watch Hill with its many shops and harbor activity. One of the remaining carousels in the country is found here and it provides a great opportunity to relive your youth. From here you can take excursions to Mystic Seaport, Newport, and Block Island. Barbara and Michael are gracious innkeepers and assure a memorable stay. *Directions:* From Boston take I-95 to the Westerly area, exiting at Route 1A to the inn on the right. Watch for house numbers as the inn is not easily visible.

THE VILLA
Innkeepers: Barbara & Michael Cardiff
190 Shore Road
Westerly, RI 02891, USA
Tel: (401) 596-1054, (800) 722-9240
Fax: (401) 596-6268
6 rooms
Double: $155–$285
Open: all year, Credit cards: all major
karenbrown.com/ne/rithevilla.html

Places to Stay–Rhode Island

Vermont
Places to Stay

Addison (near Middlebury) — Whitford House — Map: 3

A little-traveled two-lane road leads you to one of the most captivating country inns you'll ever stay in. Set on a knoll overlooking the Adirondack Mountains, 15 minutes from the town of Middlebury, Whitford House is surrounded by rich farmland. Inside the inn, in addition to the extraordinarily delightful innkeepers, there's a heart of a home you'll never forget. You'll love its comfortable living rooms, the charming dining room, the open kitchen, and the use of old barn wood for walls, cabinets, and bookcases, which adds to the country appeal. There are four bedrooms, three in the main house and one in a guest cottage, furnished with queen and king beds. In the guesthouse there is a queen sofa bed in the living room as well a king bed in the bedroom that can be converted into twins. There's a brick patio outside the cottage, making a perfect place for you and your friends to watch the sun set over the Adirondacks. A full breakfast is served and when the menu calls for maple syrup, you'll know it came from the maple trees on the property. With advance notice a chef can be brought in to produce a five-course dinner, and that would indeed be special. This is an inn you'll always remember and want to return to as often as possible. *Directions:* From Boston, take I-93 to I-89 to exit 3 in Vermont near Bethel. Follow Route 107 to Route 100 to Route 125 to Middlebury to Route 22A. Refer to a local map for detailed directions to the inn.

WHITFORD HOUSE
Innkeepers: Bruce & Barbara Carson
912 Grandey Road
Addison (near Middlebury), VT 05491, USA
Tel: (802) 758-2704, (800) 746-2704
Fax: (802) 758-2089
3 rooms, 1 cottage
Double: $110–$250
Dinner available with prior reservation
Open: all year, Credit cards: MC, VS
karenbrown.com/ne/whitford.html

Places to Stay – Vermont

Andover   Rowell's Inn   Map: 3

Built in 1820 as a stagecoach stop by Major Edward Simons, the historic Rowell's Inn sits right up front on a small country road and waits to greet you as a guest. In 1910 the the inn changed hands and the elegant tin ceilings, cherry and maple dining-room floors, central heating, and indoor plumbing were added. This is not a fancy inn, but rather one in which you will be very comfortable for a night's rest as you visit this portion of Vermont. Bedrooms have private bathrooms and are nicely furnished. The Miss Caitlin Room has a brass queen bed with canopy, blue flowered wallpaper, wonderful wide-plank floors, a wood-burning fireplace, and a bathroom with a tub and hand-held showerhead. The Miss Juliette Room has both a double and a twin bed. On the third floor the F. A. Rowell Suite has a double bed, a trundle bed, a claw-foot tub, and a towel warmer (for me one of life's nicest amenities). The Major Simons Suite has a king bed and a ceiling fan. As one would expect, there's a dark, wonderfully atmospheric tavern room—it's easy to imagine the gatherings there almost 200 years ago. This room contains a most incredible wood-burning stove—I'd like to have brought it home. The inn's restaurant serves breakfast and a four-course dinner with a single entree. Note that there are no telephones or TVs in the rooms. *Directions:* On Route 11 connecting Route 7 and I-91. The inn is 7 miles west of Chester and 7 miles east of Londonderry.

ROWELL'S INN
Innkeepers: Michael Brengolini & Susan McNulty
1834 Simonsville Road
Andover, VT 05143, USA
Tel: (802) 875-3658, (800) 728-0842
Fax: (802) 875-3680
7 rooms
Double: $120–$175
Open: all year, Credit cards: all major
karenbrown.com/ne/rowells.html

Arlington   West Mountain Inn   Map: 3

West Mountain Inn sits way up on a hill with glorious views down the long winding driveway to the valley below. There are 150 acres on which to roam, with wildflowers, a bird sanctuary, hiking trails, and the Battenkill River where you might want to try your fishing skills. Accommodation in the main house is in twelve bedrooms and three suites. The Booker T. Washington room has original butternut paneling, your choice of either king or twin beds, and views of neighboring mountains and pastures. The Rockwell Kent suite has a native-butternut cathedral ceiling in the king-sized bedroom and a spacious living room with fireplace. There are three townhouses at the historic mill, which may be rented with or without meals. Each of these has a living room with satellite TV, kitchen, master bedroom, and a cozy guestroom. The restaurant serves hearty country breakfasts and elegant six-course dinners seven days a week. Whether it's winter or summer or the peak time of foliage when all of New England comes ablaze, this inn is a great place to be. *Directions:* Leave Route 7 north at exit 3, turning left at the end of the ramp. Take the access road to the end and turn right on Route 7A into Arlington. Drive 1 mile then turn left on Route 313 for ½ mile, go left on River Road, over the green bridge, and into the inn's driveway on the left.

WEST MOUNTAIN INN
Innkeeper: The Carlson Family
River Road
Arlington, VT 05250, USA
Tel: (802) 375-6516, Fax: (802) 375-6553
12 rooms, 3 suites, 3 townhouses
Double: $179–$294*
 *Includes breakfast & dinner
Open: all year, Credit cards: all major
Select Registry
karenbrown.com/ne/westmountain.html

Barnard (near Woodstock)   Maple Leaf Inn   Map: 3

You really must stay at the Maple Leaf Inn to appreciate all the thoughtful touches that Gary and Janet lavish on their guests, from the surprise gift on your bedside pillow to the lovely stenciling unique to each guestroom (all king-sized). Although newly built, this beautiful three-story, gray-and-white inn with wraparound porch has a traditional feel and incorporates a few signature antique pieces. On the first floor you find an inviting library, a lovely sitting room, and an attractive dining room with oak tables set in front of the fireplace and Janet's gorgeous samplers on the walls. Also on this floor is a beautiful L-shaped guestroom with a high cathedral ceiling. Second-floor rooms are decorated and themed by season. We settled into Autumn Woods with its bed set against the wall to maximize the angle of the fireplace, windows on three sides, and decadent bathroom with Jacuzzi tub. Winter Haven, the most expensive room, with a true two-person Jacuzzi, is a feminine room in creams and whites with a precious winter village scene stenciled above the windows, mantle, and door. On the top floor Sweet Dreams has a lovely four-poster bed, a double rocker to dream in, and stenciling with glow-in-the-dark stars. Breakfast, served in the dining room, is a gourmet bounty. *Directions:* From Woodstock turn off Route 4 in town onto Route 12 north. Travel 9 miles to the Maple Leaf Inn located on the right side, ¼ mile before the Barnard General Store.

MAPLE LEAF INN
Owners: Janet & Gary Robison
P.O. Box 273, Route 12
Barnard (near Woodstock), VT 05031, USA
Tel: (802) 234-5342, (800) 516-2753
Fax: none
7 rooms
Double: $190–$260
Open: all year, Credit cards: all major
Select Registry
karenbrown.com/ne/vtmapleleafinn.html

Barnard (near Woodstock)   Twin Farms   Map: 3

Absolute perfection—your own farmhouse home in Vermont on 300 acres with country charm, urban sophistication, ingenious decoration, and every amenity in the world—at a price, but unique. In the evening guests come together for cocktails, wine, and lively conversation in the Barn Room, a large but warmly gracious room with fireplace and groupings of comfortable sofas and chairs. The dining room has vaulted ceilings with yet another blazing fire. There is no menu, but you will be dazzled by the chef's imaginative creations using the very freshest and finest ingredients. Meals leave your senses satiated and you are ready to linger over a brandy in the pub. There are four guestrooms in the main house and several cottages connected by winding roads (but otherwise serenely separate) each with its own style of decor and each in its own setting. I loved the Meadow Cottage, a Moroccan fantasy inside a Vermont clapboard structure—it's nothing short of a desert king's traveling palace. There's wonderful tile, a cozy sitting area in front of the fire, and a majestic bedchamber with hand-wrought bronze columns supporting a tented ceiling. The bathroom echoes this decor with its large tub, shower, and plush amenities. The inn also has a fitness room, spa, guest entertainment center, and everything else you might want. *Directions:* Please contact the hotel for directions.

TWIN FARMS
Manager: Michael Beardsley
Barnard (near Woodstock), VT 05031, USA
Tel: (802) 234-9999, (800) 894-6327
Fax: (802) 234-9990
6 suites, 9 cottages
Double: $950–$2600*
 *Includes all meals
Closed: Apr, Credit cards: all major
karenbrown.com/ne/twinfarms.html

Brandon — Lilac Inn — Map: 3

The Lilac Inn is nestled in the Champlain Valley, surrounded by the Green Mountains and the Adirondacks, on the prettiest street in the region, in the small historic town of Brandon, chartered in 1746. Built in 1909 as a summer cottage for Albert Farr; the Greek Revival style home, with a five-arched façade, rivaled the finest homes in Brandon. The inn's nine guestrooms have been discreetly modernized so as not to distract from the historic character of the home. Each room is unique and filled with treasures from over thiry years of collecting. There are two dining rooms, the casual tavern and the more formal West Garden Room, whose menu focuses on the creative use of Vermont produce and has won numerous awards for the inn. Built around a cobblestone courtyard, embraced by two acres of landscaped grounds with cascading ponds and Vermont stonewalls, the inn's lovely setting and excellent reception facilities make it a popular choice for weddings. Brandon is situated near the major ski mountains and near Lakes Champlain and Dunmore, with rivers and streams creating great opportunities for fishing, swimming, and boating. Other attractions nearby include golfing and all the activities of the college town of Middlebury. Shelburne Museum is within an easy day's visit. *Directions:* From the north or south follow Route 7 to Brandon then take Route 73 east to the inn.

LILAC INN
Innkeepers: Shelly & Doug Sawyer
53 Park Street
Brandon, VT 05733, USA
Tel: (802) 247-5463, (800) 221-0720
Fax: (802) 247-5499
9 rooms
Double: $145–$325
Open: all year, Credit cards: all major
karenbrown.com/ne/vtlilacinn.html

Bridgewater Corners — October Country Inn — Map: 3

Think casual, think relaxed, think of a place where you can put your feet up, read a book, and be totally natural and without pretense. Think October Country Inn! In this quaint, ten-bedroom inn, a 19th-century farmhouse, you'll find sincere hospitality and delicious food. This is the kind of inn where they will put an extra bed in the room for that third person traveling with you. Some of the upstairs bedrooms are under the eaves but they're quite spacious enough for a good night's rest. Rooms have flowered wallpapers and a variety of brass, iron, and wooden headboards. Be sure to save some time to sit by the fire in the living room: a table behind the sofa had so many games on it, I couldn't figure out which I'd play first. This inn is noted for its food and its reputation has spread far and wide, although breakfast and dinner are offered only to resident guests. There's a swimming pool on the grounds, gardens for walking in, and plenty of diversions nearby—skiing, golf, cycling, summer theatre, and antiquing, to name just a few. One of the guests wrote in the inn's guest book, "I think I'll stay forever and send for my family. Maybe…". *Directions:* From Woodstock drive 8 miles west on Route 4 to the junction with Route 100A. Continue on Route 4 for 200 yards, take the first right (opposite Long Trail Brewery) then right again to the inn.

OCTOBER COUNTRY INN
Owners: Edie & Chuck Janisse
Upper Road, P.O. Box 66
Bridgewater Corners, VT 05035, USA
Tel: (802) 672-3412, (800) 648-8421
Fax: (802) 672-1163
10 rooms, Double: $115–$195
Breakfast & dinner served to guests only
Closed: Apr & first 3 weeks of Nov
Credit cards: all major, Select Registry
karenbrown.com/ne/octobercountryinn.html

Burlington — Lang House — Map: 3

The Reed family constructed this Victorian mansion in 1881 and today it continues to provide the warmth, welcome, and service that were present in that earlier era. Lang House's eleven bedrooms, each with private bath, are decorated in the style of the mansion as it once was. They are large and comfortable, with space for you to unpack and spread out, and space for you to read, either in bed or in a comfortable chair with a good reading light. My room, the Hayward, had a queen bed with fishnet canopy, good reading lights, an armoire for my clothes, and a comfortable chair in which to curl up for a nap. The innkeepers serve a delicious breakfast with a choice of entrée: the gingerbread waffles were new to me and were very tasty with Vermont (of course!) maple syrup. From the inn you can walk to town, to the shops, and to the several educational institutions that are found here in Burlington. Because the town is located on Lake Champlain there is a lot of activity along the edge of the shore. Ferries cross the lake to New York State, saving you lots of driving time and giving you a nice break in a day of driving. Just south is the Shelburne Museum, a "must" for all ages. *Directions:* From I-89 take exit 14W, Route 2, which turns into Main Street. As you come down the hill, the inn is on your right just before the traffic light.

LANG HOUSE
Owner: Kim Borsarage
360 Main Street
Burlington, VT 05401, USA
Tel: (802) 652-2500, (877) 919-9799
Fax: (802) 651-8717
11 rooms
Double: $135–$195
Open: all year, Credit cards: all major
Select Registry
karenbrown.com/ne/langhouse.html

Burlington   Willard Street Inn   Map: 3

When an historic home in what was a city's grandest neighborhood is made into an inn welcoming guests from near and far, everyone wins. Such is the case with the Willard Street Inn, an imposing Georgian/Queen Anne Revival-style mansion built in 1881 in the hill section of Burlington with views out to Lake Champlain. This is a home of high ceilings, richly ornate varnished woodwork, and massive staircases. Bedrooms are very large and while they all begin with their Victorian heritage, they are individually decorated. Victorian Cabernet is, as you would expect, warm and inviting; Nantucket creates the feeling of being at the shore; and the Tower Room in the turret with the blues of its sitting area and the views of the lake will spoil you without a doubt. The Woodhouse Suite has a loveseat facing a gas stove and in its bathroom a two-person shower. Breakfast is served in the solarium with its black-and-white marble floor at tables spaciously set apart from one another. Enjoy a cup of afternoon tea in the English round garden, walk in the woodland or herb gardens, and play a game of croquet or bocci ball with other guests. From the inn you can walk to all of the activities of Burlington, including its Church Street Marketplace. Further afield you can visit the Shelburne Museum and Shelburne Farms and cruise on the lake. *Directions:* From Boston, take I-89 north to exit 14W to Route 2 west to Willard Street. Turn left to the inn on the right.

WILLARD STREET INN
Innkeepers: Gordon & Bev Watson
349 S. Willard Street
Burlington, VT 05401, USA
Tel: (802) 651-8710, (800) 577-8712
Fax: (802) 651-8714
14 rooms
Double: $135–$235
Open: all year, Credit cards: all major
Select Registry
karenbrown.com/ne/willard.html

Chelsea Shire Inn Map: 3

Chelsea, a town with history from the early 19th century, is in the real Vermont that existed before the pace of our world demanded shopping centers, movie complexes, and everything convenient. You reach Chelsea down winding country roads past farms, dairies, streams, pristine schools, and white clapboard, community churches. The historic Shire Inn, offering guests six bedrooms, helps you to rediscover the soul of our country. The Windsor is a large room on the second floor with a canopied queen bed, fireplace, wing chair, rocker, and both shower and tub. Four windows look out the front and the side of the building. The Bennington, a large second-floor room, has a king bed, fireplace, wing chair, rocker, and bathroom with stall shower. There are three smaller rooms on the second floor and a large room with fireplace on the first. The inn serves dinner and you can bet that the food will receive the same personal attention that's given to every detail by the attentive innkeepers. Before you leave be sure to take a photo of the beautiful winding staircase—it's New England at its finest. *Directions:* Leave I-89 at exit 2 (Sharon). Turn left, go 150 yards to the stop sign, turn right onto Route 14 for 7 miles, then go right on Route 110 for 13 miles to Chelsea. Leave I-91 at exit 14, go left on Route 113 and drive 23 miles to the end. Turn left and go 200 yards to the inn.

SHIRE INN
Innkeepers: Karen & Jay Keller
Main Street
Chelsea, VT 05038, USA
Tel: (802) 685-3031, (800) 441-6908
Fax: (802) 685-3871
6 rooms, Double: $115–$245
Open: May through Oct, weekends only in Jan & Feb
Credit cards: all major
Select Registry
karenbrown.com/ne/shireinn.html

Places to Stay–Vermont

Chittenden — Fox Creek Inn — Map: 3

The inn's publicity material urges you to "just think of it as a cruise ship in port for a few days" and the Fox Creek Inn is indeed a self-contained, secluded little world. Such is its tradition—it was once the "getaway" home of William Barstow, one of Thomas Edison's collaborators, who came here with his family to get away from the bustle of urban life. The common areas are warm and friendly: my favorite is the den with its large windows and stone fireplace. The largest bedroom would be my first choice: it's 23 by 18 feet in size with five windows on one side, a fireplace, a dressing room with a large closet, and a ceiling fan. The bathroom has a two-person Jacuzzi, a two-person shower, a two-sink vanity, and a fireplace. Room 4 was another of my favorites with its two green wingback chairs, hunter-green walls with cream trim, and a floral comforter in greens and pinks. These same colors are echoed in the floral wallpaper. Some of the bedrooms in this inn are located on the first floor for those who do not want to climb stairs. You can choose the options of bed and breakfast or bed, breakfast, and dinner. *Directions:* The inn is 10 miles northeast of Rutland. From Rutland take Route 7 north or Route 4 east and follow state signs to the inn.

FOX CREEK INN
Innkeepers: Ann & Alex Volz
49 Chittenden Dam Road
Chittenden, VT 05737, USA
Tel: (802) 483-6213, (800) 707-0017
Fax: (802) 483-2623
8 rooms, 1 suite
Double: $190–$409
Closed: Apr & Nov, Credit cards: all major
Select Registry
karenbrown.com/ne/vtfoxcreekinn.html

Craftsbury Common   Inn on the Common   Map: 3

Craftsbury Common, in Vermont's famous Northeast Kingdom, is one of those absolutely perfect villages, a charming collection of white clapboard houses with green shutters framed by towering oaks and stands of pine trees. This quaint rural setting offers a gentle reminder of simpler times gone by. The Inn on the Common, considered the crown jewel of the kingdom, has 16 beautifully decorated guestrooms spread over three meticulously restored Federal houses. Rooms have private baths and many fine furnishings, including hand-stitched quilts, artwork, and heirloom antiques. The grounds feature lush gardens, manicured lawns, a swimming hole, and views of the Green Mountains. In winter, guests enjoy snowshoeing and cross-country skiing on expertly groomed trails then return to cozy up next to the fireplace in the lounge or in their own rooms (five have fireplaces). The Trellis dining room offers creative country cuisine in a romantic candlelit setting with soft music and an extensive wine cellar. With over 28 combined years of hospitality experience, new owners Jim and Judi Lamberti promise to make you feel at home during your stay. *Directions:* From north or south take I-91 to exit 26 (Orleans). Follow Route 58 west for 4 miles to Irasburg. Turn left on Route 14 south and drive for 12 miles. Watch for the inn's sign. Turn left on North Craftsbury Road, drive past Sterling College, and you come to the inn's office on the left.

INN ON THE COMMON
Innkeepers: Judi & Jim Lamberti
1162 North Craftsbury Road
P.O. Box 75, Craftsbury Common, VT 05827, USA
Tel: (802) 586-9619, (800) 521-2233
Fax: (802) 586-2249
16 rooms
Double: $149–$259
Closed: Apr, Credit cards: all major
Select Registry
karenbrown.com/ne/vtinnonthecommon.html

Dorset   Barrows House   Map: 3

There are two things in Vermont that are just about perfect: one is the charming town of Dorset—quintessential New England—and the second is the hospitality of Linda and Jim, the owners and innkeepers of this wonderful property, Barrows House. This is an historic inn of nine buildings scattered about on eleven acres. The inn has a swimming pool, tennis courts, lawn games, bicycles, cross-country ski equipment, and a sauna. Not only are the bedrooms complete with every amenity, but the front desk has a supply of "forgotten" items such as hairdryers. Halstead House, located up the hill in the woods, is the most remote accommodation. The suite here has a small bedroom with a queen bed, handmade quilt, and braided rugs on the floor, and the bathroom features a two-person whirlpool tub. In the sitting room there's a loveseat in front of the wood-burning fireplace, TV/VCR, small fridge, and a bar sink. There's also a small patio for summer relaxation. The Stable Suite #2 in the old hay loft has wide floorboards, window seats in the bedroom, bathroom, and sitting room, cathedral ceilings, a gas fireplace, old barn beams, a king canopy bed, and a TV/VCR in the sitting room. The restaurant serves breakfast and dinner every day. By the way, this is a great family inn where well-behaved guests of all ages are always welcome. *Directions:* Located on Route 30, about 6½ miles north of the center of Manchester, just a block short of the Dorset town green.

BARROWS HOUSE
Innkeepers: Linda & Jim McGinnis
Route 30
Dorset, VT 05251-0098, USA
Tel: (802) 867-4455, (800) 639-1620
Fax: (802) 867-0132
18 rooms, 7 suites, 3 cottages
Double: $150–$255
Open: all year, Credit cards: all major
Select Registry
karenbrown.com/ne/barrowshouse.html

Places to Stay—Vermont

Dorset   Cornucopia of Dorset   Map: 3

Located in what some say is the most charming village in America, the Cornucopia of Dorset, a bed and breakfast inn, is just a minute's walk from Dorset's village green. It fits in beautifully with the white clapboard homes of this community and its flowerboxes and bountiful baskets of impatiens add outside charm and color. The inn is lovingly decorated with furnishings that make you want to settle in with a good book in front of the fireplace and an afternoon cup of tea—all the more enjoyable in the brisk air of the fall after you have walked about the village and poked around in its few shops. The air-conditioned guestrooms are traditionally furnished, as you would expect in a restored 1880 Colonial. Four are in the main house and all of these have corner fireplaces. The beds are four-posters or canopied and have wool mattress covers, down pillows, and fluffy down comforters. There is also a cottage with loft bedroom and skylight, living room with cathedral ceiling and fireplace, fully equipped eat-in kitchen, large bath, and private deck. The inn serves delicious, candlelit breakfasts with freshly squeezed orange juice and gourmet entrees. Sterling silver, linens, and fresh flower arrangements add to the attractive ambiance of the dining room. *Directions:* The inn is located 6 miles north of Manchester on Route 30, on the right as you enter the village of Dorset.

CORNUCOPIA OF DORSET
Innkeeper: Donna Butman
3228 Route 30
P.O. Box 307, Dorset, VT 05251, USA
Tel: (802) 867-5751, (800) 566-5751
Fax: (802) 867-5753
4 rooms, 1 cottage
Double: $180–$300
Open: all year, Credit cards: all major
karenbrown.com/ne/cornucopiaofdorset.html

Places to Stay–Vermont

Goshen — Blueberry Hill Inn — Map: 3

The Blueberry Hill Inn invites you into their special, tranquil world in the Green Mountain National Forest, a world of quiet, fresh air, lovely food, and luxurious accommodations. In the main house, built in 1813, there are four bedrooms, two with double beds and two with twins. The Greenhouse has three rooms, each with a double bed and twin beds in a loft; and there are four Pondside rooms, each with a queen bed. There is a cottage decorated with colonial furnishings—primarily antiques and antique quilts—with a double room and two twins. The inn is a recreation destination, with skiing being the greatest attraction. Just a few minutes away is Lake Dunmore where you can swim and windsurf and boat. However, I could just as easily be perfectly content with doing nothing but read, relax, and take a walk into this pristine world. The inn has great trekking and trail guides for its guests. The cooking is gourmet here and meals are a real treat, with flowers from the inn's gardens decorating the plates of food. What a great visual feast this makes the dining experience! For 21 years the inn has been baking cookies and putting them in the cookie jar for guests and non-guests alike. Now cookies are available by mail to those who wish to order a memory of a time spent at Blueberry Hill Inn. *Directions:* Off Route 73 east of Brandon, follow Forest Road. Off Route 125, 1 mile east of Ripton, follow Forest Road for 6 miles to the inn.

BLUEBERRY HILL INN
Innkeepers: Shari Brown & Tony Clark
Goshen, VT 05733, USA
Tel: (802) 247-6735, (800) 448-0707
Fax: (802) 247-3983
11 rooms, 1 cottage
Double: $250–$320*
  *Includes breakfast & dinner
Open: all year, Credit cards: all major
karenbrown.com/ne/blueberry.html

Grafton — Old Tavern — Map: 3

The Old Tavern at Grafton makes one of those architectural statements that you never forget—its façade is both wide and tall and it has an appealing porch that just beckons you to sit and relax. Guestrooms are found in the main tavern and two cottages and there are also four guesthouses, most with full kitchens, which can each accommodate up to eight people. The Old Tavern prides itself on not having phones or TVs in the rooms so that guests can truly relax during their visit. I saw several of the rooms, which have flowered wallpapers and private baths with all the amenities, and are traditionally decorated in a comfortable style. The attractive dining room is traditional in its decor, with a lovely sideboard and tables set for two, four, or six and there is café serving lunch and light suppers. Your room rate includes a full country breakfast and afternoon tea. What's especially charming about this inn is its tavern pub, a short walk down the hall from the main building. Its two stories exude New England charm with old barn-board walls, hand-hewn timbered beams, and lots of cozy seating in front of the large wood-burning fireplace. The Old Tavern has its own stables so you can make arrangements to bring your horse—you could both have a great vacation in this New England town! The inn offers discounts to senior citizens and repeat guests. *Directions:* Take exit 5 off I-91. Grafton is located at the intersection of Routes 35 and 121.

OLD TAVERN
Innkeeper: Kevin O'Donnell
Main Street
P.O. Box 9, Grafton, VT 05146, USA
Tel: (802) 843-2231, (800) 843-1801
Fax: (802) 843-2245
40 rooms, 7 suites, 4 guesthouses ($620–$890)
Double: $135–$390
Closed: Apr, Credit cards: all major
karenbrown.com/ne/vtoldtavern.html

Jamaica Three Mountain Inn Map: 3

Three Mountain Inn has all you'll want for as long a time as you can be a guest. This romantic 1790s country inn on the main street of the little town of Jamaica, just under the shadow of the Green Mountains, is ideally located for access to skiing, but also great for Fall foliage, not far from shopping, and perfect for wandering. The living room with its large fireplace is warm and welcoming and the dining rooms are simply but tastefully furnished—what's complex is the tasty food that comes from the kitchen. The traditionally furnished bedrooms all have private baths and telephones. I stayed in Jamaica, a suite whose living room had a gas fireplace, a sofa and two wing chairs for reading, and Colonial-print wallpaper. The bedroom, painted pale, creamy yellow, had tables with good reading lights on either side of the four-poster queen bed. The Arlington, just down the hall, was furnished with a queen bed, an armoire, a sofa, and a wing chair, and had pale-cream-painted walls; an added luxury was a two-person spa tub. Even though this is a sleepy mountain town, I'd probably choose one of the back rooms to be sure of a night's rest that is as refreshing as the style and welcome of the innkeepers. *Directions:* From Brattleboro take I-91 to exit 2 and go north on Route 30. From Manchester take Route 30 south.

THREE MOUNTAIN INN
Innkeepers: Jennifer & Ed Dorta-Duque
Route 30
P.O. Box 180, Jamaica, VT 05343, USA
Tel: (802) 874-4140, (800) 532-9399
Fax: (802) 874-4745
14 rooms, 1 cottage
Double: $145–$325
Open: all year, Credit cards: all major
Select Registry
karenbrown.com/ne/threemountaininn.html

Lower Waterford — Rabbit Hill Inn — Map: 3

Afternoon tea was being served as I arrived at Rabbit Hill Inn—just what I had been thinking I would like. This was just one example of the way the innkeepers and staff here seem to anticipate your every need—they have honed the art of personal service to absolute perfection, with many thoughtful touches like transforming your bedroom with candlelight and soft music when you return to it after dinner. There are nineteen rooms and suites with private bathrooms in two historic buildings—most have fireplaces and some have whirlpools tubs, but all are individual and special. I stayed on the second floor of the main building in the Canopy Chamber, a corner room with views of the White Mountains and the inn's gardens. The queen bed was waiting to share with me a perfect night's rest, the gas fireplace had a chaise longue in front of it with pillows to make me comfortable, and on the bed was a note from the staff asking if there was anything else I might want. The room also had a desk, a Boston rocker, and access to a lovely porch. The inn's dining room serves delectable, award-winning, five-course dinners. Rabbit Hill's 15 acres provide you with lawn games, a swimming pond, trails for hiking and skiing, fishing, and canoeing. *Directions:* From I-91, take exit 19 to I-93 south. Leave at exit 1, turning right onto Route 18 south for 7 miles to the inn. From I-93 north, take exit 44, turning left onto Route 18 north. Drive 2 miles to the inn.

RABBIT HILL INN
Innkeepers: Leslie & Brian Mulcahy
Route 18
Lower Waterford, VT 05848, USA
Tel: (802) 748-5168, (800) 762-8669
Fax: (802) 748-8342
19 rooms
Double: $220–$345
Closed: early Apr & early Nov, Credit cards: all major
Select Registry
karenbrown.com/ne/rabbithillinn.html

Places to Stay–Vermont

Ludlow — Andrie Rose Inn   Map: 3

The Andrie Rose Inn is found on a quiet side street in the town of Ludlow in four buildings, and since each building has a small number of rooms, you never feel as if you are a guest in a large establishment. With 23 rooms you can expect and receive various sizes of rooms with queen, king, or double beds. There are suites and accommodations offering a kitchen, which may have a stove, garbage disposal, dishwasher, a washer and dryer, and even a gas grill on the deck. The Manchester can sleep up to ten while the Weston and Woodstock suites can accommodate as many as twelve guests. Here and there in some of the rooms are spa tubs, steam showers, and fireplaces. The inn's website provides details on its varying accommodations and is a great way to find just what you want. On Friday and Saturday evenings the inn serves dinner by reservation. In the main lodge there is a welcoming living room with a fireplace, which is a great place to meet other guests and relax either before or after dinner at the inn or in one of the town's restaurants. There is also a separate TV room with a large screen. Walk to the town's shops, drive to the nearby mountain, enjoy the surrounding countryside—all are within easy reach of the Andrie Rose Inn. *Directions:* From New York, take I-91 north to exit 6 in Vermont then follow Route 103 north to Ludlow. Turn left on Depot Street and right on Pleasant Street to the inn.

ANDRIE ROSE INN
Innkeepers: Michael & Irene Maston
13 Pleasant Street
Ludlow, VT 05149, USA
Tel: (802) 228-4846, (800) 223-4846
Fax: (802) 228-7910
23 rooms
Double: $120–$330
Closed: Apr, Credit cards: all major
karenbrown.com/ne/andrierose.html

Places to Stay–Vermont

Ludlow   The Governor's Inn   Map: 3

The Governor's Inn was built in 1890 as a private home on Ludlow's village green by a Vermont governor for his bride. It has now been converted to an inn, described by your hosts, Jim and Cathy Kubec, as "a haven for enjoying life's pleasures and as a base for exploring Vermont." The inn welcomes guests into nine bedrooms on its three floors. There are double, queen, and king beds in the rooms, each of which has a private bath. On the third floor The Suite, with views of the slopes of the nearby ski mountain, has a queen bed, a gas fireplace, a separate living room with cable TV, and a whirlpool tub in the bathroom. Also on the third floor, Jessica's Room has a king bed, a gas fireplace, cable TV, a large skylight, and once again views of the nearby mountain. Food is the focus of much attention at the inn. In addition to a full breakfast in the morning and tea in the afternoon, there is a fixed-price multi-course gourmet dinner, prepared by the chef/owner and offered most weekends with advance reservations. The Governor's Inn also offers a series of cooking seminars several times a year beginning with a Friday afternoon arrival and concluding after lunch on Sunday. These classes are both demonstrations and hands-on for the participants. The inn is less than a mile from the Okemo Ski Mountain. *Directions:* Take I-95 to I-91 to exit 6 to Route 103 north to Ludlow.

THE GOVERNOR'S INN
Innkeepers: Jim & Cathy Kubec
86 Main Street
Ludlow, VT 05149, USA
Tel: (802) 228-8830, (800) 468-3766
Fax: (802) 228-2961
9 rooms
Double: $159–$299
Open: all year, Credit cards: all major
Select Registry
karenbrown.com/ne/vtgovernor.html

Places to Stay–Vermont

Manchester   Inn at Ormsby Hill   Map: 3

Perched on a hill with sweeping views of the valley below and the Green Mountains, the Inn at Ormsby Hill is a restored 1764 manor house listed on the Register of Historic Places. In this inn attention to detail is everywhere, in the decor of the common rooms and the bedrooms, and in the dining room where Chris is the master of her trade. Simply scrumptious breakfasts are served in the attractively decorated conservatory with its views out to the surrounding mountains. The living room made me feel completely at home—I could either curl up by the fire or simply relax in the luxurious surroundings. The ten guestrooms have canopied beds, fireplaces, spa tubs for two and, if you are visiting in the summer, air conditioning. All the rooms are great, but one of my favorites is wallpapered with a red-and-white print, has a gas fireplace with a small hooked rug in front, two comfortable chairs with a great reading light, a canopied bed, and a spa tub for two in the bathroom from which you can see the fireplace. There's a porch out back with old wicker furniture and a painted board floor, perfect for a second cup of breakfast coffee and a peaceful reverie. Innkeepers Chris and Ted are pros and I am sure that staying with them in the Manchester area will make for memories that will bring you back often. *Directions:* In Manchester Center, at the junction of Routes 11, 30, and 7A, take historic Route 7A south. The inn is approximately 3 miles along on the left.

INN AT ORMSBY HILL
Innkeepers: Chris & Ted Sprague
1842 Main Street
Manchester, VT 05255, USA
Tel: (802) 362-1163, (800) 670-2841
Fax: (802) 362-5176
10 rooms
Double: $205–$380
Open: all year, Credit cards: MC, VS
Select Registry
karenbrown.com/ne/ormsby.html

Manchester   The 1811 House   Map: 3

When you enter The 1811 House, which has been operating as a hostelry since 1811, you will feel as if you have stepped back in time. Within the walls of the original building and the adjacent cottage are 13 guestrooms, the most romantic with fireplaces and one with a private balcony. I loved the cottage room that takes up the entire second floor and has a cathedral ceiling: from the bed you can see the fireplace and there's a comfortable pair of leather chairs for sitting and reading. Suites are defined as having a sitting area, but any of the fireplace rooms are extremely cozy. The Jeremiah French Suite with its canopied bed set on old plank floors in front of a wood-burning fireplace is wonderful. The common rooms have wood-burning fireplaces and are furnished with English and American antiques, prints, and Oriental rugs. There's an inviting little pub with bar stools snuggled up to the highly polished dark-wood bar and a group of tables by the windows. One of the innkeepers has a passion for single-malt Scotch whiskies and there's a collection of them that will far exceed your ability to taste. Scottish ale is also on tap. This property is deceiving in that it sits right on the main street but has 7 acres of land with a pond and gardens. From anywhere out back the views to the picturesque Green Mountains are yours to enjoy. *Directions:* In Manchester Center, at the junction of Routes 11, 30, and 7A, take Route 7A south. The inn is about 1 mile along on the left.

THE 1811 HOUSE
Innkeepers: Marnie & Bruce Duff, Cathy & Jorge Veleta
Route 7A, P.O. Box 39
Manchester, VT 05254-0039, USA
Tel: (802) 362-1811, (800) 432-1811
Fax: (802) 362-2443
11 rooms, 2 suites, Double: $140–$280
No restaurant: fully licensed British pub
Closed: Christmas & the week before Christmas
Credit cards: all major, Select Registry
karenbrown.com/ne/vt1811house.html

Places to Stay–Vermont

Mendon (Killington) — Red Clover Inn — Map: 3

The Red Clover Inn is a retreat away from the cares of the world and we're glad that the original owner sought such a perfect spot for building in the 1840s. This inn truly feels like a private home. The beamed-ceilinged keeping room is most inviting with its fireside sofas and wonderful leather wingbacks. Guestrooms, all air-conditioned, with private bathrooms, king or queen beds, and lovely mountain views, are in two buildings—seven in the farmhouse and seven newer rooms in the carriage house. The three newest rooms are especially deluxe and extremely spacious, with king beds, whirlpool tubs from which you can see the gas fireplace, and beamed ceilings. Carriage house rooms have TVs and some have VCRs. On Fridays and Saturdays, guests are invited to enjoy an elegant candlelit dinner featuring a menu sumptuous in content and presentation. The inn is conveniently located near the major ski areas of central Vermont. In the summer hiking and horseback riding are popular, while downhill and cross-country skiing are the sports of choice in the winter. Less strenuous activities include antiquing and attending concerts and plays. *Directions:* Five miles west of Killington, turn left from Route 4 onto Woodward Road and drive ½ mile to the inn on the left. Five miles east of Rutland, turn right from Route 4 onto Woodward Road and drive half a mile to the inn on the left.

RED CLOVER INN
Owners: Bill Pedersen & Tricia Treen Pedersen
7 Woodward Road
Mendon (Killington), VT 05701, USA
Tel: (802) 775-2290, (800) 752-0571
Fax: (802) 773-0594
14 rooms
Double: $145–$350
Open: all year, Credit cards: all major
Select Registry
karenbrown.com/ne/redcloverinn.html

Newfane — Four Columns Inn   Map: 3

Newfane is a "must-visit" beautiful New England town and has been one of my favorites for 40 years or so. The historic green and all the houses that surround the county courthouse stand as they have since the 1840s and behind the courthouse you find the Four Columns Inn. The inn is a popular base for sightseeing in this area, and if you'd like to visit during foliage time (generally the first half of October), you'll need to make reservations as much as a year ahead. There are 15 guestrooms with gas fireplaces, private baths (some with two-person spa tubs or two-person showers), and telephones—the TV is in the common room. My personal favorite was room 12, with its king pencil-post cherry-wood bed and a fireplace open on one side to the bedroom and on the other to the bathroom. There's an attractive sitting area with two comfortable chairs, a painted armoire, and views of woods. The inn's restaurant produces impeccable, creative cuisine blending New American, Asian, and French traditions into taste sensations (once again, reservations are needed well in advance, even for houseguests). Presentations are so spectacular that it's hard to decide whether dinner looks better or tastes better. *Directions:* Leave I-91 at exit 2 in Vermont and turn left onto Western Ave for half a mile then turn left onto Cedar Street. At the third stop sign turn left onto Route 30 north for 11 miles. The inn is on Newfane Green behind the county courthouse.

FOUR COLUMNS INN
Innkeepers: Debbie & Bruce Pfander
P.O. Box 278
Newfane, VT 05345, USA
Tel: (802) 365-7713, (800) 787-6633
Fax: (802) 365-0022
15 rooms, 6 suites
Double: $150–$350
Closed: Dec 24 & 25, Credit cards: all major
Select Registry
karenbrown.com/ne/vtfourcolumnsinn.html

Places to Stay–Vermont

Shelburne — Heart of the Village Inn — Map: 3

Aptly named, this inn is located right on Route 7 in the middle of Shelburne where you can walk to shops and restaurants or drive a short distance to the Shelburne Museum. It's an 1886 Queen Anne Victorian with front doors made out of tiger oak. There are two common rooms for guests to relax in, complete with fireplace, scrolled woodwork, and comfortable armchairs. The inn's nine very comfortable bedrooms, several of which can be made into twins, are divided between the main house and the carriage barn. I stayed in the Fletcher Room with a queen bed, a chair to relax in by the window, a skylight, and a full private bath with tub and shower. Though the rooms may be decorated in Victorian style, they lack nothing for the comfort of the guest: air conditioning, TVs, data ports, and telephones are standard. A great American breakfast is served in the mornings from 8 to 10:00am so you can partake at your pleasure. In the afternoon after a day of busy activity, return to the inn for a cup of tea and a cookie—just enough to tide you over till you walk to one of the neighboring restaurants. Hospitality is high on the list of reasons to stay at this inn and the innkeeper makes sure that you are more than welcome. The inn is on the main street and double glazing makes the rooms quieter, but you're still aware that you are in town. *Directions:* From Boston, take I-93 to I-89 to exit 13 to Route 7 south. Drive about 4½ miles to the inn on the left.

HEART OF THE VILLAGE INN
Innkeeper: Pat Button
5347 Shelburne Road
Shelburne, VT 05482-0953, USA
Tel: (802) 985-2800, (877) 808-1834
Fax: (802) 985-2870
9 rooms, Double: $130–$245
Open: all year, Credit cards: all major
Select Registry
karenbrown.com/ne/heart.html

Places to Stay – Vermont

Shelburne — Inn at Shelburne Farms — Map: 3

It would be hard to imagine a more spectacular setting than that of the Inn at Shelburne Farms, which sits in a 1,400-acre estate overlooking Lake Champlain and the Adirondack Mountains. The grounds are a creation of Frederick Law Olmsted, the architect who designed New York's Central Park. The estate is owned by a nonprofit organization devoted to preserving, maintaining and adapting its historic buildings and landscape for teaching and demonstrating the stewardship of natural and agricultural resources. The dramatic, 60-room Queen Anne mansion has 24 guestrooms, 17 with private bathrooms, which are individual in their decor and vary dramatically in price and comfort. The most popular rooms are on the second floor, facing the lake and decorated with fine antiques. Of those, the W. Seward Webb bedroom has William Morris wallpaper and a massive double bed, while the handsome Empire Room has furnishings, drapes, and wall coverings of the Empire period. Tucked under the eaves of the third floor overlooking the garden are the least expensive rooms. Apart from touring Shelburne Farms itself, also plan to visit the Shelburne Museum with its 37 historic buildings housing exhibits from 300 years of life in America. *Directions:* Leave I-89 at Vermont exit 13 onto Route 7 south for 5 miles as far as the light in the center of Shelburne. Turn right onto Harbor Road to the first stop sign and go left into Shelburne Farms.

INN AT SHELBURNE FARMS
Manager: Karen Polihronakis
1611 Harbor Road
Shelburne, VT 05482, USA
Tel: (802) 985-8498, Fax: (802) 985-8123
24 rooms, 2 cottages
Double: $105–$380*
 *Breakfast not included
Open: mid-May to mid-Oct, Credit cards: all major
karenbrown.com/ne/vtinnatshelburne.html

Places to Stay–Vermont

Stowe — Green Mountain Inn — Map: 3

Stowe is one of Vermont's most renowned ski and mountain resorts yet its history goes back long before skiing became popular. The Green Mountain Inn, the first inn in town and listed in the National Register of Historic Places, is part of that early history. The core of the inn still retains a feeling of days of old and when you walk through the door you become part of the history and its memory. Enter into the lobby and receive a warm Vermont welcome then wander into the library and salon, intimately sized rooms warmed by a crackling fire. The large dining is the setting for the hot and cold breakfast buffet and afternoon refreshments. Downstairs you find a popular, cozy bar and grill, The Whip, where you can enjoy a variety of good-value meals. As you climb the stairs from the entry you enjoy a constantly changing panorama of Vermont in the numerous original watercolors by Walton Bodgett, which run the length of the stairwell. In the main house, bedrooms vary dramatically in size, but all enjoy good lighting, wonderful baths, very comfortable beds, and decorative details, such as stenciling. Additional rooms are found in the Mill House and two newly constructed buildings, the Mansfield House and the Sanborn House, both built and decorated in a traditional style with very luxurious rooms offering all the modern amenities. *Directions:* Route 100 turns to Main St. as it travels through the heart of old Stowe. The Green Mountain Inn is on Main St.

GREEN MOUNTAIN INN
Owner: The Gameroff Family
Innkeeper: Patti Clark
18 Main Street, Stowe, VT 05672, USA
Tel: (802) 253-7301, (800) 253-7302
Fax: (802) 253-5096
83 rooms, 17 suites, 5 townhouses
Double: $119–$409*
 *Breakfast not included: $11.95
Open: all year, Credit cards: all major
karenbrown.com/ne/vtgreenmountaininn.html

Places to Stay–Vermont

Stowe — Stone Hill Inn — Map: 3

Amy and Hap created Stone Hill Inn, often called the best accommodation in Stowe, with the aim of offering guests the perfect blend of romance, ambiance, and privacy. Set above the road to the ski mountain, this inn attracts not only skiers, but also more particularly, guests who want a romantic getaway. Off the entry is a games room, a large room with a gas fireplace, sofas, game tables, and a guest pantry where hors d'oeuvres are served. Each of the nine guestrooms, all with identical amenities, opens onto the central garden and uses handsome, regal materials for bedcovers and drapes. I was disappointed in the furniture, which provides the guest with just a pair of armchairs and a covered circular table. A two-sided fireplace is open both to a side wall in the bedroom and the luxurious bath (two sinks, large Jacuzzi tub, separate shower). The most dramatic room and my favorite is the long, narrow breakfast room, which stretches out into the yard and is surrounded on all sides by a full expanse of windows. The tariff seems a bit high, but Stone Hill Inn affords a small, intimate-size inn in a lovely location with privacy and luxury to match. *Directions:* Traveling I-89, take exit 10 for Route 100 north. Go 11 miles to Stowe and at the blinking light go left on Route 108. Drive 3 miles, turn right on Houston Farm Road, then take the first driveway on the left.

STONE HILL INN
Owners: Amy & Hap Jordan
89 Houston Farm Road
Stowe, VT 05672, USA
Tel: (802) 253-6282, Fax: (802) 253-7415
9 rooms
Double: $265–$390
Closed: beg-Apr to beg-May & mid-Nov
Credit cards: all major
Select Registry
karenbrown.com/ne/vtstonehillinn.html

Waitsfield — Inn at the Round Barn Farm — Map: 3

The Inn at the Round Barn Farm, sitting in 245 lovely acres of mountains, meadows and ponds, promises romance, relaxation, and an escape from reality. On the day of my visit the first welcoming touch I encountered was a tureen of hot soup for returning skiers in the small but cozy library. The dining room, where you savor Anne Marie's wonderful breakfasts, has windows on both sides looking out to the surrounding hills and tables set in various sizes. The guestrooms are all very different from one another in their decor but all have private bathrooms, original pine floors, rich wallpapers, and plush robes. I stayed in the Abbott Room, a suite with a king four-poster with feather bed, a TV hidden in an armoire, a living room with a gas fireplace, an oversized two-person corner whirlpool tub, and separate bathroom steam shower and two-person vanity. Hand-hewn beams and plenty of windows complete the scene. An unusual amenity here is the 60-foot lap pool, which extends into a greenhouse filled with flowering plants. The inn has its own groomed, marked snowshoe center and downhill skiing is just minutes away. The inn's Round Barn hosts weddings, conferences, concerts, and art exhibits. *Directions:* Take I-89 south to exit 10, then Route 100 south for 14 miles. (From I-89 north take exit 9 onto Route 100B south for 14 miles.) Turn onto Bridge Street, through the covered bridge, and bear right at the fork. The inn is 1 mile further on the left.

INN AT THE ROUND BARN FARM
Innkeeper: Anne Marie DeFreest
1661 East Warren Road
Waitsfield, VT 05673, USA
Tel & fax: (802) 496-2276
11 rooms, 1 suite
Double: $140–$315
Closed: last half of Apr, Credit cards: all major
Select Registry
karenbrown.com/ne/theinnatroundbarnfarm.html

Warren Pitcher Inn Map: 3

Throw away the books on decorating—start thinking outside the box and book into one of the Pitcher Inn's fabulously decorated and themed rooms, whether it's The School Room, The Trout Room, The Lodge, The Hayloft, or The Ski Room. I suppose that the most spectacular has to be The Lodge with its massive four-poster bed with eagles sitting on top of the headboard and Egyptian, Greek, and Masonic-lodge influences. Its starry ceiling overhead with the constellations in place for Christmastime is just plain wonderful. Add a bathroom with marble slab walls, a steam room, a deep soaking Jacuzzi, and you are in heaven. The Ski Room uses relics from ski areas—old bamboo poles, skis, ticket windows, a bedspread made from ski jackets. Your entrance to the room is a stone walkway set into the carpet. The inn's common rooms have plush furniture which you just sink into. The downstairs lounge with its stone fireplace and Adirondack style—is our kind of place. The dining room serves magnificent food in a bright and elegant room whose tables are set with crisp white linens and sparkling silver and glasses. The handcrafted Windsor chairs make for a refined elegance. *Directions:* I-89, I-91, I-93, and I-95 will all bring you to the vicinity of the inn. From I-89 north take Route 100 south to Warren where you find the Pitcher Inn on Main Street in the center of the village.

PITCHER INN
Manager: Robyn Shannis
275 Main Street
P.O. Box 347, Warren, VT 05674, USA
Tel: (802) 496-6350, (888) 867-4824
Fax: (802) 496-6354
9 rooms, 2 suites
Double: $330–$600
Open: all year, Credit cards: all major
Relais & Châteaux
karenbrown.com/ne/pitcherinn.html

Places to Stay–Vermont

West Dover   Deerhill Inn   Map: 3

The Deerhill Inn and Restaurant sits perched high on a hill with views out to the ski areas of Haystack and Mount Snow. The downstairs living room is shared by non-resident guests coming for dinner but there is an upstairs living room that's reserved for inn guests. Decorating here is done with flair, incorporating lots of flowers and vines, and in fact Waverly Fabrics chose one of Deerhill's bedrooms as the room of the year in 1996. The inn has 15 guestrooms, a full-service bar, and a swimming pool. All bedrooms, four with king beds, have private baths, some have fireplaces, and some have superb views of the mountains. Balcony rooms enjoy one-person jetted tubs. The Library Suite has two rooms, with a king bed in the bedroom and a convertible sofa in the living room, which also has a TV and lovely mountain views. Queen bedrooms are cozy and quaint, some decorated in blue and pink, some in green and yellow, others in pastels. Room L2 (one of the inn's two rooms with a loft) has a queen canopied bed with mosquito netting and is decorated with an Oriental theme. The restaurant presents imaginative modern American cuisine featuring seasonally fresh local ingredients in a charming dining room with a fireplace, hand-painted murals, and spectacular views. *Directions:* From I-91 take exit 2 to Route 9 west, driving 20 miles to Route 100 where you go north. Drive 6 miles to Valley View Road and go up the hill for 200 yards.

DEERHILL INN
Innkeepers: Michael Allen & Stan Gresens
Valley View Road
P.O. Box 136, West Dover, VT 05356, USA
Tel: (802) 464-3100, (800) 993-3379
Fax: (802) 464-5474
13 rooms, 2 suites
Double: $165–$350
Open: all year, Credit cards: all major
Select Registry
karenbrown.com/ne/deerhillinn.html

West Dover — Inn at Sawmill Farm — Map: 3

The Inn at Sawmill Farm is imbued with old New England style and decor. You feel the warmth of this property as you climb the stairs to the reception area and the adjoining common room with its charming timbered ceilings, barn-board walls, and that ever-present New England fireplace. The bedrooms are swathed in floral fabrics and you're likely to find that the decor in your room is coordinated with a single pattern and color. Rooms are large and have all the amenities that you expect in a first-class inn. A new suite by the trout pond has a large living room, bedroom, windows overlooking the pond, and a wraparound deck. There's a world-class restaurant on the premises with a 28,000-bottle wine cellar. A very sophisticated menu offers five-course dinners with ingredients all prepared in very individual styles. With a great selection of cold and warm appetizers, dinner at this inn is a real pleasure. Breakfast time is no less grand, with a hot entree to give you a good start to the day's activities. Be sure to spend some time in the old tavern in the barn where the real charm of this New England inn is everywhere around you. The inn is located in the heart of Southern Vermont with more activities than you could dream of, every sport imaginable, and with more antique shops than you can visit. *Directions:* Leave I-91 at Vermont exit 2. Take Route 9 west to Route 100 north about 6 miles to the village of West Dover—the inn is on the left after the church.

INN AT SAWMILL FARM
Innkeeper: Brill Williams
Route 100 & Crosstown Road
P.O. Box 367, West Dover, VT 05356, USA
Tel: (802) 464-8131, (800) 493-1133
Fax: (802) 464-1130
21 rooms, Double: $450–$900*
 *Includes breakfast & dinner
Closed: Apr 1 to May 24
Credit cards: all major
karenbrown.com/ne/theinnatsawmill.html

West Townshend — Windham Hill Inn — Map: 3

The Windham Hill Inn sits on 160 acres at the end of a country road on a rise with views all around. Inside the inn, there are lovingly decorated living rooms to make you feel instantly as if you've just returned to see an old friend. Fireplaces and comfortable chairs beckon and windows give magnificent views of ancient apple trees, gardens, and lawns. There are 21 guestrooms, most with fireplaces, several with large soaking tubs. I stayed in the White Barn in a first-floor room with a pot-bellied stove sitting in the corner, two luxuriously overstuffed chairs, and a sliding door to its own private deck. The bed was king-size, and the bath had a two-person whirlpool tub and a shower with two showerheads—a wonderful extravagance that made me linger just a few moments longer. The inn has an excellent dining room and the chef prepared a memorable dinner while I was there. The dessert of pear and apple with homemade ice cream and a swirl of crisp cookie was as spectacularly presented as it was delicious. The wine list is award-winning and extensive. Tea is served from 2 to 5:30 pm, and a cheese board at 5:30 every day. The innkeepers are caring and want to be sure that your every moment will create a memory. The inn has an excellent conference/event center. *Directions:* Take I-91 north to Brattleboro, exit 2, to Route 30 and drive 21½ miles northwest to West Townshend. Turn right onto Windham Hill Road, drive 1-3/10 miles, and follow the sign to the inn.

WINDHAM HILL INN
Innkeepers: Marina & Joe Coneeny
311 Lawrence Drive
West Townshend, VT 05359, USA
Tel: (802) 874-4080, (800) 944-4080
Fax: (802) 874-4702
21 rooms, Double: $195–$430
Closed: early Apr & Christmas week
Credit cards: all major
Select Registry
karenbrown.com/ne/windhamhillinn.html

Weston — Inn at Weston — Map: 3

This National Historic Register inn has thirteen rooms in three buildings—the Markham House dating to 1848, the Coleman House (1830), and a charming country barn—all nestled on 6 acres of woods, lawn, and gardens on the banks of the West River. Within walking distance are the quaint village of Weston's village green, the famous Vermont Country Store, art galleries, the Playhouse, museums, antique shops, and more. The inn's common rooms are welcoming and comfortably furnished and there's a pub that just waits for your presence. The dining room offers dinners that will tantalize all your senses. I was able to see two guestrooms: the Waite had a king cherry-wood bed, a pot-bellied gas stove, a TV, a whirlpool bath from which you could peek into the bedroom, and a steam shower. Flowered wallpaper completed the decor. In the Parkhurst there was also a king bed, wingback chairs in front of the fireplace, TV, and a whirlpool bath. There are two suites in the carriage house. Since taking over as innkeepers, Bob and Linda have incorporated their love of flowers into the property improvements. They have built an orchid greenhouse to house their collection, which is displayed throughout the inn, while a gazebo offers a romantic spot for summer and fall dining. *Directions:* Take I-91 north to Route 103 west through Chester to Londonderry. Turn right on Route 100 to Weston and to the inn on the left.

INN AT WESTON
Owners: Bob & Linda Aldrich
Route 100
Weston, VT 05161, USA
Tel: (802) 824-6789, Fax: (802) 824-3073
11 rooms, 2 suites
Double: $185–$335
Open: all year, Credit cards: all major
karenbrown.com/ne/weston.html

Windsor   Juniper Hill Inn   Map: 3

Set on a hillside surrounded by ancient pines, the Juniper Hill Inn is a handsome estate overlooking historic Windsor. You enter into the Great Hall, an enormous, very attractive room with soft-yellow walls—gorgeous against honey oak walls and flooring—where guests enjoy beverages and snacks in the afternoons. Off the hall is the pretty dining room with walls painted a deep burgundy and tables dressed with white linen set in front of the fireplace, where a full breakfast and four-course dinners (reservations only) are served. To the other side of the Great Hall is the sitting room, a more intimate salon with the only television available for guests. I fell in love with the library, a cozy room with a gas fireplace, lots of books, and a game table. Two very private guestrooms are found upstairs from the library: room 21, once occupied by Teddy Roosevelt, enjoys a handsome four-poster bed and a wood-burning Franklin stove, while room 20, pretty in a red wallpaper, offers a claw-foot tub and private porch. Of the other guestrooms number 2 is one of the most dramatic with its handsome four-poster bed, pretty flowered paper, fireplace, claw-foot tub, and balcony. The inn makes a great base for exploring the lovely Upper Connecticut River Valley and is also popular for weddings. *Directions:* From I-91 take exit 9 and travel south on Rte 5 for 2½ miles to Juniper Hill Road. Turn right and travel ½ mile up the hill (left at the fork) to the inn.

JUNIPER HILL INN
Owners: Susanne & Robert Pearl
153 Pembroke Road
Windsor, VT 05809, USA
Tel: (802) 674-5273, (800) 359-2541
Fax: (802) 674-2041
16 rooms, Double: $115–$200
Closed: 2 weeks in Apr & 2 weeks in Nov
Credit cards: MC
Select Registry
karenbrown.com/ne/vtjuniper.html

Places to Stay–Vermont

Woodstock — Charleston House — Map: 3

As Route 4 takes a gentle bend and angles into the heart of downtown Woodstock, you see the Charleston House, a Greek Revival townhouse with a handsome brick and shuttered façade. From the side entrance you pass into the elegant dining room where guests enjoy a candlelit country breakfast. Continue on into the front living room where guests often settle in front of the fire. The only guestroom on the first floor, The Antique Store, is a cozy room with a high four-poster queen bed covered by pretty quilts. Climb the stairs from the living room to four more of the original guestrooms. A lovely front corner room, Pomfret Hills, is decorated in a pretty, soft-green floral and has a handsome four-poster bed and lots of windows. One of the smallest rooms, Hillary Underwood (named for the original owner) is simple in decor and its bathroom, although private, is located across the hallway. Gables, tucked under the eaves, enjoys a claw-foot tub and Good Friends, the only twin-bedded room, is decorated in blues. In an addition behind the main building are four luxurious guestrooms. Here we were able to see only one of the two ground-floor suites, Mount Peg, a handsome, spacious room with a dramatic four-poster bed, fireplace, and Jacuzzi tub in the bathroom. *Directions:* Take Route 4 into Woodstock and the Charleston House is on the east side, just across from the junction of Route 12 as it turns north.

CHARLESTON HOUSE
Owners: Dieter (Dixi) & Willa Nohl
21 Pleasant Street
Woodstock, VT 05091, USA
Tel: (802) 457-3843, (888) 475-3800
Fax: none
9 rooms
Double: $115–$235
Open: all year, Credit cards: all major
karenbrown.com/ne/vtcharleston.html

Places to Stay—Vermont

Woodstock   Jackson House Inn & Restaurant   Map: 3

Woodstock, Vermont is one of those New England towns designed with such charm and quaintness that you would think that one mastermind had created it. It's one of those places that has to be on your tour of New England. The Jackson House, just outside town, is a great place for a stopover. With its yellow exterior it beckons you inside where you'll find great examples of late-Victorian architecture with floors of cherry and maple setting off the fine furniture, walls, and moldings. Its traditionally decorated guestrooms include six one-room luxury suites with fireplaces, thermal massage tubs, and views of the gardens. Period antiques are used throughout most of the inn, adding to your enjoyment. I loved the third-floor Francesca room, decorated in muted tones of taupe, with its deck overlooking the landscaped grounds. The Mary Todd Lincoln room is much more Victorian in feel, with a high-back Victorian bed of the Lincoln period, a marble-topped table, tufted-velvet chair, and an exquisite Casablanca ceiling fan of bronze, copper, rosewood, and French-cut crystal. The inn has a very fine dining room and celebrated chef, which have garnered much praise. *Directions:* From Boston take I-93 to I-89, leaving at Route 4 west. Leave at exit 1 in Vermont for Woodstock. The inn is on the far side of the town on the right.

JACKSON HOUSE INN & RESTAURANT
Innkeepers: Carl & Linda Delnegro
114-3 Senior Lane
Woodstock, VT 05091, USA
Tel: (802) 457-2065, (800) 448-1890
Fax: (802) 457-9290
9 rooms, 6 suites
Double: $195–$380
Open: all year, Credit cards: all major
karenbrown.com/ne/vtjackson.html

Index

A

A Cambridge House, Cambridge, 130
A Little Inn on Pleasant Bay, South Orleans, 175
Abigail Stoneman Inn, Newport, 201
Acadia National Park, 62
    Cadillac Mountain, 63
    Loop Road, 63
    Otter Cliffs, 63
    Schoodic Peninsula, 63
    Thunder Hole, 63
Adair, Bethlehem, 186
Addison (near Middlebury)
    Whitford House, 210
Adele Turner Inn, Newport, 202
American Revolution, 35
Andover
    Rowell's Inn, 211
Andrie Rose Inn, Ludlow, 228
Antique Shops, Lower Maine, 56
Antiques and Accommodations, North Stonington, 77
Antiquing, 11
Applegate Inn, Lee, 141
Arlington, 47
    West Mountain Inn, 212
Ashland
    Glynn House Inn, 184
Ashley Falls, 45
Ashley Manor, Barnstable, 120

B

Bagley House Inn, Durham, 98
Bar Harbor, 64
    Inn at Bay Ledge (The), 89
    Manor House Inn, 88
    Ullikana, 90
Barnard (near Woodstock)
    Maple Leaf Inn, 213

Barnard (near Woodstock) continued
    Twin Farms, 214
Barnstable, 27
    Ashley Manor, 120
    Cobb's Cove Inn, 121
Barrows House, Dorset, 222
Bartlett, 68
Bath, 59
    Kennebec River Ride, 59
    Maine Maritime Museum, 59
Beach House (The), Kennebunk Beach, 102
Beach Plum Inn and Restaurant, Martha's Vineyard—Menemsha, 151
Beacon Hill Hotel & Bistro, Boston, 122
Bedford
    Bedford Village Inn, 185
Bee and Thistle Inn, Old Lyme, 79
Belfry Inn & Bistro, Sandwich, 171
Bennington, 47
Berry Manor Inn, Rockland, 115
Bethlehem, 68
    Adair, 186
Blantyre, Lenox, 143
Block Island
    1661 Inn & Hotel Manisses (The), 200
Blue Hill
    Blue Hill Inn, 91
Blueberry Hill Inn, Goshen, 224
Boothbay Harbor, 60
    Five Gables Inn, 92
Boston, 17
    Back Bay, 19
    Beacon Hill, 18
    Beacon Hill Hotel & Bistro, 122
    Boston Common, 19
    Boston Pops, 21
    Capitol Building, 18

Boston continued
  Charles Street Inn, 123
  Charlestown
    USS Constitution, 22
  Children's Museum, 20
  Clarendon Square Inn, 124
  Commonwealth Avenue, 19
  Copley Square, 19
  Faneuil Hall, 18
  Fifteen Beacon, 125
  Financial District, 20
  Freedom Trail, 18
  Harrison Gray Otis House, 19
  Isabella Stewart Gardner Museum, 20
  John Hancock Tower, 19
  Lenox (The), 126
  Museum at the John F. Kennedy Library, 20
  Museum of Fine Arts, 20
  Museum of Science, 20
  New England Aquarium, 22
  Newbury Street, 18
  North End, 20
  Old South Meeting House, 18
  Old State House, 18
  Paul Revere House, 20
  Public Garden, 19
  Quincy Market, 18
  SPNEA Headquarters, 19
  State House, 19
  Subway, 18
  Symphony Orchestra, 21
  Theatre District, 21
  Tourist Information, 22
  Trinity Church, 19
Brandon
  Lilac Inn, 215
Bretton Woods, 68
Brewster, 27
  Brewster By The Sea, A European B&B, 127
  Captain Freeman Inn, 128

Brewster continued
  Isaiah Clark House, 129
Bridgewater Corners
  October Country Inn, 216
Brook Farm Inn, Lenox, 144
Brunswick, 59
  Bowdoin College, 59
    Museum of Art, 59
Bufflehead Cove, Kennebunkport, 103
Burlington, 49
  Lang House, 217
  Willard Street Inn, 218
Buttonwood Inn, North Conway, 197
By the Sea B & B, Plymouth, 163

C

Cambridge, 21
  A Cambridge House, 130
  Botanical Museum, 22
  Harvard Memorial Church, 22
  Harvard Museums of Cultural and Natural History, 22
  Harvard University, 21
  Harvard Yard, 22
  Massachusetts Institute of Technology, 21
  Radcliffe College, 21
Camden, 61
  Camden Maine Stay, 93
  Camden Windward House (The), 95
  Hartstone Inn, 94
  Library, 61
  Main Street, 62
Cape Ann, 55
Cape Cod, 26
Cape Cod Canal, 26
Cape Cod National Seashore, 27
Cape Porpoise, 57
Captain Farris House, South Yarmouth, 176
Captain Freeman Inn, Brewster, 128
Captain Jefferds Inn, Kennebunkport, 104
Captain Lord Mansion, Kennebunkport, 105

Captain's House Inn, Chatham, 131
Car Rental, 11
Casco Bay, 58
Castle Hill Inn & Resort, Newport, 203
Charles Street Inn, Boston, 123
Charleston House, Woodstock, 245
Charlotte Inn, Martha's Vineyard—Edgartown, 148
Chatham, 27
    Captain's House Inn, 131
Chelsea
    Shire Inn, 219
Chester, 39, 48
Chesterfield
    Chesterfield Inn, 187
Chittenden, 49
    Fox Creek Inn, 220
Christopher Dodge House, Providence, 206
Clarendon Square Inn, Boston, 124
Cliffside Inn, Newport, 204
Cobb's Cove Inn, Barnstable, 121
Cohasset, 25
Colby Hill Inn, Henniker, 193
Concord, 36
    Concord's Colonial Inn, 132
    Hawthorne Inn, 133
    Museum, 37
    Old North Bridge, 36
    Old North Bridge Visitor Center, 36
    Orchard House, 37
    Ralph Waldo Emerson Home, 37
    Sleepy Hollow Cemetery, 37
    Walden Pond, 37
Concord's Colonial Inn, Concord, 132
Connecticut River Valley, 39
Conway, 67
Copper Beech Inn, Ivoryton (Essex), 72
Cornucopia of Dorset, Dorset, 223
Craftsbury Common
    Inn on the Common, 221
Crawford North, 68

Credit Cards, 4
Crocker House Country Inn, Hancock Point, 101
Crowne Pointe Historic Inn, Provincetown, 165

D

Damariscotta, 61
Daniel Webster Inn, Sandwich, 172
Deep River, 39
Deer Isle, 62
    Pilgrim's Inn, 96
Deer Isle–Sunset
    Goose Cove Lodge, 97
Deerfield
    Deerfield Inn, 134
Deerhill Inn, West Dover, 240
Dennis, 27
    Isaiah Hall Bed & Breakfast Inn, 135
Desert of Maine, 59
Devonfield, Lee, 142
Dockside Guest Quarters, York, 118
Domaine (Le), Hancock, 100
Dorset, 48
    Barrows House, 222
    Cornucopia of Dorset, 223
Driving Times, 12
Dunscroft by the Sea, Harwich Port, 139
Durham
    Bagley House Inn, 98
    Three Chimneys Inn, 188
Duxbury, 25
    Powder Point Bed & Breakfast, 136

E

East Haddam, 39
    Goodspeed Opera House, 39
Eastham, 27
    Whalewalk Inn, 137
Emerson Inn By The Sea, Rockport, 167
Enfield
    Enfield Shaker Inn, 189

Essex, 39, 55
    Griswold Inn (The), 70

F

Falmouth
    Maison Cappellari at Mostly Hall (La), 138
Fernside Inn (The), Princeton, 164
Fifteen Beacon, Boston, 125
Five Gables Inn, Boothbay Harbor, 92
Four Columns Inn, Newfane, 233
Fox Creek Inn, Chittenden, 220
Francestown
    Inn at Crotched Mountain, 190
Franconia, 68
Freeport, 59
    L. L. Bean Store, 59

G

Gateways Inn & Restaurant, Lenox, 145
Glen, 68
Gloucester, 55
    Beauport, 55
    Cape Ann Historical Museum, 55
    Hammond Castle Museum, 55
Glynn House Inn, Ashland, 184
Goose Cove Lodge, Deer Isle–Sunset, 97
Goose Rocks, 57
Gorham, 68
Goshen, 49
    Blueberry Hill Inn, 224
Governor's Inn (The), Ludlow, 229
Grafton, 48
    Old Tavern, 225
Great Barrington, 45
Green Guide to Antiquing in New England, 11
Green Mountain Inn, Stowe, 236
Green Mountains, 48, 64
Greenville, 64
    Lodge at Moosehead Lake, 99

Greenwich
    Homestead Inn–Thomas Henkelmann, 71
Grey Rock Inn, Northeast Harbor, 112
Griswold Inn (The), Essex, 70

H

Hancock
    Domaine (Le), 100
    Hancock Inn, 191
Hancock Point
    Crocker House Country Inn, 101
Hancock Shaker Village, 46
Harbor Light Inn, Marblehead, 147
Hart's Location, 68
    Notchland Inn, 192
Hartstone Inn, Camden, 94
Hartwell House, Ogunquit, 113
Harwich Port
    Dunscroft by the Sea, 139
Hawthorne Hotel, Salem, 170
Hawthorne Inn, Concord, 133
Heart of the Village Inn, Shelburne, 234
Henniker
    Colby Hill Inn, 193
Historic Jacob Hill Farm B & B Inn, Providence, 207
Hob Knob Inn, Martha's Vineyard—Edgartown, 149
Holderness
    Manor on Golden Pond, 194
Home Hill Inn, Plainfield, 198
Homestead Inn–Thomas Henkelmann, Greenwich, 71
Hyannis, 27
    John F. Kennedy Summer Home, 27
Hydrangea House Inn, Newport, 205

I

Icons, 5
Inn at Bay Ledge (The), Bar Harbor, 89
Inn at Castle Hill, Ipswich, 140
Inn at Crotched Mountain, Francestown, 190
Inn at Harbor Head (The), Kennebunkport, 108

Inn at National Hall, Westport, 85
Inn at Ormsby Hill, Manchester, 230
Inn at Richmond (The), Richmond, 166
Inn at Sawmill Farm, West Dover, 241
Inn at Shelburne Farms, Shelburne, 235
Inn at Stockbridge, Stockbridge, 177
Inn at Stonington, Stonington, 83
Inn at Sunrise Point, Lincolnville Beach (Camden), 110
Inn at the Round Barn Farm, Waitsfield, 238
Inn at Thorn Hill and Spa, Jackson, 196
Inn at Weston, Weston, 243
Inn on the Common, Craftsbury Common, 221
Innkeepers
    Professionalism, 6
Inns
    Bathrooms, 2
    Breakfast, 2
    Cancellation Policies, 3
    Check-in, 3
    Children, 4
    Comfort, 4
    Credit Cards, 4
    Criteria for Selection, 5
    Reservations, 6
    Responsibility, 7
    Restaurants, 7
    Room Rates, 8
    Smoking, 8
    Socializing, 8
    Websites, 9
    Wheelchair Accessibility, 9
Intervale (North Conway)
    New England Inn, 195
Introduction, 1
    About Inn Travel, 2
    About Itineraries, 10
Ipswich
    Crane Estate, 55
        Great House, The, 55
    Inn at Castle Hill, 140

Isaiah Clark House, Brewster, 129
Isaiah Hall Bed & Breakfast Inn, Dennis, 135
Isaiah Jones Homestead, Sandwich, 173
Itineraries, 10
    Boston: A Grand Beginning, 17
    Byways of Coastal Maine, The, 51
    Cape Cod, Nantucket, Martha's Vineyard & Newport, 24
    Fall Foliage Routes, 12
    Route 7 & Much More, 42
    Sturbridge & the Connecticut Shore, 34
Itineraries, Fall Foliage
    Northern New Hampshire & Northern Vermont, 66
Itinerary Maps, 14
Ivoryton (Essex)
    Copper Beech Inn, 72

J

Jackson
    Inn at Thorn Hill and Spa, 196
Jackson House Inn & Restaurant, Woodstock, 246
Jackson Village, 68
Jacob's Pillow Dance Festival, 46
Jamaica, 48
    Three Mountain Inn, 226
Juniper Hill Inn, Windsor, 244

K

Kancamagus Highway, 68
Kennebunk Beach
    Beach House (The), 102
Kennebunkport, 57
    Bufflehead Cove, 103
    Captain Jefferds Inn, 104
    Captain Lord Mansion, 105
    George Bush Summer Home, 57
    Inn at Harbor Head (The), 108
    Maine Stay Inn at the Melville Walker House, 106
    Old Fort Inn, 107
    White Barn Inn, 109

L

Lancaster, 68
Lang House, Burlington, 217
Ledyard
    Stonecroft Country Inn, 73
Lee
    Applegate Inn, 141
    Devonfield, 142
Lenox
    Blantyre, 143
    Brook Farm Inn, 144
    Gateways Inn & Restaurant, 145
    Wheatleigh, 146
Lenox (The), Boston, 126
Lexington, 35
Lilac Inn, Brandon, 215
Lincolnville Beach (Camden)
    Inn at Sunrise Point, 110
Litchfield, 44
    First Congregational Church, 44
Littleton, 68
Lodge at Moosehead Lake, Greenville, 99
Lodges at Old Sturbridge Village, Sturbridge, 179
Longfellow's Wayside Inn, Sudbury, 181
Lower Waterford, 68
    Rabbit Hill Inn, 227
Ludlow, 48
    Andrie Rose Inn, 228
    Governor's Inn (The), 229
Lyme, 39

M

Maine
    Places to Stay, 87
Maine Stay Inn at the Melville Walker House, Kennebunkport, 106
Maison Cappellari at Mostly Hall (La), Falmouth, 138
Manchester, 47
    1811 House (The), 231
    Inn at Ormsby Hill, 230

Manchester Center, 47
Manor House Inn, Bar Harbor, 88
Manor House, Norfolk, 76
Manor on Golden Pond, Holderness, 194
Mansion House, Martha's Vineyard—Vineyard Haven, 152
Maple Leaf Inn, Barnard (near Woodstock), 213
Maps
    Itinerary Maps, 14
Marblehead, 54
    Harbor Light Inn, 147
Martha's Vineyard, 29
    Edgartown, 30
    Gay Head, 30
    Oak Bluffs, 30
    Vineyard Haven, 30
Martha's Vineyard—Edgartown
    Charlotte Inn, 148
    Hob Knob Inn, 149
    Point Way Inn, 150
Martha's Vineyard—Menemsha
    Beach Plum Inn and Restaurant, 151
Martha's Vineyard—Vineyard Haven
    Mansion House, 152
    Thorncroft Inn, 153
Massachusetts
    Places to Stay, 119
Mayflower II, 25
Mayflower Inn, Washington, 84
Mendon, 49
Mendon (Killington)
    Red Clover Inn, 232
Minuteman National Historic Park, 37
Minutemen, 36
Mohegan Island, 61
Montpelier, 68
Morgan's Way Bed & Breakfast, Orleans, 162
Mount Desert Island, 62
Mount Equinox, 47

Mystic
    Steamboat Inn, 74
    Whalers Inn, 75
Mystic Village Seaport, 38
    Charles W. Morgan, 38
    Children's Museum, 38
    Stillman Building, 39

N

Nantucket Island, 29
    Nantucket Historical Association, 29
    Old Gaol, 29
    Old Mill, 29
    Oldest House, 29
    Three Bricks, 29
    Whaling Museum, 29
Nantucket Island—Nantucket
    Pineapple Inn, 154
    Seven Sea Street, 155
    Union Street Inn, 156
    White Elephant, 157
Nantucket Island—Siasconset
    Summer House, 158
Nantucket Island—Wauwinet
    Wauwinet (The), 159
New Canaan, 44
    Silvermine Guild of Artists, 44
New England Inn, Intervale (North Conway), 195
New Hampshire
    Places to Stay, 183
New Marlborough
    Old Inn on the Green & Gedney Farm, 160
Newburyport, 56
Newcastle, 61
    Newcastle Inn, 111
Newfane, 48
    Four Columns Inn, 233
Newport, 30
    Abigail Stoneman Inn, 201
    Adele Turner Inn, 202

Newport continued
    Castle Hill Inn & Resort, 203
    Cliffside Inn, 204
    Hydrangea House Inn, 205
Norfolk
    Manor House, 76
North Adams
    Porches Inn, 161
North Conway, 67
    Buttonwood Inn, 197
North Stonington
    Antiques and Accommodations, 77
    Randall's Ordinary, 78
North Woodstock, 68
Northeast Harbor, 64
    Grey Rock Inn, 112
Norwalk, 44
Notchland Inn, Hart's Location, 192

O

October Country Inn, Bridgewater Corners, 216
Ogunquit, 56
    Hartwell House, 113
Old Bennington, 47
    Battle Monument, 47
    Grandma Moses Schoolhouse, 47
    Old First Church, 47
Old Fort Inn, Kennebunkport, 107
Old Inn on the Green & Gedney Farm, New Marlborough, 160
Old Lyme, 39
    Bee and Thistle Inn, 79
Old Mystic
    Old Mystic Inn, 80
Old Tavern, Grafton, 225
Orleans, 27
    Morgan's Way Bed & Breakfast, 162

P

Pacing, 14
Paul Revere, 35
Penobscot Bay, 61
Pilgrim's Inn, Deer Isle, 96
Pineapple Inn, Nantucket Island—Nantucket, 154
Pitcher Inn, Warren, 239
Pittsfield, 46
Places to Stay
    Maine, 87
    Massachusetts, 119
    New Hampshire, 183
    Rhode Island, 199
Plainfield
    Home Hill Inn, 198
Plymouth, 25
    Burial Hill, 26
    By the Sea B & B, 163
    Hobbamock's Homesite, 26
    Mayflower II, 25
    Mayflower Society Museum, 26
    Plymouth Rock, 25
Point Way Inn, Martha's Vineyard—Edgartown, 150
Pomegranate Inn, Portland, 114
Porches Inn, North Adams, 161
Portland, 57
    Museum of Art, 58
    Pomegranate Inn, 114
Powder Point Bed & Breakfast, Duxbury, 136
Princeton
    Fernside Inn (The), 164
Providence, 31
    Brown University, 31
    Capitol Building, 31
    Christopher Dodge House, 206
    Historic Jacob Hill Farm B & B Inn, 207
    John Brown House, 31
    Rhode Island School of Design, 31
    State House, 31
    Waterfire, 31
Provincetown, 27
    Crowne Pointe Historic Inn, 165
Publick House Historic Inn, Sturbridge, 180

Q

Quincy, 25

R

Rabbit Hill Inn, Lower Waterford, 227
Rand McNally Maps, 14
Randall's Ordinary, North Stonington, 78
Red Clover Inn, Mendon (Killington), 232
Red Lion Inn, Stockbridge, 178
Rhode Island
    Places to Stay, 199
Richmond
    Inn at Richmond (The), 166
Ridgefield, 44
    Aldrich Museum of Contemporary Art, 44
    West Lane Inn, 81
Rockland, 61
    Berry Manor Inn, 115
    Farnsworth Art Museum, 61
Rockport, 55
    Emerson Inn By The Sea, 167
    Seacrest Manor, 168
    Yankee Clipper Inn, 169
Rowell's Inn, Andover, 211

S

Sagamore Bridge, 26
Saint Johnsbury, 68
Salem, 54
    Chestnut Street, 54
    Hawthorne Hotel, 170
    House of Seven Gables, 54
    Peabody Essex Museum, 54
    Pioneer Village, 54
    Witch Museum, 54
Salisbury, 45

Sandwich, 27
    Belfry Inn & Bistro, 171
    Daniel Webster Inn, 172
    Glass Museum, 27
    Heritage Plantation Museum, 27
    Isaiah Jones Homestead, 173
Seacrest Manor, Rockport, 168
Seven Sea Street, Nantucket Island—Nantucket, 155
Sheffield, 45
Shelburne, 49
    Heart of the Village Inn, 234
    Inn at Shelburne Farms, 235
    Museum, 49
Shire Inn, Chelsea, 219
Simsbury
    Simsbury 1820 House, 82
Society for the Preservation of New England Antiquities, 19, 55
South Egremont
    Weathervane Inn, 174
South Mountain Concert Festival, 46
South Orleans
    A Little Inn on Pleasant Bay, 175
South Yarmouth
    Captain Farris House, 176
Southwest Harbor, 64
Squire Tarbox Inn, Wiscasset, 117
Steamboat Inn, Mystic, 74
Stockbridge, 46
    Berkshire Playhouse, 46
    Chesterwood, 46
    Inn at Stockbridge, 177
    Norman Rockwell Museum, 46
    Red Lion Inn, 178
Stone Hill Inn, Stowe, 237
Stonecroft Country Inn, Ledyard, 73
Stonington, 62
    Inn at Stonington, 83
Stowe
    Green Mountain Inn, 236

Stowe continued
    Stone Hill Inn, 237
Sturbridge, 37
    Lodges at Old Sturbridge Village, 179
    Old Sturbridge Village, 37
    Publick House Historic Inn, 180
Sudbury
    Longfellow's Wayside Inn, 181
Summer House, Nantucket Island—Siasconset, 158
Sunset, 62

T

Tanglewood Music Festival, 46
Thorncroft Inn, Martha's Vineyard—Vineyard Haven, 153
Three Chimneys Inn, Durham, 188
Three Mountain Inn, Jamaica, 226
Townshend, 48
Twin Farms, Barnard (near Woodstock), 214
Twin Mountain, 68

U

Ullikana, Bar Harbor, 90
Union Street Inn, Nantucket Island—Nantucket, 156
USS Constitution, 22

V

Vermont
    Places to Stay, 209
Villa (The), Westerly, 208

W

Waitsfield, 49
    Inn at the Round Barn Farm, 238
Warren, 49
    Pitcher Inn, 239
Washington
    Mayflower Inn, 84
Waterford
    Waterford Inne, 116
Wauwinet (The), Nantucket Island—Wauwinet, 159

Index

Weather, 15
Weathervane Inn, South Egremont, 174
Website
    Karen Brown Website, 9
Wedding Cake House, nr Kennebunkport, 57
Wells, 56
West Dover
    Deerhill Inn, 240
    Inn at Sawmill Farm, 241
West Lane Inn, Ridgefield, 81
West Mountain Inn, Arlington, 212
West Townshend, 48
    Windham Hill Inn, 242
Westerly
    Villa (The), 208
Weston
    Inn at Weston, 243
Westport
    Inn at National Hall, 85
Whalers Inn, Mystic, 75
Whalewalk Inn, Eastham, 137
Wheatleigh, Lenox, 146
White Barn Inn, Kennebunkport, 109
White Elephant, Nantucket Island—Nantucket, 157
White Mountains, 64, 68
Whitford House, Addison (near Middlebury), 210
Willard Street Inn, Burlington, 218
Williamstown, 46
    Sterling and Francine Clark Institute, 46
    Theatre, 46
Windham Hill Inn, West Townshend, 242
Windsor
    Juniper Hill Inn, 244
Wiscasset, 60
    Squire Tarbox Inn, 117
Woodstock, 48
    Charleston House, 245
    Jackson House Inn & Restaurant, 246

Y
Yankee Clipper Inn, Rockport, 169
Yarmouth Port, 27
York, 56
    Dockside Guest Quarters, 118
York Harbor, 56

Travel Your Dreams • Order Your Karen Brown Guides Today

Please ask in your local bookstore for Karen Brown's Guides. If the books you want are unavailable, you may order directly from the publisher. Books will be shipped immediately.

- _____ *Austria: Charming Inns & Itineraries* $19.95
- _____ *California: Charming Inns & Itineraries* $19.95
- _____ *England: Charming Bed & Breakfasts* $18.95
- _____ *England, Wales & Scotland: Charming Hotels & Itineraries* $19.95
- _____ *France: Charming Bed & Breakfasts* $18.95
- _____ *France: Charming Inns & Itineraries* $19.95
- _____ *Germany: Charming Inns & Itineraries* $19.95
- _____ *Ireland: Charming Inns & Itineraries* $19.95
- _____ *Italy: Charming Bed & Breakfasts* $18.95
- _____ *Italy: Charming Inns & Itineraries* $19.95
- _____ *Mexico: Charming Inns & Itineraries* $19.95
- _____ *Mid-Atlantic: Charming Inns & Itineraries* $19.95
- _____ *New England: Charming Inns & Itineraries* $19.95
- _____ *Pacific Northwest: Charming Inns & Itineraries* $19.95
- _____ *Portugal: Charming Inns & Itineraries* $19.95
- _____ *Spain: Charming Inns & Itineraries* $19.95
- _____ *Switzerland: Charming Inns & Itineraries* $19.95

Name _____ Street _____

Town _____ State_____ Zip _____ Tel _____

Credit Card (MasterCard or Visa) _____ Expires: _____

For orders in the USA, add $5 for the first book and $2 for each additional book for shipment. Overseas shipping (airmail) is $10 for 1 to 2 books, $20 for 3 to 4 books etc. CA residents add 8.25% sales tax. Fax or mail form with check or credit card information to:

KAREN BROWN'S GUIDES
Post Office Box 70 • San Mateo • California • 94401 • USA
tel: (650) 342-9117, fax: (650) 342-9153, email: karen@karenbrown.com, www.karenbrown.com

KAREN BROWN wrote her first travel guide in 1976. Her personalized travel series has grown to 17 titles, which Karen and her small staff work diligently to keep updated. Karen, her husband, Rick, and their children, Alexandra and Richard, live in Moss Beach, a small town on the coast south of San Francisco. They settled here in 1991 when they opened Seal Cove Inn. Karen is frequently traveling but when she is home, in her role as innkeeper, enjoys welcoming Karen Brown readers.

JACK BULLARD researches for Karen Brown's guides to New England and the Mid-Atlantic. Jack grew up in New England and after completing his graduate education there spent fifteen years in international consulting in marketing and finance, and then ten years as executive director of two Boston law firms. He managed another law firm before owning The Inn at Occidental in the Sonoma wine country north of San Francisco for ten years. He now lives in Newport, Rhode Island and remains close to the world of hospitality—consulting, designing and decorating.

JANN POLLARD, the artist responsible for the beautiful painting on the cover of this guide, has studied art since childhood, and is well known for her outstanding impressionistic-style watercolors, which she has exhibited in numerous juried shows, winning many awards. Jann travels frequently to Europe (using Karen Brown's Guides) where she loves to paint historical buildings. Jann's original paintings are represented through The Gallery, Burlingame, CA, 650-347-9392 or www.thegalleryart.net. Fine-art giclée prints of the cover paintings are also available at www.karenbrown.com.

VANESSA KALE produced all of the property ketches and itinerary illustrations in this guide. A native of Bellingham, Washington, Vanessa spent her high school year in Sonoma California. After graduating in Art from UC Davis, Vanessa moved to southern California where she lives with her husband, Simon, and works as a freelance artist. www.vanessakale.com

Traveling To Europe?

Karen Brown's Preferred Provider of
Car Rental Services
&
Discount Air Travel

Regularly scheduled flights on major carriers to Europe
Including discounts on both coach & business class

*For special offers and discounts to Karen Brown readers
on car rentals and air fares in 2005,
be sure to identify yourself as a Karen Brown Traveler –
use your Karen Brown ID number 99006187*

Make reservations online via our website, www.karenbrown.com
Just click
"Auto Rentals" or "Discount Airfares" on our home page

Need to talk to a real person?
Call 800-223-5555

Karen Brown Presents Her Own Special Hideaways

Karen Brown's Seal Cove Inn

Spectacularly set amongst wildflowers and bordered by cypress trees, Seal Cove Inn (Karen's second home) looks out to the distant ocean. Each room has a fireplace, cozy sitting area, and a view of the sea. Located on the coast, 35 minutes south of San Francisco.

Seal Cove Inn, Moss Beach, California
toll free telephone: (800) 995-9987
www.sealcoveinn.com

Karen Brown's Dolphin Cove Inn

Hugging a steep hillside overlooking the sparkling deep-blue bay of Manzanillo, Dolphin Cove Inn offers guests outstanding value. Each room has either a terrace or a balcony, and a breathtaking view of the sea. Located on the Pacific Coast of Mexico.

Dolphin Cove Inn, Manzanillo, Mexico
toll free telephone: (888) 497-4138
www.dolphincoveinn.com

Icons Key

We have introduced the icons listed below in our guidebooks and on our website (www.karenbrown.com). These allow us to provide additional information about our recommended properties. When using our website to supplement the guides, placing the cursor over an icon will in many cases give you further details.

Air conditioning in rooms	Restaurant
Beach	Spa
Breakfast included in room rate	Swimming pool
Children welcome	Tennis
Cooking classes offered	Television w/ English channels
Credit cards accepted	Wedding facilities
Dinner served upon request	Wheelchair friendly
Direct-dial telephone in room	Archaeological site nearby
Dogs by special request	Golf course nearby
Elevator	Hiking trails nearby
Exercise room	Horseback riding nearby
Fireplaces in some rooms	Skiing nearby
Mini-refrigerator in room	Water sports nearby
Some non-smoking rooms	Wineries nearby
Parking available	